#SayHerName

#SayHerName

Black Women's Stories of Police Violence and Public Silence

The African American Policy Forum

Coauthored by Kimberlé Crenshaw
and the African American Policy Forum

Foreword by Janelle Monáe

Haymarket Books
Chicago, Illinois

Published in 2023 by Haymarket Books
P.O. Box 180165
Chicago, IL 60618
773-583-7884
www.haymarketbooks.org
info@haymarketbooks.org

ISBN:978-1-64259-494-2

Distributed to the trade in the US through Consortium Book Sales and Distribution (www.cbsd.com) and internationally through Ingram Publisher Services International (www.ingramcontent.com).

This book was published with the generous support of Collective Futures Fund, Lannan Foundation, New Orleans Saints, NoVo Foundation, Pivotal Ventures LLC, Tides Foundation, WNBA, Wallace Action Fund, and Marguerite Casey Foundation.

Special discounts are available for bulk purchases by organizations and institutions. Please email orders@haymarketbooks.org for more information.

Cover design by Julia Sharpe-Levine.

Entered into digital printing August, 2023.

Library of Congress Cataloging-in-Publication data is available.

Entered into digital printing August, 2023.

Contents

Foreword: Say Her Name
by Janelle Monáe vii
Prologue: Her Names ix

Introduction: Unheard Stories 1
Chapter 1: Breaking Silence 27
Chapter 2: Stolen Histories 63
Chapter 3: Disposable Lives 91
Chapter 4: Building Community 121
Chapter 5: In Memoriam 157
Chapter 6: Art Activism 195
Conclusion: Bearing Witness 229

Epilogue: Brokenhearted 265

Acknowledgments 287
Notes 291

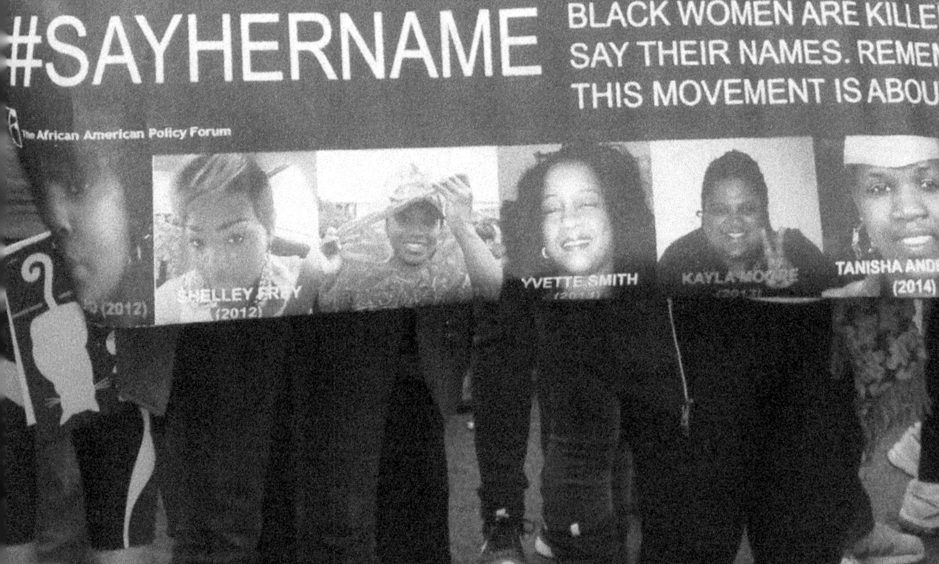

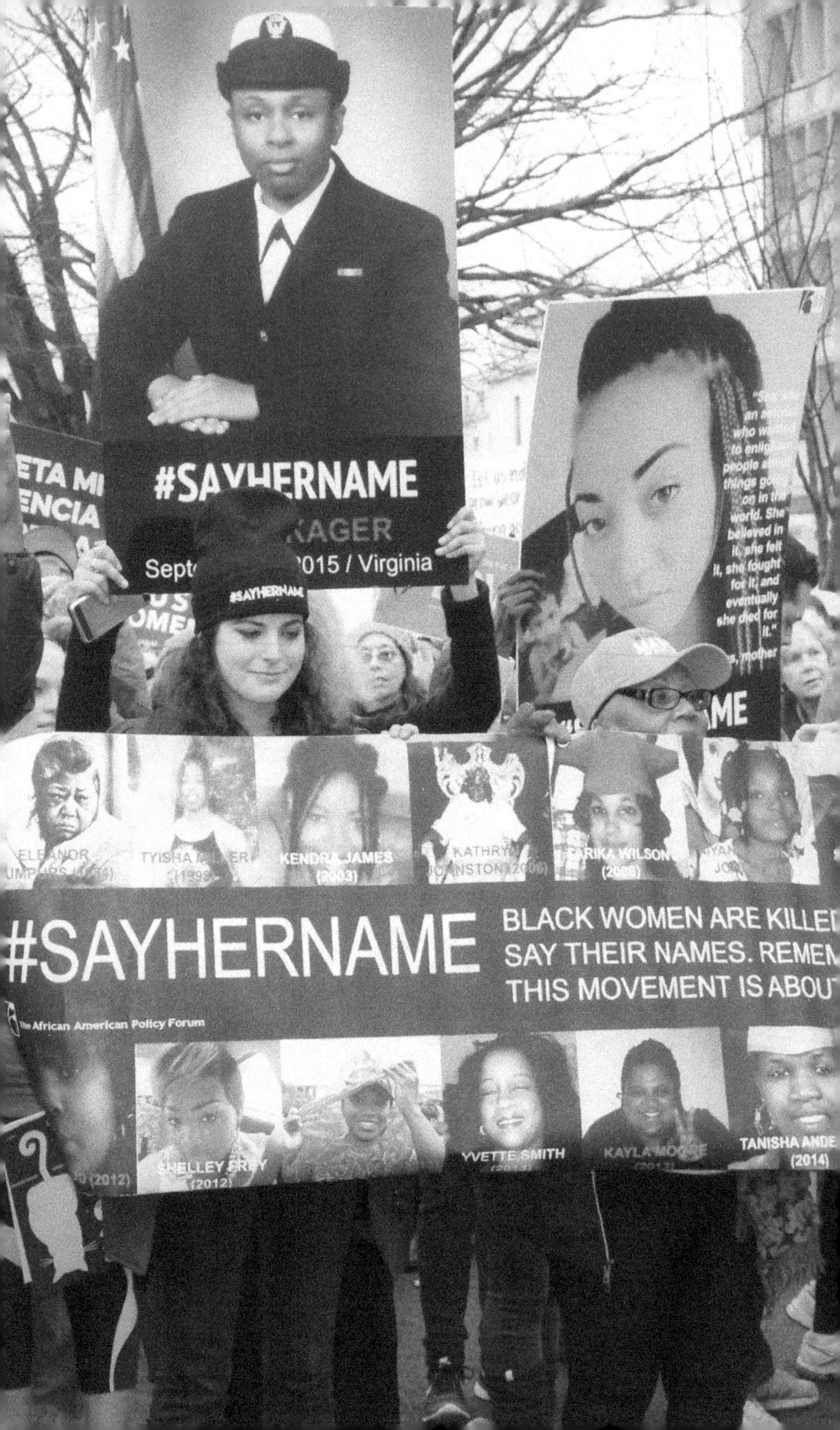
#SAYHERNAME
KAGER
2015 / Virginia
#SAYHERNAME
believed in it, she felt it, she fought for it, and eventually she died for it."
KENDRA JAMES
(2003)
#SAYHERNAME
BLACK WOMEN ARE
SAY THEIR NAMES.
THIS MOVEMENT IS
The African American Policy Forum
SHELLEY FREY
(2012)
YVETTE SMITH
KAYLA MOORE
(2014)

FOREWORD

Say Her Name

Janelle Monáe

The lack of visibility of Black women has changed—and the incredible work of Kimberlé Crenshaw, African American Policy Forum, and the #SayHerName campaign are examples of this. So is this powerful book you are about to read.

When Kimberlé invited me to one of the mothers' meetings, to hear them speak directly about their loved ones who were lost, I learned about the number of women—Black women in particular—who had lost their lives to police violence. I realized that I didn't know 90 percent of the stories. Their stories were not covered.

I felt like I was listening to my aunt, my mom, my mom's best friend, their girlfriend, my grandmother. I was watching all of them grieve right before my eyes. And when you see family hurting like that, you take on a different level of responsibility. It becomes personal. They are family. These are our sisters. We need to take care of each other.

I knew we had an opportunity to use our voices to speak truth to power, to bring more eyes and ears to these stories. I felt a personal responsibility to uplift the names of these women and raise more awareness. To uplift their names so that history won't repeat itself.

That's why I recorded the song "Say Her Name (Hell You Talmbout)." I could have done it alone, but I know the impact when you lock arms with other Black women. When we're all together, there is an infinite source of power.

I reached out to Kimberlé and the mothers, asking for the blessing to perform a rallying cry, a spoken ritual, speaking their names with other women in my industry—not as celebrities, not as artists, but as daughters, as sisters, as family. We came together on a human-to-human level, sister-to-sister level, to honor these names.

How can we amplify their names? How can we bring more awareness to their cases? And how can we bring joy to the hearts and minds of these families? These families live this tragedy every single day. How can we lift some of the work off their backs? How can we give the scores of women and girls whose names are not as well known as Sandra Bland and Breonna Taylor visibility, so another young Black girl's name doesn't have to be added to the scroll?

Honestly, I wish that we did not have to come together around this song. I wish it was around celebrating their lives.

I was able to join them on a call when we had a listening party with all the women in the mothers' network and their family members, and it was a different level of appreciation on their faces. *Finally, more people are recognizing my baby. That's all we want is to be acknowledged. That's all we want is for people to know how incredible my little sister was, how incredible my daughter was.*

They want their loved ones to be acknowledged. And it's an honor to be able to amplify that in my song and here in this book.

Prologue

Her Names

How does one begin a book on state violence? What words can capture the pain and anguish the loss of life inevitably engenders? How does one tell a story about that pain and anguish that is also a story about love, courage, community, resistance, and hope? And how does one capture the intersection of these stories in ways that center Black women in the ongoing efforts to make Black lives matter?[1]

While this book does not offer a definitive answer to the preceding questions, its point of departure is that we must "say her name." That simple imperative—to say her name—is more than a political slogan. It is a call to action, a movement that refuses to be silent about the numerous Black women the police have killed.

This book foregrounds the stories of these lost lives through the voices of the mothers and sisters, they left behind. In their own words, these courageous survivors tell us who their loved ones were, the circumstances that led to their untimely deaths, the impact these police killings have had on their families and communities, and their individual and collective struggles for legal accountability and justice.[2] Each chapter begins with such an account.

You will read the names Tanisha Anderson, Michelle Cusseaux, Shelly Frey, Korryn Gaines, India Kager, and Kayla Moore; Atatiana Jefferson, Miriam Carey, and Michelle Shirley, each of their lives stolen by a police officer. The mothers and sisters of these women have created a reciprocal network of support to fight for justice for their daughters, sisters, and the countless other Black women police officers have killed.

The mothers and sisters speak to us not only about the pain of their losses but also about what we call *the loss of the loss*: the grief arising from the public failure to acknowledge the police killing their daughters and siblings. Telling their stories in their own words is an act of reclamation that signals their refusal to allow police violence against Black women to remain illegible, an afterthought at best, a mere wrinkle in the fabric of anti-Black racism. Refusing to go quietly into the night of their grief, these survivors speak loudly against the silences enveloping these killings, resisting both the victim-blaming narratives and the condemnation of their loved ones to the permanent double erasure of death and anonymity.

That this book tells the story of the #SayHerName Mothers Network and the broader #SayHerName campaign is not to suggest that these projects are the only interventions against police killings of Black women. #SayHerName is one among various important organizing efforts that are all necessary, but insufficient, in the fight to end racialized and gendered state violence. Motivating the campaign is the sense that knowing these women's stories—who they were, how they lived, and why they suffered at the hands of the police—allows us to engage more deeply with the circumstances enabling their deaths and subsequent invisibility. By listening to the courageous testimonies of the #SayHerName mothers and sisters, we are able to see why Black women and girls—across gender identity, sexual orientation, religion, class, national origin, and immigration status—are disproportionately subject to police violence.

While writing about state violence is hard, reading about the phenomenon might be even harder. In that regard, it is important to say from the beginning that there is no "right" way to read this book. Because #SayHerName is many different things to survivors, activists, and communities, the book contains different voices that can be engaged in different ways. You may be reading it on your own or as part of a course or a book group or some other collective. You may choose to read it cover to cover or you may look at those chapters that resonate most with your own experiences. All these ways of experiencing the collection are vital; all of them provide different routes to #SayHerName to break a de facto conspiracy of silence about police killings of Black women. Throughout the book, it is the words of the mothers and sisters of the #SayHerName campaign—their memories, pain, and dreams—that lie at the heart of this formation. They have so much to teach us all.

At the same time, this book does not presume to know you or your relationship to the stories of state violence around which it is organized. Undoubtedly, some of you will be intimately familiar with the histories of violence recounted throughout the book. You may be a Black woman who has experienced police violence or lost a loved one to it. For others, the accounts in this book will be new, shocking, and for some, perhaps even incredulous. Its purpose is to expose everyone to how the United States has come to create and maintain the marginality of Black women, how survivors have been impacted by many of the same dynamics that contributed to the loss of their daughters and sisters, and how we must work together to challenge this reality. Through the voices of the mothers and sisters of Black women killed by the police, you will learn how #SayHerName has not only confronted Black women's precarity but also how that precarity has been written out of the public record.

The stories that begin each chapter teach us about the lives that were lost and the lives that *should* have been. We know that these stories only scratch the surface in telling us who these women were, the struggles they encountered, the suffering they endured, and the lives they leave behind. In that sense, it bears emphasizing that it is impossible to fully understand these mothers' pain or to capture the true intricacy of their daughters' lives. Still, the mothers' narratives function not only as an invaluable archival record of these women's lives beyond the atrocities they suffered but also an intersectional reckoning of Black women's trajectory toward "premature death."[3]

That reckoning demands that all of us work to disrupt the degree to which, in the collective consciousness of the nation, Black women's experiences with state violence remain unheard stories.

Michelle Cusseaux

Introduction

Unheard Stories

"No one was paying attention."

—Fran Garrett, mother of Michelle Cusseaux
(August 17, 1963–August 14, 2014)

My name is Fran Garrett. I'm the mother of Michelle Cusseaux, who was shot and killed at the hands of the police during a mental health pick-up call on August 14, 2014.

Michelle loved people, she loved life. She didn't attend the party, she was the party. She loved to travel, loved to be near water. She always gave back to others and just had such a beautiful soul. She was the youngest of three children. And you could tell at times that she was the baby. Michelle has always been a momma's girl and always promised never to leave me. She was my support. She took care of me, and I took care of her. I can still see her smiling face. Michelle was a lovable child, a lovable person, and as she grew into womanhood she became a go-to type of person. In her circle of friends and in our family, everyone would go to her for advice. She would always have very good advice for her friends and family. I was her friend. She was my friend. We laughed and talked together, cried. She would call at least a few times a day to ask me how I was doing.

She was witty, kept you laughing. Just very, very outgoing. And she never knew a stranger. Sometimes, she'd take the bus to my house. I'd get there to pick her up, and she'd have made friends with whoever else was at the bus stop. And I would end up having to take them where they had to go. She was that kind. "Momma, you have to take them."

She was a lesbian. I knew it at a very early age, and kids would call her names and stuff. She was always tomboyish, hung with her brother. I was okay with it, and I accepted it. Everyone else in the family accepted it too, and we never really had to discuss it. This is the family we're from.

Kids loved her. Michelle had no biological kids of her own, and she was like the Pied Piper to the kids in the neighborhood and her little nieces and nephews. She always had time to play with them. My great-grandson Rider always said his Titi was his best friend, and they would sing songs together. I remember the last trip we actually took right before her death. We had gone to the LA area, and the song "Happy" was out. We were all singing that song, and [Michelle and Rider were] in the back being silly, doing faces, and just entertaining each other.

Michelle had a mental health problem, and she had recently gone back to school to help others with similar mental health issues. Her goal was to open up a home for them. I could see her doing that for the rest of her life—she had her certifications and graduated second highest in her class. She enjoyed that. She's always worked with these nonprofits, helping women with kids, women with HIV, and women facing domestic violence. Michelle was a fighter, not a victim. She had life struggles, and she worked through them. And one way or another would always figure out a way to get through it, over it, or under it. She'd never just sit down to have a pity party.

Michelle's brother, my son David Cusseaux, was an activist and a former altar boy. Just an all-around kid, good-natured. He was killed in a drive-by shooting in the early eighties. He was leaving my mom's home and taking a friend his jacket. A kid that he kind of mentored who was a blind boy, and he was taking this kid his coat. On the way, he encountered a group of men coming from Berkeley. Someone had done something to their dog earlier that day in East Oakland. They became irate, went home, got weapons, came back, and just started to shoot anybody they saw walking the streets in Oakland. He just happened to be at the wrong place at the wrong time, and he was murdered. He was twenty-one. That was in '84.

The murder of her brother sent Michelle downhill, and her mental health suffered.

The morning of August 14, 2014, I got a call from Michelle's mental health counselor, who told me that Michelle had just made a threatening call to the agency's office. They had forgotten to send a cab for Michelle's doctor's appointment, and she was extremely agitated. Normally in instances like this, they would send a team of mental health professionals from the agency to go check on her and maybe bring her to my house.

That particular morning, I was out of town. I had gone to California for the parole hearing of the man who killed my son decades earlier. I'd seen this particular gentleman grow through the years, and I had accepted his apology. Two lives were lost that night: my son's and this young man's; his life was just gone after years in prison. I had gone to the suitability hearing a few years before that, and I recommended to the board that this young man continue about four or five more years in prison. This time when I got back, I saw a change—a great change. I discussed this with Michelle, and we agreed that he should be released. I was in California to recommend his release to the parole board and to offer him my assistance with resources, referrals, and reentry back into society the morning before Michelle was killed. I told her over the phone that I had accepted the gentleman's apology and I forgave him. I explained that to her, and she was okay with it.

It hurts me so because that day it happened I had just finished talking to her, and at some point, the police came, and that upset her and scared her. And they said she was on the phone. They themselves told me that she was on the phone trying to call me. She was trying to call her momma. "I will call my momma." She always felt that her mother could resolve any and everything. That's how much she loved me and believed in me. I could make mountains move. And other times I think about this, her last minutes and trying to call me, and she couldn't get through. She couldn't get through to me. I know she was fighting. And all them at her door and banging on it, and then this officer trying to get her to open up her door. I hate to cry, but I keep reliving it.

I finally found out because Michelle's neighbor phoned me in Oakland to let me know the police were there at Michelle's house. I asked the neighbor to put me on the phone with one of the officers, but the police refused to speak with me. Shortly thereafter, I found out that Michelle had been shot.

It didn't have to be that way. This was a mental health call, and they sent eight police [officers] with guns drawn and dogs in the car. Things were calm at first. The first seven officers to arrive at

Michelle's house were from our community. They had been talking to Michelle through the security door, having a calm conversation.

Then Sergeant Percy Dupra, an officer from another district who was filling in for someone, arrived on the scene. Within six minutes, Michelle was dead. Sergeant Dupra came upstairs and demanded that they pry open her front door. Then he shot her. He came to do what he came to do. In six minutes, all this happened, and a life was gone. A life was taken. And he took that life.

I'm not sure what he saw when he saw my daughter. I'm thinking he just saw a lesbian woman at this point—a crazy, Black, gay lady. She was not outraged or screaming; the other officers said she was quiet. She told them to just go away, that she was okay. She was not screaming, cursing, or anything. She said, "Let me call my momma," because she knew that her mother could help the situation.

I imagine she had a look of shock, a look of fright, on her face. She's in her own home, the safety of her own home. Now she's surrounded by all these policemen, and now one is cursing at her through the door, "Open the fucking door!" and all this, and he's "sick of her shit." He's not going to "take her shit." With five to seven police coming to her door, and all of this is because of a pick-up order from her mental health provider who sent the police. Fear. Fear.

They think that we're angry when we're only attempting to explain ourselves. They accuse us of just being angry Black women. That's how we're classified, as just being angry. Then for Sergeant Dupra to say he shot my daughter because he was scared of the look on her face. It's just so unreal. They pried open her door and went in, and he's the one who feared for his life? She's five foot five or something, weighing about 120 pounds, had just a hammer in her hand. [Eight] police officers feared for their lives? It's really far-fetched. It's unbelievable.

Five days after Michael Brown was killed, Michelle Cusseaux was killed in Phoenix, Arizona, with a population of about 10 to 12 percent African Americans. And no one was paying attention. I don't know what it would have been, a blurb in the newspaper, maybe not even in the newspaper. But me being her mother—and the person that I am—I refused. Somebody is going to recognize that the police have murdered my daughter in her home. I had to come up with a way to demand their attention and that was it—to bring a casket to city hall. I got a few people to assist me in carrying her coffin, and that's what we did. We marched through town.

People in the office buildings started to peek out. They didn't know what [this] commotion was. That got the attention. I wanted justice. Michelle had been murdered by the police, and I wanted justice. And then the press came out. So that started the ball rolling in Phoenix. After that it snowballed, and we got the recognition that we wanted. The mayor and the attorney general came out to my home to apologize. The police chief apologized and asked me what I wanted. Everything that I had asked for we just about got, except for drug test testing of police. I wanted the police tested right after an incident to see if they're under the influence of steroids. But, no, thanks to the union, they fought it, and we didn't get that. We did get more body cams. We got that intervention squad that we requested. And bottom line, after an internal police procedure, Sergeant Percy Dupra was found guilty of violating Michelle's civil rights.

When I said the police were found guilty, trust me, it was not of murdering my daughter. It was not in court. His own department knew that he had used excessive force. He had been on the force for seventeen years. So, of course, they protected their own. I wanted him fired. They did not fire him, so he could move forward and keep his pension. They put him immediately back on the force in a different position. It was like a slap on the wrist. I fought hard for that because I felt as if he needed to be at least suspended for a few days with no pay. They didn't see fit to do that. He was demoted back out on the streets. I really couldn't fathom that.

Justice for Michelle would be ongoing. It wouldn't just be justice for Michelle, but justice for all women killed by police officers in their homes. We are human. We are damsels in distress. We have issues. We have problems. Just don't come out with guns in hand and shoot us. Until laws are changed and amendments are made, there will be no justice for Michelle or anyone else.

I want people to say her name and know that my daughter was a person, a very lively person—she was loved by her family and friends—and that Michelle did exist and is still here with me [in spirit] today. Now we're fighting for our daughters' names to be in the newspaper, in bold print: KILLED, MURDERED BY THE POLICE. *It needs to be made known that these things happened. I am so thankful for the organization AAPF and #SayHerName. I say my daughter's name, I keep it out in the public. I'm not ashamed. I want the world to know she was killed, she was murdered by the police, and this is how and why.*

What gets me through is the need to know that I fought for her, I didn't let her death be in vain. And I do it for the population that she cared for—to make it better for them. Back then, police in uniforms were the first responders. Today somebody else in Phoenix would respond to a mental health wellness order, to help them through what it is that they're going through, to talk to them and to calm them down. And I could see Michelle just beaming and grateful that we have moved this far in making the changes. Because if she were alive, she would've been working to do those things. She would have been front and center on this one. I can hear her telling her story: "Due to them taking my life, these are the changes that have occurred. It took my life for these changes to come about."

She was just my friend, and I miss her so. As I'm getting older, I see certain things going on in my life that wouldn't be this way if she was here. I wouldn't have to go through certain things. I wouldn't have to do certain things. I just truly miss her. But I keep seeing the smile on her face, and it keeps me going.

Fran Garrett

I am standing in an air-conditioned auditorium thinking about Michelle Cusseaux and the countless other Black women killed by the police whose deaths "no one was paying attention" to. My audience on this balmy spring day is mostly made up of public interest lawyers, students, and faculty. I am remembering the courage that Michelle's mother, Fran Garrett, exhibited after Phoenix police killed Michelle in her own home. Michelle's story, like those of too many others, would have ended when Sergeant Percy Dupra stole her life had she not been born to a tenacious mother who refused to let her daughter's name be forgotten. Fran was determined that her daughter's life and death would not be reduced to obscurity, another statistic that no one counted. Michelle was killed just five days after a cop gunned down Michael Brown in Ferguson, Missouri. After seeing the community protests taking shape there, Fran decided to march Michelle's casket to Phoenix City Hall. In this brave act of protest, she joined a powerful tradition of Black women resisting and denouncing the state violence that directly threatens them and all too often destroys their families.

Fran's march to the Phoenix City Hall was a flare in the night. Fran's radical act—literally placing her daughter's casket at the door of municipal power—not only demanded that Michelle be seen but also rendered visible the police killings of other Black women. The sorrowful procession of Michelle's coffin to city hall left a searing image that spoke to the many ways in which Black women's fate has been left in the hands of police while their stories have been marginalized and sometimes erased.

While Michael Brown's killing justifiably sparked a wave of nationwide protests over lethal police shootings of Black men, the killing of Black women like Michelle had yet to be memorialized in widespread activations and denunciations. Fran offered a powerful and moving witness to the fact that Black women were also losing their lives in circumstances that spoke to the disregard of Black life and family bonds. There was no sound reason for their stories to be banished to the shadows of our collective consciousness, mere afterthoughts in the litany of savagery that has come to constitute anti-Black state violence. Fran's act reminded us all of the obvious fact that slain women's mothers don't grieve for them any less, their children don't cry for them any less, their siblings don't mourn them any less, and we should not protest their killings any less than we do the killings of their brothers, fathers, and sons.

Six months later, as I look out at the audience, I wonder who among them will know Michelle Cusseaux's name. Would they know of any other daughters who were stolen like Fran's was? Or was the erasure of these horrific losses difficult to interrupt because of the reflexive ways that the very notion of anti-Black police violence defaults almost exclusively to our endangered sons? To make the patterns of erasure visible—and audible—I invite the audience to join me in doing something new. I ask those audience members who are able to do so to stand. I tell them, "When you hear a name you don't recognize, take a seat and remain seated." I promise to invite the last person standing to tell the seated audience what they know about the person whose name no one else recognized. Then I call out the names, slowly, deliberately, and loud enough for even those seated at the very back of the auditorium to hear: Eric Garner, Mike Brown, Tamir Rice, Philando Castile, and Freddie Gray. I'm always a bit surprised when one or two people don't recognize even those first few names, but fewer than a handful have taken their seats by the time I lift up Freddie Gray. The vast majority of people recognize these men and know the common risks that link their fates: they are Black and did not survive an encounter with the police. I pause for a moment and ask the audience to look around. The room is quiet and still. People take in what they have demonstrated: group literacy about the vulnerability of Black people to police violence. At the moment, it seems a completely obvious reading of social knowledge that is minimally necessary to ground any conceivable collective action. I continue. I say "Michelle Cusseaux." And then comes that *whoosh* of dozens, sometimes hundreds, and sometimes thousands, of people taking their seats. It is the sound of silence.

The sounds of people taking their seats mount as I continue the roll call: "Tanisha Anderson, Aiyana Stanley-Jones, Kayla Moore, India Kager, Shelly Frey, Korryn Gaines." One person is left standing after India Kager, but I continue anyway so people can hear more names. At last, I release that last person from any obligation to speak. I remind everyone that I'm a law professor after all, but I only say that the last person standing will tell us something about the name that they recognize to ensure everyone's honesty throughout the exercise. There are nervous titters as the last person takes their seat. This moment releases some of the tension in the room. Yet the point still hangs over us. The silence about Black women who have been killed by the police has distorted our collective capacity to respond. We cannot address a problem we cannot name. And we cannot name it if the stories of these women are not heard.

The African American Policy Forum's (AAPF) #SayHerName campaign began in earnest against the background of this profoundly disturbing reality: the deaths of Black women who were killed by the police barely registered a blip in the national news. Fran and so many others were grieving and protesting the loss of their loved ones all too often without the support and recognition of their communities, the media, and sometimes even their own families. Something had to change. AAPF had been founded to elevate the gendered dimensions of racist oppression in order to ground a more fully inclusive commitment to racial justice.

A critical precursor in the establishment of #SayHerName was AAPF's Breaking the Silence town hall series.

Beginning in 2014 in Atlanta, AAPF traveled to fourteen cities to partner with organizers, advocates, and elected representatives to hold public hearings on the status of women and girls of color. In providing community platforms for Black women and girls to testify about their experiences and vulnerabilities, state violence emerged as a tragically under-addressed issue. For the first time in many of these cities, community members, families, activists, and thought leaders learned from women and girls firsthand about the discrimination, subordination, and violence they had experienced. Yet these conditions were escaping public attention. As we had already learned in our attempts to broaden the prevailing frameworks surrounding the school-to-prison pipeline, if the conditions don't fit the prevailing frames of reference, it is extremely difficult to draw attention to an unfolding crisis. We published our study *Black Girls Matter: Pushed Out, Overpoliced, and Underprotected* to raise awareness of an under-addressed dimension of zero-tolerance policies in public schools. Our data showed shockingly high levels of disparity between Black girls and white girls when it came to suspensions, expulsions, and other disciplinary events. In fact, the disparity between Black girls and white girls was greater than the disparity between Black boys and white boys, but very little of the discourse about how these policies endangered the future of Black youth specifically addressed girls.

Telling these truths was the foundational objective of the town halls, but they became more salient in the face of My Brother's Keeper, a presidential initiative on Black youth in crisis that excluded girls altogether. Building on the obvious fact that Black boys faced a range of obstacles that undermined their well-being, the program did not infer the same issues for girls. The silence about Black girls' vulnerability to punishment, violence, and involvement in the criminal justice system became foundational to the misinformed belief that Black girls were not also suffering and could afford to wait until a later date for empathetic interventions. The town halls became a perfect vehicle for Why We Can't Wait, a coalition of feminists of color across gender that sought to paint a more robust picture of how male-centric anti-racism was insufficient to meet the crisis facing our youth. Thousands of people flocked to these hearings both to testify and/or listen to the many dimensions of disempowerment that escaped the attention it deserved. And in that context, several participants spoke about system involvement, dehumanizing conditions of confinement, overreliance on policing strategies in response to social problems, and finally the vulnerability of women and girls of color to draconian policing practices, largely justified as essential to the war on drugs.

Survivors of police violence and family members of victims raised names of Black women killed by police. Rekia Boyd, for example, was killed by an off-duty cop who never served a day in

prison for firing into a crowd of young Black people in Chicago. Her brother, Martinez Sutton, gave gut-wrenching testimony about how the Chicago police disregarded Rekia's life, leaving an audience of hundreds stunned and bereft. On the precipice of the Black Lives Matter protests, the vulnerability of Black women to police violence had found expression within Breaking the Silence and Why We Can't Wait, leaving those who were involved primed to lift up women and girls as the movement against anti-Black police violence unfolded. The more town hall participants discussed underreported and underanalyzed state violence against Black women, the more visible the intersectional picture of state violence against Black women became. By functioning as a consciousness-raising space in which to foreground the unheard stories of Black women's exposure to state violence, the town halls had the potential to generate public attention, motivate political resistance, and effectuate social change. In addition to being compelling in their own right, the stories spotlighted during the town halls revealed that, far from being isolated acts by "bad apple" cops, state violence was part of a broader intersectional story of racial patriarchy working itself out on the bodies of Black women.

From the outset, the #SayHerName campaign has sought not only to recognize and memorialize the deaths of Black women killed by the police but also to confront, contest, and dismantle the interlocking systems of state power that continue to routinize and normalize those killings. The deceptively simple imperative to "say her name" has been a critical component of that work that operates on different levels.

On one level, the directive to say her name is a plea for equality of attention to ensure that violence against Black women be treated with the same urgency and awareness as violence against their brothers. But even the simple act of name-saying raised a host of challenges involving the actual capacity to *do so*. So many names were unknown because of the same imbalanced dynamics of gender recognition that called the #SayHerName project into being in the first place.

By uncovering these neglected stories and giving them names, faces, and personal histories, we sought to reverse this long-standing pattern of malign neglect in real time—to restore these overlooked victims of state violence to a position of honor and equity in spaces where lost lives are being protested. That seemingly straightforward imperative required more than a demand. We needed to explain just why and how Black women victims of state violence had, for generations, not played a significant role in the narrative of the lethal policing of the Black community. That realization opened onto another one: We had no readily familiar ways of imagining the risks associated with Black women's encounters with police.

The public records—media accounts, court documents, public hearings, discourses in public spheres—contained precious few accounts of the risks of violence and death faced by girls sleeping on their grandmothers' couches, femmes in the throes of a mental health crisis, or a great-grandmother defending herself in a botched drug raid. Stories that begin with a 911 call for help and end in the stolen lives of mothers, daughters, grandmothers, and sisters don't fit the available narrative frames for recognizing police violence.

The absence of public recognition of the foregoing acts of violence created a political organizing problem. When the templates of racial justice struggles don't fit the facts, it can be difficult to understand, interpret, or even remember the stories. In order to show up for women like Tanisha Anderson, Kayla Moore, and so many others, we had to develop and advance a counternarrative to explain how they had become forgotten in the first place and then train ourselves and our audience to see and remember the patterns of police encounters that led to these deaths.

AAPF's first report on our campaign, *Say Her Name: Resisting Police Brutality Against Black Women*, memorialized the names of Black women and girls killed by the police and elevated recognizable narratives. The report was launched in May 2015 in advance of a day of action organized by Black feminist and queer activists across the nation.[1]

After the #SayHerName vigil in New York's Union Square, AAPF launched the Mothers Network, a group of Black women who had survived the killing of their daughters and sisters. Building on connections and strengths that families found in their shared experiences, we made a dedicated effort to provide healing spaces for survivors and to elevate their demands for justice.

Since then, this Mothers Network has come together for critical focus groups and planning sessions. Those gatherings have facilitated the activism that survivors have pursued in honor of their loved ones, including lobbying for police reform both on Capitol Hill and at the local level, and assessing ways to offer support to new members of the sisterhood of women who've lost mothers, sisters, and daughters to police violence. As both a network of relatives and a public awareness campaign, #SayHerName has supported mothers and their allies in hosting teach-ins, vigils, and protests. Since 2014, the #SayHerName Mothers Network has gathered annually for support, solace, relaxation, and agenda setting. Together, we have curated rituals of remembrance to honor the lives that should have been and our determination to change the conditions surrounding their deaths.

Neither grieving nor remembrance are straightforward propositions in the #SayHerName community. The devastating trauma of Black women's stolen lives has garnered so little public acknowledgment and attention that the hard work of mourning is often deprived of any healing ritual. As we listened more deeply to the social and psychological dimensions of losing women to police violence, we began to understand how being unaware that Black women, too, are killed by the police might generate a sense

of shame around the killings of their loved ones. When the prevailing discourse fails to acknowledge that police murder happens to women, their survivors can fall prey to a lurking anxiety that the victims themselves must somehow be to blame for their exceptionally terrible fates. If anti-Black police violence is conceptualized as an exclusively male phenomenon, then what is left to infer about the Black woman who is killed?

Even if a surviving mother doesn't harbor such thoughts, she may grapple with the thought that *others* might. Too often survivors recounted how the media, investigators, and even loved ones question how a Black woman "got herself killed." Consequently, a critical part of the work at #SayHerName is to give isolated and grieving survivors a desperately needed reality check. Through one another's experiences, mothers affirm that their daughters did not bring their deaths upon themselves. Sisters have been able to remember their siblings not as agents in their own deaths but as people who were killed simply because of who they were,

where they were, or who they happened to be with. Collectively bearing witness to one another, they—and we—create and sustain an awareness that we need not succumb to a raced and gendered blame game, nor need we carry memory and trauma in isolation. We are not alone.

In saying their names, we break this silence. We not only challenge the taboo surrounding the public recognition of police murders of Black women but also counter the violence done by the lies, fabrications, and racist and misogynist representations of Black women spread by the police and the mainstream media. In this sense, #SayHerName functions as a critical site of historical recovery in the face of myth and a trenchant disregard of the truth.

The family testimonies of the mothers and sisters lend vital context and background to the many disturbing images readily viewable on the internet. In the decontextualized settings of YouTube or Instagram, this cruel footage—images of Black girls thrown across a classroom floor or pinned to the ground; a mentally disabled woman beaten in the face with closed fists; a woman hog-tied and dragged out of a police car; an elderly and disabled grandmother paraded nude inside a police precinct—elicits raw shock on its own.

The testimony of #SayHerName fleshes out these stark, enraging montages with the stories of the Black women and girls victimized by state violence every day in our country. This recovered history destabilizes and decenters myths about Black women that have been cynically fabricated and leveraged to justify violence against them. Genuinely *seeing* Black women and girls disarms the hateful images of them in white supremacist propaganda—as either female versions of the fabled "superpredator," wielding superhuman and alarmingly threatening physical powers or as scheming, dependent "welfare queens," per the racist coinage of Ronald Reagan.

Once these stereotyped and caricatured depictions of Black women and girls are deprived of their power, we can see the images anew in their full, tragic proportions. Look once more at those social media videos, and pay attention to the real stories they tell. Girls as young as seven and women as old as ninety-three have been killed by police. They have been slain in their living rooms and on the streets, in their cars and in their bedrooms, in front of their children and in front of their parents. They have been killed when they or their family members have sought help, they have been killed when men they were with were targeted, and they have been killed when they were alone. They have been killed driving while Black, shopping while Black, being homeless while Black, having a mental disability while Black, or having a domestic dispute while Black. They have been killed while using a cell phone, turning into the National Security Agency (NSA) parking lot, or driving near the White House with an infant strapped in the back seat. They have been killed for being lesbians who "look like men" or for having romantic relationships with men who have been criminalized. The same set of factors, including non-normative gender identities, that make certain bodies vulnerable to a range of exclusions and violence in wider society put Black women at heightened risk of state violence. Their shared Black identity conveys one very distinct and pressing perception of threat to armed police officers, one that tends either to crowd out or lethally reinforce. In that regard, it bears emphasizing that the relative status of this group of victims as women and girls does virtually nothing to counter the excuses police give for the use of deadly force against them.

Police have described Black women as possessing an extraordinary strength, as utterly tireless, or as wordlessly posing a mortal threat to officers by the simple look of their faces. No matter their actual physical or mental condition, their age or circumstances, these women were never seen as anything close to what their white counterparts might be taken for: as damsels in distress; women in crisis; or frightened, confused, and endangered fellow human beings.

This vulnerability to police violence is an experience girls and women killed by police share with Black men. What they do *not* share in common with their fallen brothers is the same public attention, communal outcry, or political response. This is not to say that Black men have received too much attention. They have not. It is to say that while Black male encounters with state violence have served as a battle cry for contesting police power, Black female encounters—with few exceptions—have not. The erasure of Black women regardless of the circumstances speaks to the consequences of the deaths occurring outside of the readily available narrative of anti-Black police violence. There were no mass demonstrations over the 2015 death of Natasha McKenna while in custody in Fairfax, Virginia, even though her killing at the hands of six officers who swarmed, shackled, hooded, and tasered her four times was filmed and released to the public. This absence supposedly affirmed the claim that the officers had operated in an entirely professional manner. We have seen no sustained advocacy for Mya Hall, a Black transgender woman who was killed by the NSA in Baltimore just days before the killing of Freddie Gray. Nor was there public attention for Tanisha Anderson, who was killed by the same police force that took Tamir Rice's life just nine days later. The #SayHerName campaign was launched to fill in the blanks about police violence against Black women as a necessary step in changing the reality of police violence against Black women. In order to do so, this book describes how the campaign centers their survivors.

#SAYHERNAME
AFRICAN AMERICAN POLICY FORUM

Shelly Frey

Chapter 1

Breaking Silence

**"When is she coming?
When is she gonna call?"**
Sharon Wilkerson, mother of Shelly Frey
(April 21, 1985–December 6, 2012)

My name is Sharon Wilkerson. I'm from New Orleans, Louisiana. My daughter Shelly was twenty-seven when she was murdered in Houston, Texas.

Shelly was my firstborn. Everyone loved Shelly, she was such a loving person. You didn't see her upset because she was always smiling. She was a very happy kid. Even when she became a young woman, she still had that same sweet spirit.

She had two daughters, Chassidy and Cherish. She loved taking care of them. The baby girl, Cherish, had sickle cell, so Shelly stayed at home to take care of her. Her kids were her life. She was always focused on what she needed to do to make things better for her girls, because they were her world. So now I pick up the pieces, and now they're my world.

One thing she did love—she loved to sing. She also enjoyed cooking, and she loved doing hair and makeup. She wanted to finish beauty school and open up her own business. She loved to talk. I think she gets that from me because I love to talk. But she loves to talk, and she loves putting a smile on her client's face. Excuse me. She loved putting a smile on her client's face. If she could help somebody, she would do it. She loved making other people beautiful and making them feel good about themselves. Women having low self-esteem, men telling them "you ain't nothing." She wanted to show women that they were beautiful, that they were going to be somebody. Her dream was to help others.

She was the life of the party—always happy, always cracking jokes. Everybody used to call her Big Bertha, and we knew that if Big Bertha was coming, we was going to have a good time.

When her grandmother passed right before [Hurricane] Katrina, it was hard. She was the first grandkid, so it kind of took a toll on her. Then her grandfather passed. Had Katrina not happened, she would've stayed in New Orleans. Whenever she would come home to visit, she always wanted something with rice and gravy. She loved gravy, and now the girls love gravy. I grew up on that, I don't want any more gravy. But the grandkids love rice and gravy. I said, "Y'all get that from your mom because that's how she was." Everybody knew if Shelly was coming to town, she wants something with rice and gravy, and that's what we would fix her. They're the same way. I'm like, "I don't want that." "Well, we want that." "Okay, that's fine. If I fix it, you're going to eat it." And they would eat it. Big appetite, just like their mom had.

She was concerned about my illness, so we would talk every day all day. She would always call and want to know if I took my medicine that morning. "Mom, you don't sound so good, you sure you're okay?" She would keep me up on how the baby was doing, the one that had sickle cell disease. We talked every day, four or five times a day. Because she was in Houston, and I was in New Orleans, a six-hour drive. I'd say, "Don't you come down here." "Well, I have to come see for myself, because I don't believe you're doing fine." Sometimes she'd call me and she would be right outside. I'd say, "Don't you drive down here," and then I'd hear somebody open the door. "I told you I was coming to check on you," she'd say.

Shelly was a giver. She would give everything away. She would take her shirt off her back and give it to somebody I didn't even know. She gave it away till we had to go somewhere:

"Shelly, where's your jacket?"

"Oh, so-and-so have it."

"Why?"

"Well, she asked to wear it."

I said, "But you didn't ask me, did you?"

So that's the type of person she was. And even when she was murdered, she was the same way, and she trusted everybody. She trusted everybody. I would always tell her that a mother can tell whether their friends are sincere with them. And I would tell her, I said, "They not your friends." I even said that about her sister-in-law. "They're not your friends because when you were shot, this young lady pulled in front of the door and left you in the car." And did not call 911 to come and get her. So she died in front of her sister-in-law's house.

I talked to her in the morning the day she was murdered. She called me and said, "Mom, guess what?"

"What?"

She said, "I'm moving back home."

"You're coming home to stay?"

"Yeah, I'm coming home."

I was so excited, telling everybody that my grandkids was coming back home.

I was supposed to call her back later, but I ended up getting busy, and I didn't get to talk to her again that day. Then at around 11:00 or 11:30 at night, I got a phone call: "Your daughter was murdered."

And I was like, "But she said she was coming home." I couldn't understand that and was like, "You sure?"

"Yes. Shelly was just murdered."

I said, "You sure it was her?"

"Yeah, we sure it's her. I think you should come—your grand-kids is crying for you."

My other daughter had just come home from college, and she was the one that drove us to Houston. And I kept saying, "This can't be right." And my life hasn't been the same since.

It turns out that Shelly was in Walmart with both of her sisters-in-law. This off-duty police officer was doing a detail at Walmart, and someone went up to the security guard or the police officer and told him that they believed the three young ladies were stealing. So on their way out, he tried to stop them. As he tried to stop them, one of the young ladies hit him with her purse. After she hit him, she ran, so then he ran behind her. By that time, my daughter was in the passenger seat, the other young lady and her two kids was in the back seat. The lady that hit him ran into the driver's seat, and as she did, he jumped in between the door and the car.

He then shot into the car—not once, but twice. They was saying that the police officer only shot once, but the autopsy showed he had shot twice. The kids was all hysterical, screaming, asking him not to shoot, but he did anyway. He said he was fearing for his life, so that's why he had to shoot. You couldn't get the license plate number? You couldn't just shoot out a tire? You had to shoot in the car? Was it that serious? He's saying he had to take off the security guard hat and put the police hat on. They didn't have a weapon, they didn't have anything, so why would you even do that? You're going off hearsay. He didn't have any proof.

The young lady who was driving drove to her house, and went upstairs saying that she couldn't go to jail. So she drove home. At that time, my daughter was in the passenger seat fighting for her life, asking her, "Can you just bring me to the hospital?" And she wouldn't.

One of the witnesses said: "Your daughter lived for a while. By the time the paramedics got there, they said she was fine. They left. Then she sat in the car for eight hours."

The auntie that had my grandbabies brought them to the scene, so that messed up the oldest one, to see her mom sitting in the car and sitting for so long her body started swelling. She witnessed all that. Her mom was a tall slim person and by her sitting in the car, her body swelled. So they had a private investigator question a seven-year-old . . . seven years old. I guess he was thinking maybe she was one of the kids that was in the car. We still don't know why he did that, why he questioned her. Still no answers today.

That was a hard car ride. That was hard. My middle girl was eight months pregnant, she took that ride with us. And then to get there and nobody have any answers for you . . . nobody wants to talk to you. The police officers don't want to talk to you. You got private investigators parked outside watching the house—and when you go to the car and ask them what they want, they pull off. Nobody really wants to tell you what was going on. You go to the police station, nobody wants to talk about it. Then I find out they're questioning my seven-year-old granddaughter. She don't know what's going on.

All she knows is that her mom's dead in the car. Dead. My grandbaby was just traumatized. The two-year-old, she didn't know what was going on at the time. But the seven-year-old, she knew.

So it's like these officers and them didn't care. They didn't care. Then you watch it on the news, and they got all these lies coming across the screen. It was horrible. So we really didn't know what was true and what wasn't true.

When I was going through that, I was angry. I was bitter. I just needed someone to talk to. I needed someone who had been through what I've been through, so they could share with me how they made it through. What did they do? I was so angry. I was even angry at God, because I felt like, "God, why did you have to take her from me? It wasn't her time." I didn't understand it, and so I was bitter. I was angry, and it was just so much. It was stuff I didn't understand. There's a lot of stuff today I still don't understand.

I'm seeing a psychiatrist because three months after my dad died, my husband left. He wasn't her dad. He said he couldn't handle me being depressed. I thought I would lose my mind with all of that back to back. I was a daddy's girl so that was another part of me that left. I really needed my dad and husband at that time, I was left with the two grandbabies. They still ask for him.

Shelly's oldest daughter picked up her hobby of doing hair and makeup. The nine year old, she makes up a lot of songs. So she just walks around our house just singing, and these were things their mom did. Each one of them have something of her. I see so much of her through them, and I know I have to be strong for them. They depend on me. All they have is me, so I have to do what I have to do for them. So I try to be strong for them, I don't let them really see me break down. They always on me, "No more sugar. Did you take your medication?" I don't want them to have to worry about that.

The oldest one is being bullied now. I'm trying to teach her to be the bigger person and just walk out, walk away, but it's easier said than done. . . The kids are talking about her mom, her mom this, her mom that. And I tell her, "They don't even know your mom. So whatever they say don't matter. It don't matter. You don't have to fight back because, in the end, this is going to follow you."

I try to stay active now because before I used to just sit in the house and cry. Now I'm very seldom in the house, I'm always doing something. I used to wear dark clothes, I was depressed. I quit doing my hair. I didn't do make up. I wouldn't put clothes on. And I was like, "I have to get out of this because these little girls need me." And if I leave, who is going to take them? And you know what, that used to be their question, "Momma if something happens to you, where are we going?" That made me get out of bed.

Shelly died in 2012, and I got the call from #SayHerName in 2014, so that was two years I didn't have no support. I've met so many women through #SayHerName that have lost daughters who've left grandkids behind.

That's the hardest part of it. What do you tell these kids when they're too young to understand? The two-year-old would say, "When is Momma coming to get us?" We're all waiting on her to come through the door, but she's never coming through the door.

I still feel like I'm babysitting sometimes. I sit there, and it's like, "Okay, when is she coming? When is she gonna call?"

Our daughters were taken from us. Our whole world changed. They weren't just murdered, they were taken, and we can't get them back. They can't come back. You did more than just murder her—you took a part of us, someone we birthed, we carried for nine months. You just came and snatched it away from us like nothing.

What I'll never understand is why he had a gun in the first place. I doubt they have armed security guards in Bloomingdales. What was so serious about the situation that he had to shoot? What was so urgent? It's not like they had stolen the Mona Lisa or something. It wasn't that serious.

They get into the car, where their two young children are waiting for them. As they start to drive off, an armed security guard shoots twice into the front window, striking Shelly in the neck. Hours later, she's pronounced dead.

I've wondered about the guard dog who killed Shelly. Walmart lapdog is more accurate. Louis Campbell—Reverend Louis Campbell he turned out to be. Found out he has a church in Houston. A killer and a minister.

I wonder, Reverend Campbell, what scripture you will quote when you meet your maker. How you will explain to God that when he told you to feed and care for our children, you chose to kill them instead, with a Bible in one hand and gun in another. Oh I pray that I don't have to wait that long to see you pay. Oh yes, each day I pray on it. But if I do have to wait to see it, Lord knows I want a front row seat on that judgment day just to see Shelly open up that gate and kick your sorry ass right into hell. For killing Shelly AND for not having one ounce of compassion for any of us left behind.

Sharon Wilkerson

Since 2015, African American Policy Fourm (AAPF) audiences—civil rights groups, women's rights organizations, professors, students, psychologists, sociologists, social justice activists, and even progressive members of Congress—have remained *unable* to continue to stand for Black women killed by police because they did not know their names. They are not alone.

AAPF's #SayHerName campaign took shape in what was effectively the first demonstration of the sounds of silence; a real-time lesson sprung in the midst of the Eric Garner protests in December 2014. Tens of thousands of protesters took to the street in New York in the aftermath of the non-indictment of Daniel Pantaleo, the New York City police officer who was filmed choking Garner, an unarmed Black man, to death while ignoring his pleas that he couldn't breathe.

We were heartbroken and outraged by the flood of police killings of Black people in the preceding months. And we were demoralized to hear the age-old justifications presuming to explain why, in virtually every instance, the taking of those lives was judged to be legally and morally legitimate. Like others, we were driven to the streets in disgust at the stolen lives of not only

Eric Garner but also of Tamir Rice and Mike Brown. We lifted up their names, and the names of others before them, in our chants and demands. The cacophonous march intended to ensure that everyone would know their names, that their lives mattered, and that the failure to achieve even basic accountability for their killings was utterly unacceptable.

But in stark contrast with those with whom we stood shoulder to shoulder, we were also compelled to lift up other names—those of Michelle Cusseaux, who, as you might remember from the introduction, was killed five days after Michael Brown; Tanisha Anderson killed ten days before twelve-year-old Tamir Rice; Aiyana Stanley-Jones, a seven-year-old child who was killed in a botched raid by the Detroit police in 2010; and Shelly Frey, whose story opens this chapter.

As we marched, we chanted their names and many others, interchanging the names of those everybody knew with those only few of us did. The silence that met our efforts to include

the names of women and girls sharply underlined the need to #SayHerName—an imperative that prompted us to step outside the crowd and climb a scaffold, banner in hand. From there, as marchers passed, we demanded our collaborators in struggle see these sisters, that they register their loss, and that they bear witness to each woman's tragic absence by saying her name.

The struggle to know their names cannot just be attributed to simple disinterest in or hostility toward Black women per se, but it is a reflection of a long-standing failure within anti-racist politics to grasp that Black women, like Black men, are subjects of anti-Black state violence.

The dynamics that relegate to obscurity the lives of Black women killed by the state are products of the intersectional failures that breed debilitating silences, and blind spots, in our

efforts to confront lethal state violence. They stem from an anemic understanding of how oppression based on gender and sexuality combines with oppression based on race to create different modes of discrimination against Black communities. This is not to say that the prevailing politics that shape how police violence is understood are non-intersectional. Quite the contrary: anti-Black violence that is both state sanctioned and extrajudicial, ranging from police killings to private vigilantism, has long been understood through an implicitly intersectional lens that attends to the ways that Black masculinity has been viewed as inherently threatening to the racial order. The problem is that this intersectional prism is insufficiently attentive to gendered dimensions of vulnerability apart from the experiences of men and boys. The result has been a persistent cycle of compounded loss that prevents us from properly elevating Black women killed by the state because their lives and deaths are classified outside the dominant model of lethal policing. That misclassification means the loss does not galvanize communities, elected officials, policy makers, and media to respond. There can be no demands for accountability for lost lives if the fact of that loss is itself hidden.

As a countermeasure, #SayHerName has created channels of ritual, research, and remembrance that aim to recover the stories of Black women's experiences of racist police violence and to address the multiple forces that enable that violence and the various silences that follow it.

#SayHerName takes its charge from Black feminists across generations who confronted a long history of public and private violence—including sexual and reproductive violence—that dates back to Black women's arrival on these shores. Like their male kinfolk, Black women across the generations have faced the constant threat of legally sanctioned racial violence, but in addition they have borne the consequences of their particular vulnerabilities being displaced or denied within solidarity politics and popular representation. Both of these persistent, first-order obstacles are structural and representational features of their intersectional vulnerability.

The media's prevailing story lines in reports of anti-Black police violence reinscribe that vulnerability by underreporting accounts of police violence that involve Black women. All too often, this erasure of Black women carries over into the conventional conduct of feminist and anti-racist politics.

This constellation of practices that exiles or omits the vulnerabilities and losses of Black women cannot merely be reformed or wished away. It too is grounded in a historical pattern of willful forgetting of, and inattentiveness to, particular features of anti-Black racism that consistently elide and downplay the experiences of Black women. This pattern is deep-seated and stretches across institutions, representational politics, and coalitional strategizing. The overlapping vulnerabilities and precarities facing Black women implicate not only state power but also the internal politics of the multiple groups in which they are situated. For that reason, #SayHerName draws upon a multiplicity of voices to pay genuine attention to the lethal policing of Black women and girls and to demand its end.

It is worth mentioning that it is precisely because of the fact that the killing of Black women does not provoke the kind of news coverage and political responses that could catalyze a justice movement to confront and remedy the precarity of Black women's lives that the heightened public attention that greeted the deaths of Breonna Taylor and Sandra Bland didn't materialize into a broader contestation of state violence against Black women. Their fatal encounters with the police were treated as exceptional.

But the hard truth of the matter is that Taylor's and Bland's deaths were not at all unusual. Consider, for example, the familiar frame of "driving while Black." That frame is intended to capture the risks that Black Americans face in a regime that permits police to surveil Black people on the flimsiest of pretexts. Driving while Black, as a subset of all potentially lethal police encounters, shows how even casual encounters produce a disproportionate risk of fatal outcomes for Black citizens. The point to emphasize here is that Black women are not exempt from this risk. In addition to Sandra Bland, there is a long list of other Black women who have experienced traffic encounters as sites of state violence that too many did not survive: Alexia Christian (2015), Mya Hall (2015), Gabriella Nevarez (2014), Miriam Carey (2013), Shantel Davis (2012), Malissa Williams (2012), Sharmel Edwards (2012), Kendra James (2003), and LaTanya Haggerty (1999). If near-total police impunity for the use of deadly force, even in the context of traffic stops, did not exist, these women, like their male counterparts, would still be alive today.

And therein lie three critical insights. The first is that, because of stereotypes of African Americans as dangerous and criminal, Black people as a group are more susceptible to surveillance and disciplinary interactions with the police than any other demographic.[1] The second is that among women as a group, Black women, because of those very same stereotypes, are more likely than other women to be surveilled and to come in contact with police. The third is that specifically racialized forms of misogyny contribute to the way Black women are treated during these encounters. These three insights help to explain Sandra Bland's violent traffic stop. In that encounter, Bland did nothing more than question why she was required to put out her cigarette in her own car. In fact, she was not required to do so. Yet her assertion of her right resulted in the officer dragging her out of her car, shouting "I will light you, light you up" while he did so.

Bland's encounter embodied the lethal dimensions of intersectional vulnerability. There is every reason to believe that the violence the officer mobilized against Bland and her subsequent arrest were the products of both racist stereotypes of Black people as lawbreakers and gendered stereotypes of Black women as unruly. Both race and gender hierarchies are enforced by disciplinary practices that subject those perceived to be in need of discipline to enhanced surveillance, social control, and violence. Sandra Bland experienced each of these dimensions as a Black woman, and, in that regard, Bland's traffic stop encounter is a powerful reminder that the greater Black people's exposure to police interactions under conditions of anti-Black racism, the greater their exposure to the possibility of violence. As legal scholar Devon W. Carbado explains, "If the police have fewer opportunities to stop and question Black people, they have fewer opportunities to kill us."[2] Gender does not exempt Black women from this risk; it shapes its contours. That is why it is important to pay attention to *all* the ways in which Black women are exposed to police contact, because those contact moments place Black women on a trajectory toward premature death.

But part of the difficulty Black women confront is that their enhanced exposure to policing is often obscured by the fact, in general, that men are more likely to encounter police than women, and Black men are the demographic most likely to experience lethal force. Naming this problem is not to say that we should drop the project of contesting Black male exposure to state violence. As I have stated before and want to stress again, the prevalence of police violence against Black men remains a crisis that demands outrage and critical intellectual work to highlight their particular susceptibility—across gender identity, sexual orientation, class, and other axes of difference—to state violence.[3] That, in turn, means that the killing of Black men *is* also an intersectional issue. Yet we do not often see that Blackness is an exacerbating risk factor for women as well as men. Part of the aim of the #SayHerName project is to get us to do precisely that.

To the extent that we take the racial dimensions of Black women's intersectional vulnerability seriously, we are much more likely to place Black women's experiences with state violence on our anti-racist agendas. Doing so would help us see that because of the intersection of legally sanctioned state violence and anti-Blackness, Black women, and not just men, have found themselves in the necrological position of desperately gasping for air:

I can't breathe. These were George Floyd's last words.
I can't breathe. These were Eric Garner's last words.
I can't breathe. These were Kayla Moore's last words.
I can't breathe. These were Barbara Dawson's last words[4]

The foregoing reality is just one of reasons Black women's names should be in the roll call of lost Black lives, and one of the reasons why Black women's experiences more generally should shape the content and trajectory of anti-racist thinking, practices, and interventions.

Contestations over police violence are not the only domain in which Black women struggle for visibility and recognition. The marginalization of Black women's experiences extends to the wider dynamics of criminalization and punishment in the American justice system. For too long, critics of the carceral state have overlooked the disproportionate vulnerability of Black women and girls relative to other women. For example, in research data and policy making that set out to document disproportionate vulnerability to policing, Black women are often airbrushed out of the picture. In the news media, stories about the racial impact of the war on drugs, the criminalization of poverty, and the school-to-prison pipeline frequently lack Black women.

Some justify the elision of Black women in discourses about carcerality by arguing that things are far worse for Black men. There are a number of ways in which one might counter that understanding, including the fact that it is important to compare the carceral vulnerability of Black women to the carceral

Photo by Paul Becker

vulnerability of other women (rather than comparing Black women to Black men). While it is true that in all racial groups in the United States men are killed in higher numbers by the police than women, Black women stand out as the women who are particularly vulnerable to police violence. Black women make up just over 10 percent of the female population in the US, yet they account for one-fifth of all women killed by the police and almost *one-third of unarmed women killed by the police.*[5] In fact, Black women are the only race-gender group to have a majority of its members killed while unarmed. Nationwide data from the Fatal Interactions with Police Study (FIPS) research project published in 2018 indicated that from May 1, 2013, to January 1, 2015, 57 percent of Black women were unarmed when killed. Odis Johnson, lead researcher for the project, summed it up this way: "Our analysis finds that the 'hands up, don't shoot' slogan of the post-Ferguson movement becomes most relevant when you also 'say her name.'"[6]

Our analysis finds that the "hands up, don't shoot" slogan of the post-Ferguson movement becomes most relevant when you also "say her name."

The collective disregard of Black women's experiences is a vicious cycle that leads too many to assume that women and girls are not at risk. Ordinary activities that heighten their exposure to police encounters place Black women at risk in ways that echo the vulnerability of Black men. The war on drugs, which justifies heightened surveillance of Black people both in public and in private, has similarly placed Black women at risk—a situation exacerbated by class inequality and segregation. In the crucible of these intersecting susceptibilities, gender does not inoculate women from the rapid escalation of violence—likely fueled by race-based fear—that culminates in lost lives.

By contrast, the familiar narratives about anti-Blackness in relation to police violence foreground how perceptions of Black masculinity may be an exceptional triggering factor in the escalation of police violence. The assumption that many police officers are threatened emotionally by Black masculinity may lead some observers to infer that the *less-threatening* characteristics typically associated with femaleness will help forestall any such escalating effect. Yet the patterns of police violence suggest that none of the assumptions that might otherwise militate against the lethal use of force seem to override the fears associated with Blackness. Certainly being a woman doesn't insulate Black women from punitive policing; otherwise Bland would still be alive. Being elderly doesn't seem to give police officers pause. Although older women as a group are rarely seen as presenting a grave threat to the security of police, Black women don't seem to be able to age out of the perception that they are threats, as the tragic deaths of ninety-two-year-old Kathryn Johnston and ninety-three-year-old Pearlie Golden remind us. Nor does being unhoused, middle-aged, and mentally incapacitated allow Black women to escaped these lethal, catch-all justifications for the use of deadly force, as the fatal shooting of fifty-five-year-old Margaret Laverne Mitchell—a petite widow who was shot in the back while pushing her shopping cart away from an officer in Venice Beach, California—shows.

And while the home is meant to be a sanctuary, it provides Black women no safety from state violence. If it did, Breonna Taylor's, Michelle Cusseaux's, Atatiana Jefferson's, and Kayla Moore's lives might have been spared.[7] Even when Black women seek 911 emergency services for circumstances that fall far outside the bounds of hazard-driven "law enforcement," they have found themselves immediately treated as the objects of lethal force—as the families of Anderson and Jefferson remember. This is the case for domestic life writ large for Black Americans; the ease with which the police can engage Black people in their homes suggests that a Black person's home is not their castle, to borrow the phrasing of Oliver Wendell Holmes's landmark opinion on privacy.[8] Court transcripts from inquiries into lethal police invasions of Black homes typically resolve on the shooting officer's casual claim that "I feared for my life"—a tacit acknowledgement from our legal system that Black homes are viewed as looming threats to civic order rather than as sanctuaries of domestic virtue.

In all these encounters, law enforcement officers have framed Black women in the same way they frame Black men: as dangerous, threatening, and posessing superhuman strength. These stereotypes drown out and override the asymmetries and terrors of women's encounters with police—circumstances that often render them vulnerable, confused, or frightened. Recall the haunting, terrified words of Natasha McKenna—naked, alone, and defenseless—whose last plea was to remind officers that they "promised not to kill" her. Watching the video of the nude and hooded young woman being strapped to a restraining chair and tasered multiple times was a clear sign of Black women's non-normativity. It's hard to imagine this level of profound inhumanity being deployed against any woman who was properly seen as a "damsel in distress."

Not even the trope of motherhood functions to protect Black women. Police officers with eager trigger fingers haven't cared if a Black woman is a mother and whether their violence against her places her children at risk. If they did, India Kager, Korryn Gaines, and Miriam Carey would still be with us.

Simply put, the "separate spheres" model of womanhood (the notion that women's exclusion from the public realm of paid work, politics, and economics is compensated by their central role as wives and mothers within the sanctified space of the home) does not countermand the use of lethal policing force against

Black women. The traditional idea that motherhood—based on an ideal of bourgeois white femininity—could insulate mothers in the company of young children from state-sanctioned violence has never been the case for Black mothers or their children. Black women's familial bonds seem largely irrelevant to the police who have taken their lives. Mothers like Tarika Wilson have been killed while tending to their infants. Daughters like Gaines and Anderson have been taken as police forced their mothers and siblings to stand down and helplessly watch. As Black motherhood is discounted, so is the sanctity of Black children's lives. In fact, the racially disproportionate use of lethal force is greater for children than it is for adults.[9] The safety of children—a supposedly universal value in policing and in war—is null and void in the racialized "war on drugs," as Aiyana Stanley-Jones's tragic death illustrates.

The point I am stressing about racialized gender violence is key to the #SayHerName campaign: Regimes of gender that might trigger protection for white women in the context of policing operate differently for too many Black women.

One of the reasons Black women and girls' vulnerability along the preceding lines escapes public attention relates to when and how we see gender at work. A persistent problem in anti-racist organizing, politics, and thinking is the internalization of narratives about anti-Black racism that are inflected with harmful assumptions about gender. At the root of this problem is the degree to which some stories—those principally involving male victimization—are treated as representative of the whole; while other stories involving nonmale gendered vulnerabilities become imbued with particulars that render them "not really" or "not only" about race. This male-centric way of thinking obscures the fact that, as noted above, discourses about Black men are every bit as gendered as discourses about Black women. Notwithstanding this reality, racism as framed through the prism of maleness has been taken to be archetypal both within and outside of Black discourse. The end result is that Black men are positioned as the typical subjects of anti-Black racism, a positioning that forwards the notion that Black women are the atypical subjects of such violence.

This typicality/atypicality dynamic is especially salient in how the particular precarity of Black maleness has historically served as a warning to the entire Black community that they are all vulnerable. The brute objective of Black subjugation has long been understood to be containing, disciplining, punishing, and annihilating Black masculinity, and so this gendered expression of anti-Black racism becomes a stand-in for Black people across gender.

The male-centric parameters of anti-racism are not the only conditions that contribute to the marginalization of Black women's narratives of police violence. When whiteness serves as the default baseline for some feminisms, the many ways that patriarchy plays out for Black women through white supremacy are also obscured. The topic of state violence, especially police violence against women, has not fully surfaced within mainstream feminist agendas partly because women as a group are less likely than men to be killed by police, and those women who *are* killed are disproportionately Black.[10] Typically, Black women's violent encounters with the state are at best marginalized and at worst overlooked as not a feminist concern.

Indeed, to the extent that the wider culture has developed a broad story line about women, violence, and policing, white women and girls occupy center stage. At the nexus of vulnerability and policing, Black women's disproportionate susceptibility to police violence falls far from view.

In fact, in matters of domestic partner and interpersonal violence, police are commonly faulted, at least implicitly, for their failure to protect vulnerable women, particularly when they're white. This is implicit in the mainstream movement against intimate partner violence. Even the growing awareness of the correlation between officers with records of interpersonal violence and the use of force hasn't been enough to bring police violence against Black women firmly onto the feminist agenda.[11] This isn't exactly surprising, given the way that the police and media are galvanized to report on and protect white women.

The late Gwen Ifill, a renowned Black woman journalist, coined the term "missing white woman syndrome" to denote the media obsession with the plight of white women and their parallel disregard for Black women and other women of color.[12] This term, which emphasizes the uneven attention paid to the disappearance or deaths of conventionally attractive, young, and often wealthy, white women also captures the orientation of the police. The culture-wide preoccupation with the well-being of white women works to marginalize women of color who are targets of violence, whether in private or public. Black women are rarely the subjects of an anguished search when they go missing; as a Black female former officer in Oakland, California, acknowledged, police work was never finished in cases involving missing white girls until the victim had been recovered; searches for Black girls were too often cut short and abandoned by the end of the work day.[13] As some of the mothers cited above have noted, even when their daughters were in distress, police did not treat them as "damsels in distress"; they treated them as threats to their own safety, as legitimate targets of violence. Moreover, Black women's deaths at the hands of police rarely prompt the sympathetic wall-to-wall media coverage that crime stories involving white women do.

In contrast, we saw the full application of the damsel-in-distress narrative in the case of the fatal police shooting of Justine

Ruszczyk Damond by now-former police officer Mohamed Noor in Minneapolis, Minnesota, in 2017. The media coverage not only strongly condemned the police killing of Damond (something they far too often fail to do when the victims are Black women); they also doted on sympathetic facts about her, a white Australian immigrant who taught yoga and meditation and was about to be married. Damond had called 911 to report a possible sexual assault and had rushed to the cruiser to meet police officers, which prompted both Noor and his partner to fear they were being ambushed.[14]

According to the testimony of Noor, a Black officer, he fired after noting his white partner's terrified expression. But the usual split-second justification of lethal force that police are routinely granted in cases involving victims of color did not prevail in Noor's defense. The unreasonableness of Noor's assessment appeared, at least to some, to rest on Damond's race and gender, an inference suggested by the prosecutor Amy Sweasy's incredulous interrogation of him on the witness stand: "Her whole blonde hair, pink T-shirt and all, that was all a threat to you?"[15]

The resulting outrage about Damond's killing—locally, nationally, and abroad—not only resulted in a rare murder conviction of an officer for a killing in the line of duty but also led to the swift resignation of Police Chief Janee Harteau, who had weathered the storm after the 2015 police killing of Jamar Clark, a young Black man.[16] This almost unprecedented punishment of a police officer for a homicide committed while on duty—and the wider

demands for police accountability surrounding Damond's death—didn't translate to the scores of cases in which Black women and girls were killed by (usually white) police officers. The incredulity with which so many observers received Noor's claim that Damond could possibly be read as a threat to him and his partner did not extend to Black women who were killed inside their homes, including those whose stories are told in this book.

The media frenzy in response to Damond's death lies at the other end of the ongoing media silence surrounding Black women's deaths at the hands of police. Even in the post–Breonna Taylor era of heightened public attention to police violence, media outlets continue to downplay stories about police violence against Black women and girls.[17]

This extreme case of lethal policing marks just one of the ways that our culture routinely discounts Black women and girls. Rekia Boyd, a twenty-two-year-old Black woman who was shot and killed in 2012, was not accorded sympathy similar to that of white women by the jury that acquitted her killer, an off-duty cop who fired through his window directly into a crowd of young Black people. Although Boyd, like Damond, was innocent of any wrongdoing, a jury accepted Dante Servin's claim that he reasonably feared for his life.

Martinez Sutton, Boyd's brother, notes the unequal distribution of compassion and accountability between white and Black women in his heartbreaking testimony at the Breaking the Silence town hall hearings in 2015:

> Down the road, a couple of months later, a white woman went to go buy drugs from the projects. She got thrown from a window. The state paid her an enormous amount of money, made sure she was taken care of. She's still

living to this day. A while later, a woman's dog got shot by the police. They immediately fired the police officer, compensated her, and said their apologies. Do you want to know what they said to me? Close your eyes and you'll see exactly what they said to me. Nothing.[18]

If movements to end police murders of Black people have too often failed to center gender, police killings of Black women have *also* been surprisingly muted on the rare occasions that anti-Black state violence has found its way to the center of women's organizing. Members of the #SayHerName Mothers Network encountered this marginalization of concern for Black women's death at the 2017 Women's March in Washington. The march brought people together from across the country to protest the election of a racist, sexist president and to broaden the mainstream understanding of women's rights to embrace an intersectional social justice agenda. March organizers had rightly incorporated the

many police killings of Black people that devastated marginalized communities as one of the issues on the Women's March agenda.

Still, three years after the 2014 Eric Garner vigil and protest, where the demand to #SayHerName emerged, the persistent silence around Black women's vulnerability to police violence created a disappointing moment. When the mothers of #SayHerName were informed that there would be a point in the march where the issue of police violence would take center stage, they rallied to join the march, enthusiastically and proudly marching in their daughters' memories. Their mood was hopeful and their spirits were buoyed in anticipation that, at long last, the world would hear their daughters' names. They spoke about what it would mean for their grief to be recognized and their lonely fight for justice to be acknowledged and uplifted. But the unity they sought was absent that day as they watched from the crowd while mothers of sons killed by police filled the stage. Their disappointment was immense. They did not begrudge any other mother who was invited to represent their loved one—they were all in a sisterhood of sorrow—but for them, the irony of their daughters' invisibility at a moment in which anti-Black police violence was being centered was just too much to bear. They asked to leave.

Vicky Coles-McAdory, one of the early members of the Mothers Network, led the other mothers in their decision to leave the march. Vicky, whose niece India Beatty was shot to death by police in Virginia in 2016, later recalled:

> We had been fighting all day to get to that stage to hear our babies' names being uplifted and remembered in front of hundreds of thousands of people who had maybe been lied to about their situations, who didn't understand their situations, who did not realize and

> understand that our babies were everything to us. They had families. They were mothers, they were sisters, they were nieces. They were partners. They were a part of families whose chains had been broken.
>
> So that left us to feel like our babies were sacrificed. We no longer live to make our babies understand the importance of being fair and being loving and being understanding and forgiving to others. Now our purpose is to bring attention to our children who are unlawfully murdered because people who were supposed to protect them didn't understand who they were and what they mean to so many others.

The mothers' expectations that a women's march would lift up their daughters as an expression of racial consciousness and sisterhood did not materialize. Determined to recover and regroup, they rededicated themselves to telling the world about the loved ones they'd lost. And we at the AAPF recommitted ourselves to supporting their efforts by having difficult conversations with allies and friends about how our movements sometimes unwittingly overlook Black women and girls and their survivors. The moment challenged allies to go beyond the idea that a gender-sensitive positioning of anti-Black police violence in the women's movement might sufficiently meet the mark by reconceptualizing the issue through mothers' right to the survival of their children. This, of course, is a wider understanding of anti-Black police violence through the prism of reproductive freedom: Black mothers should be free to have and raise their children free of the worry that they will be taken from them by wanton acts of state-sanctioned violence. The matter should have been center stage. Gender inclusivity should incorporate mothers' rights to their daughters and their daughters' right to the lives that should have been. This is a wider view of what a Black feminist encounter with anti-Black police violence could entail. The failures to broaden the conventional framing of police violence mean that even spaces organized by and for women continue to rehearse and recapitulate a narrow conception of how and why this violence operates. As a result, even the mothers bravely setting out to situate their daughters' murders as a women's issue became marginalized at the hands of their would-be allies.

As this striking example and others show, the invocation of "motherhood" has been a particularly salient theme in the symbolic and moral discourse against police violence. The frame is a powerful one, since it draws on our culture's widespread reverence for motherhood, while also reminding Americans that victims of police violence have been loved and mothered by someone. They are all someone's children. But invocations of motherhood are not equally poised across race, leaving the challenge in generating awareness and momentum around anti-Black racism unrealized within this maternalist frame. White supremacy, patriarchy, and misogynoir operate together in ways that diminish the power of maternal imagery for mothers of Black women, undermining sympathies and receptivity to #SayHerName. The Mothers Network does not readily fit the preconceived model of maternal grief in the face of the unimaginably painful loss of sons. The challenge here is not simply a matter of remembering to say the names of women killed by the police but also to conceptualize that the longed-for child, the subject of that loss, the bond that has been cruelly broken, might be that of a beloved daughter and her mother.

But in order to resonate, this alternate mother-daughter matrix of loss has to be situated in a culture that isn't prone to disregard and devalue Black motherhood as a deficient or compromised dynamic. As matters stand, the experience of Black motherhood is broadly depicted, in the debate over lethal policing of Black communities, as tasked with mothering sons against the constant threats posed by anti-Black policing. Conceptualizing Black mothers of daughters in a similarly sympathetic moral context means that we must revise our inherited raced and gendered hierarchies of motherly longing and empathetic grief. Intersectional thinking about police violence should incorporate and broaden the solidarities among women to incorporate *all* of the ways that gender contributes to vulnerability, often in conjunction with race, to produce the specific, disproportionate dimensions of the problems that harm women.

If the Women's March of early 2017 demonstrated how Black mothers are more easily incorporated into the racial justice narrative when it is their sons who are killed, the summer of 2020 in Portland, Oregon, revealed how race shapes the symbolic

function of motherhood in mobilizing against repressive state violence.

In the aftermath of George Floyd's death, protesters in Portland, like all major cities in the country, took to the streets for weeks. President Donald J. Trump unleashed federal agents on the Oregon city, ostensibly to protect public property and impose "law and order." The agents rapidly became infamous for their use of violence, firing flash grenades and tear gas; beating protesters with batons; making dozens of arrests; and manifesting a dystopic fascist future by pulling people off the streets into unmarked vans.

On July 17, 2020, a "wall of moms" came onto the streets to stand between federal agents and protesters in downtown Portland. Images of the moms—mostly white women between twenty and fifty years old, hair tied back in ponytails and held in place with baseball caps—linking hands and chanting "Feds stay clear! Moms are here!" went viral. One video depicted a wall of white women with arms raised, singing "Hands up, please don't shoot me" to the tune of a lullaby. When the white suburban moms of Portland valiantly stood up to militarized police, their use of their symbolic racial power in service of drawing attention to the problem of anti-Black violence revealed the continuing salience of white motherhood. The same capital is not available to Black mothers who have often faced indifference when they fought to save their children from police violence. This is not an indictment of the white mothers' act of solidarity but a recognition of the continuous disparity in the moral capital of motherhood rooted in American history.

Historically, Black maternity signals to authorities threat and perversion rather than maternal authority grounded in innocence and purity. Scholars such as Saidiya Hartman and Dorothy Roberts have demonstrated that one of the foundations and legacies of slavery has been the denial of Black women's capacity for maternal care. During slavery, this denial manifested in the theft of newborns from enslaved women and the continual breakup of families; in the twentieth and twenty-first centuries it continues in evidence that Black children are at much greater risk of being removed from their families than other American children are. Underwriting this violence against Black children, families, and mothers is the white supremacist belief that Black women do not have the emotional capacity to care for their children when they are alive or to mourn them when they die.

These legacies are hard to dismiss as we witness and document the stories of #SayHerName mothers who have had their identity and labor as mothers denied again and again. Fran Garrett has spoken about how her daughter, Michelle Cusseaux, repeatedly tried to reach her while police were standing armed outside her home. Michelle's downstairs neighbor had called Fran to let her know that Michelle needed help, and herself tried to speak with officers on the scene to de-escalate the situation. But officers would neither help Michelle nor take Fran's calls, disregarding the lives at stake and the bonds that held them together.

Fran's story has echoes in the experience of Rhanda Dormeus, another leader of the #SayHerName Mothers Network, whose story opens chapter 4. Rhanda's daughter, Korryn Gaines, was also killed by police in her own home, in Baltimore in 2016. Like Fran, Rhanda pleaded with police to allow her to speak to her daughter before she was killed, and officers refused her request. Both Fran and Rhanda know firsthand how helpless family members can be in the face of officers' intent on life-threatening use of force rather than drawing on familial bonds to save lives. Neither Rhanda nor Fran were allowed to protect their children from deadly force. Unlike the wall of moms, their motherhood and love for their daughters was illegible to both law enforcement and the media as something valuable and sacred.

#SayHerName is a movement of Black mothers for their daughters against a backdrop that historically endows white motherhood with unique social capital, and an understanding of anti-Black racism that foregrounds losses of sons over losses of daughters. It is an embodied imperative to demarginalize the structured vulnerabilities of Black women to police violence. It is dedicated to interrogating the intersectional failures that leave unanticipated victims of anti-Black police violence unnamed. As an element of the #SayHerName campaign, the Mothers Network seeks accountability and protection for all those they love.

#SayHerName joins a lineage of Black women who have taken on the work to break the conspiracy of silence surrounding the police killings of Black women and girls, and to prefigure the world we want to see. Black women's care and concern for their continued victimization, and that of others, has directly animated the trailblazing work they have done as activists both in the movement for racial justice and in creating the conditions to meet these aspirations.

All of this is to say: The work of #SayHerName is not new. As long as Black people have struggled and suffered within the American project, Black women have been there, to fight for not only their right to life but for all of our lives. It is the legacy of that work that #SayHerName seeks to lift up. Doing so helps to reframe the longstanding practices of state violence against Black women into a new politics of solidarity, a politics that takes seriously the degree to which Black women's experiences in the United States continue to exist as stolen histories.

Miriam Carey

Chapter 2

Stolen Histories

"How do you shoot somebody in their back who doesn't have a gun?"
Valarie Carey, sister of Miriam Carey
(August 12, 1979–October 3, 2013)

My name is Valarie Carey. I'm the sister of Miriam Carey, and I'm a part of the #SayHerName Mothers Network.

Miriam was a beautiful girl, a beautiful young lady. She wanted to be successful in life. And, as she got older, she decided to go into the field of health, and she became a registered dental hygienist. I'm actually older than Miriam by seven years. And so there's a gap. I remember when she was a baby, because she was so round and chubby, my father nicknamed her Butterball. And I guess my favorite memories really started to develop when she got older and when we would actually hang out more. That was my little sister.

But I would say my most favorite memory, which resonates every year when I release butterflies in my sister's honor, was when we went to Niagara Falls. So, I love butterflies, and Miriam decided we should all go up to Niagara Falls for Memorial Day weekend. I think that was 2007, around that time. So, two carloads, we go up to Niagara Falls and we went to a butterfly conservatory at my request, and the butterflies just kept landing on my sisters, Amy and Miriam. And I took some beautiful shots of them. And that was one of my favorite moments. And I held onto that after she was killed to just remember her smile and how she lived her life, as opposed to how horrifically we lost her.

So, the day that Miriam was killed, it was a Thursday, October 3, 2013. I believe it was a Thursday. I was in my office preparing for an event I was hosting that evening with Terry Williams. And so, I was just really trying to get my thoughts together, what I was going to say. I'm sitting at my desk, my laptop's open, and I use AOL. And so, I saw on the main page, there was a blurb about something happening in DC. I didn't click on it because I was busy. I was in my zone, and I had a TV at the time in my office, and I didn't have it on. And then my phone started to ring. It was a little after two. My phone just started ringing incessantly from different phone numbers.

A lot of the numbers, I now know, were coming from the DC area. I actually picked up one of the calls because it was a Connecticut area code number. And at the time my sister was living in Connecticut. She had just recently moved there and purchased a co-op. And so, I answered the call because I thought maybe it's my sister. I didn't know why all these calls were coming through, but they weren't registered in my phone, so I wasn't going to answer it.

And when I answered this one particular call, there was a man on the other line, he was a reporter. He asked to speak to me, and then he started asking me questions about Miriam. What type of car did she drive? Did I know where she was at? And I just stopped and said I'm not sure where this line of questioning is going, but, before I could finish, he said, "Well, apparently you haven't been watching the news. I need you to turn on your TV to CNN." And when I turned on the news, I saw what looked to be my sister's car. I saw what looked to be my niece being held by an officer. And there was a footer that read, "Suspect killed."

In the early afternoon of October 3, 2013, thirty-four-year-old Miriam Carey drove through a police checkpoint in Washington, DC. Miriam's one-year-old daughter was in the car with her. According to Miriam's sister Valarie, the checkpoint was not clearly designated as such; it was not cordoned off or demarcated in a way that would obviously make it look like an official police checkpoint. After Miriam was confronted by Secret Service officers inside the checkpoint area, she tried to drive out of it. An off-duty officer, who was dressed in plain clothes and carrying food (and could therefore have been confused for a civilian) placed a metal barrier in her way. Miriam tried to avoid the man while she drove through the barrier, but he was knocked down before Miriam continued driving down Pennsylvania Avenue. Secret Service vehicles followed Miriams's car, which was swerving. When the car stopped at a curb, six officers surrounded it on foot, attempting to open the car doors and demanding that Miriam get out. When she drove away, officers opened fire on her car, shooting eight rounds. Eventually Miriam's car came to a raised barrier, ran into a parked car, and stopped. Two Capitol Police officers shot nine rounds each into the car. Miriam was taken to hospital where she was declared dead shortly afterward. Her young daughter survived. Miriam did not fire any shots, and there was no gun in her car. The entire event—from Miriam's original drive through the checkpoint to the final shots fired—transpired in seven minutes.[1]

I was still on the phone with the reporter, and now he's pressing for my comment . . . I said, "I need to process this." And I hung up the phone. And at that point in time, more calls came in. I called my mother. She was screaming because the reporters started calling her. I immediately knew, while I wasn't sure exactly what happened, I immediately knew that this wasn't good and I needed my most trusted counsel around me. I called one of my really good friends who's a retired first-grade detective with NYPD. I called my friend who became my attorney, who's retired from the NYPD, because I knew I needed counsel at that point. And I called my godfather who's retired from the NYPD as a lieutenant. I'm a retired NYPD sergeant.

And I sent for my mother, and I sent for my sister, Amy, to come to my house because I kind of saw something brewing, even though I didn't know exactly what was happening. More calls kept coming through, and text messages started coming from reporters. "Can you confirm whether that's Miriam in the car?" I said, "I have not been officially notified by police." There was no official notification made.

About maybe an hour after, an hour, two hours after, the initial calls started coming in, two FBI agents showed up at my door, wanting to talk to me, and I didn't let them in until my attorney arrived. And then they came in, and they would not confirm nor deny whether the person that was in the vehicle was my sister.

They said they could tell me that the person that was in the vehicle was dead, but they cannot confirm or deny whether or not it was my sister. And this whole evening, while I'm making phone calls and people are reaching out, no one can tell me whether or not that was my sister. We decided the next morning that we were going to drive down to DC so I can identify the person that we believed to have been my sister.

It would make sense that it was her since she wasn't answering her phone, and that was my niece on a television, and that was what appeared to be her vehicle. But then the news, even though I didn't give him confirmation, began running her name on TV as being the suspect and the suspect of what? Of what crime? My sister didn't commit any crimes. She was in Washington, DC, which is where she was killed, but she didn't commit any crimes.

Meanwhile, the news was broadcasting that she was a suspect. And while the FBI were at my house, questioning me about my last conversation with my sister and what her interests were, there were field agents in Connecticut searching her house. What were they searching for? They were trying to justify killing an unarmed woman, shooting her in her back while she was driving with her thirteen-month-old baby in the car. She didn't commit any crime. She was not [involved] in the commission of a crime. She didn't have a gun on her and she's never been arrested, but yet they found fit to fire twenty-six shots at her vehicle while it was moving away, shooting her in the back of her head, in the back of her back, five times.

So, the next morning . . . we, myself, my husband, my sister, and my brother-in-law, and my attorney, drive to Washington, DC. And we go to the medical examiner's office to identify what I would have thought I would've been looking at, at least a corpse. They didn't have the decency. They didn't have no courtesy. No. They showed me a picture of my sister's body, shrouded in a blue sheet, on a slab. I wasn't to take pictures of this picture. I couldn't see my sister's body. There was no police courtesy given to me at all. And so I identified a photo . . . of my sister.

Miriam's death has affected my whole family. What those people did was they dismantled a family with her death. My niece was thirteen months old at the time. My sister was not in a relationship with her daughter's father at the time of her death. However, someone in their infinite wisdom found it fit on a day that we were going to identify my sister, someone contacted my niece's father. My sister was never married to him. Not understanding how this happened, but they gave custody—they gave my niece to him on that Friday while we were identifying my sister.

I haven't seen my niece in person for five years; the last time I saw my niece was on a FaceTime . . . almost two years ago. Last year, my niece's father said he didn't want her to have any contact with us until she was of age. Miriam would have never allowed that had Miriam been alive.

My mother died in 2018 from pancreatic cancer, which I believe manifested from her sorrow. Not having answers, not getting full disclosure on her daughter's death, and not having justice for her daughter's killing. Because my sister was killed by law enforcement and I have law enforcement ties, people look at me and make comments. Why don't I know the names of the officers that killed my sister besides having to do gumshoe work on my own?

The government, those municipalities, US Secret Service, and Capitol Police have not disclosed the names of the officers involved in my sister's death. From the over three hundred pages that we FOIA'd [got from a Freedom of Information Act request], highly redacted information that shouldn't be redacted, and because I know that with the police radio transmissions, if they were released, which they have not been, will tell a full story of what exactly happened to my sister. It will tell that those officers were told to stop pursuing her. And they ignored those commands that came from a Black watch commander who was a female. This I know because of the personal investigation that I've had to do, not because of what someone else has presented to me.

So, how has it affected me? Every day . . . Every day I have to think about is today going to be another day that I push forward to ask someone to help me reopen my sister's case? I mean, the letters that were written to President Obama, who was actually our sitting president [the] day that it happened, he ignored it. He hasn't responded. He's never made a statement. This happened in his backyard. Allegedly, she was said to have rammed the White House gate, which she didn't, and that was later. The news stopped going with that narrative because that wasn't the truth.

The senators that we've written, Chuck Schumer, Kirsten Gillibrand, and so many others. The district attorney, please reopen my sister's case, which you prematurely closed within nine months. And with a two-page letter stating that you could not prove that the officers willfully took her life. They did willfully take her life. They willfully moved forward, followed her, pursued her, and shot at her, even after being told not to pursue the vehicle, which made a U-turn. And that was the catalyst to the events that occurred in Washington, DC.

So, I struggle day by day. And each year I release butterflies on her birthday in August and on her death day. But I don't want to be in an act of releasing butterflies. I want a grand jury to be held and [to] have those officers held accountable for their actions. Who exactly killed her? And why are they still sitting with their families having dinner? Enjoying Mother's Day and Father's Day. We were robbed of my sister.

When she first was killed, it was a media frenzy and people just wanted a story, and they tried to piece it together. What, why? What, why was she in DC? It didn't matter why she was in DC. She has a car. She has a driver's license, and she's a citizen. She's free to drive wherever she wants to. I would love to say, "Well, Miriam, what brought you to DC on that day?" Because I don't know, but she's not here to tell that story. So, in the beginning, when the media didn't know what they had, and I'm sure that the officers on the scene fed them . . . misdirection. There were photos of mangled police cars, along with the story as if my sister mangled those police cars, and she didn't. After going on several different news outlets—Anderson Cooper 2020, The Today Show, *Megyn Kelly—I believe that the news began to see that it's not quite what they initially tried to make it out to be. She wasn't a suspect, and then [the story] died.*

And then a year later, I think, David Montgomery from the Washington Post *did a story in maybe 2014, 2015, and he did an investigation of a story. And it was about, it was more than nine pages in a Sunday* Washington Post, *because initially they tried to justify she was going on a crazy chase through Washington, and she wasn't even driving more than twenty-five miles an hour. And so he did a really good objective piece, so did* Mother Jones. *And nothing. Nothing.*

And then last year in 2021, January 6, the insurrection. And so those individuals were actually handled with care. They were welcomed into the People's House and all the while my sister was gunned down in the People's House's backyard in 2013, [they] were told that they were protected from an alleged threat. And the representatives on October 3, 2013, stood [and] gave a standing ovation to the Capitol Police for shooting my sister. They applauded for a minute.[2]

But last year there was a little bit of interest in her story again, because I tweeted about . . . the difference. And then more people actually signed our petition that was online . . . with Change.org, which we were at 114,000 signatures, 114,000. And then I go back another day, we're down to 85,000. I don't know how you go from up to down. And then Change.org has been collecting money from people to push the petition out. That doesn't make sense to me. But with all of that being said, I had plans last year on printing out all of those signatures and bringing them to Congress and asking them: "Please reopen my sister's case."

It's exhausting emotionally. And so, I ebb and flow. But that is my goal, to have my sister's case reopened. Because those people who shot my sister, who was unarmed, she did not . . . That's . . . she didn't have a gun. How do you shoot somebody in their back who doesn't have a gun? And I understand that time goes by and people look at different situations. And I understand that each state is different. While she wasn't even in a state, she was in a District of Columbia.

However, there just seems to be a universal language that I'm seeing. That individuals that actually do commit crimes that are white and are fully, fully armed with heavy artillery are brought into custody, unharmed. And while other individuals like my sister who weren't in the commission of a crime, and even if someone was in a commission of a crime, depending on the crime, still not justification for murder. And that was murder. Police officers are supposed to enforce laws. They're not supposed to execute people. And she was executed, shot in the back of her head. Justice begins with pulling those officers to the mat, naming them publicly, having them tried for their actions and ultimately convicted. That's justice for Miriam.

In 2015 I got a call from my attorney telling me about #SayHerName. It was an event that was going to highlight and talk about women who were killed by the police. When I first heard about it and I got on a call with Dr. Kimberlé Crenshaw, I was just really thankful that someone acknowledged Miriam and wanted to say her name, wanted to amplify her and her case, because people at that point, while it was two years later, I felt . . . didn't give it . . . they . . . no one was talking about her and how horrific of a crime it was. She was a mother with a baby. It's like, we are all mothers. Thank God my niece wasn't killed.

Also in 2015, we went to Union Square and we had big posters with our loved ones' names that were killed by police, #SayHerName. And since then, I have grown to know some of the women involved in the movement of #SayHerName. And I have become a part of the Mothers Network, which has really been helpful . . . Because nobody comes around and asks how you're doing, or . . . It's been helpful.

I would really love to not have a sister to be a part of this group. It's not a group you want to be a part of. But I would say that if someone were to ever find themselves in a situation where their sister, their mother, their daughter was killed by police, #SayHerName and the Mothers Network is a loving, welcoming, empathetic space where you can actually be heard and not judged and . . . get emotional support and resources that can . . . help during the course of you navigating your plight for justice.

I would say for people who want to help share the stories, contact your local representatives. Ask that these cases be reopened. Ask that Miriam Carey's case be reopened. Get more involved in your local level of politics. Know who your representatives are and what their interests are. Are their interests actually protecting your interests? Because while today it's not you, it could possibly be you.

I'm a retired sergeant in New York. And while I have nephews that I would talk to about how to interact with the police, when you're stopped, if you're stopped how to speak to an officer, I've never ever in my life thought that I would have to think about my sisters. My sisters are professional women—a registered nurse and a registered dental hygienist. Never had a conversation with my sisters about what to do when you're stopped by the police, if you're stopped by the police, because I never feared for my sisters' lives. I feared for my nephews as men but never my sisters. So, while today, it's not you, it's not knocking at your door, it may, in the sense of your neighbor, it could be someone in your family. I never thought it would be in my family. I wasn't immune.

Valarie Carey

Since their arrival on American shores, Black women have lived lives on the whims of others. As a group, Black women have been essential to the American project; their reproductive labor under a system of coercive childbearing otherwise known as enslavement is the "but for" condition of possibility for the wealth that underwrote the American economy. Thus, while Black women's presence was indisputably essential to the various racial projects on which this nation was founded, Black women's lives have been expendable.

That history of Black women's subordination continues to be stolen in the silences around their ongoing exposure to private and state violence. Over time, the foundational failure to acknowledge Black women's experience has created many distortions and contradictions—of Black women first and foremost but also in our understanding of not only racism and sexism but also the dominant narrative of the American nation's founding and consolidation. These distortions have not gone unchallenged. Over the centuries that this regime of denial has taken root, Black feminists have powerfully contested and interrogated the terms of Black women's erasure from the nation's official histories.

#SayHerName is one in a lineage of efforts both past and present that endeavor to make this paradox visible. The movement tackles head-on the most egregious and devastating outcome of this denial—a nation that owes its very existence in large part to Black women does precious little to protect them from the forces both public and private that have punished and killed them.

#SayHerName draws sustained attention to the physical and material vulnerabilities that underlie Black women's marginalization by memorializing and continuing the work of Black women in Black freedom struggle. Sojourner Truth, Harriet Tubman, and legions of other women who fought white supremacy fashioned an organically intersectional anti-racism that confronted the gendered particulars of anti-Black violence. I have tried to capture the relationship between Black women's history and the very foundation of this nation in many ways and many contexts, including through "Respect," a spoken word poem. I wrote the piece for a special performance of Eve Ensler's *Vagina Monologues* and performed it at the Apollo Theater in Harlem at a benefit for domestic violence shelters and rape crisis centers serving Black and Latinx women in New York.[3]

Black vaginas
the hardest working vaginas in America,
and still they get no respect.
No vagina has done so much for this country
and received so little. Really.
Black vaginas built this country.
It all started right here,
between blueberry black, chocolate cream, honey brown,
praline pecan,
french vanilla,
legs.

It wasn't the Declaration of Independence,
the Constitution,
or the stars and stripes that gave birth to America.
It was the Black vagina that laid the golden egg,
or rather,
the chattel slave . . .

To move the struggle forward, #SayHerName engages in a feminist and anti-racist intervention that consistently names the specific dimensions of racist violence that have shaped and continue to threaten Black women's lives. We do this both by mapping out the conditions that gave rise to this violence and vulnerability and by collaborating in a principled and insistent fashion with contemporary tools to expose those same conditions in our present-day struggles.

A full grasp of the historical and contemporary context of Black women's vulnerability and victimization is crucial to a thorough reckoning with anti-Black violence and its tangled, destructive legacies. The "problem" of police violence is not confined to specific encounters between Black women and law enforcement, but rather it is part of a wider scope of the American state's concerted control over and strategic marginalization of Black women.

American history bears witness to a wide litany of abuses inflicted specifically on Black women: reproductive violence, sexual assault, economic exploitation, overpolicing, and underprotection. These are all state-based methods of controlling, disciplining, and assaulting Black women. The killing of Black women by law enforcement is simply the most spectacular reflection of these deep-seated historical patterns. Without reference to this still-submerged and incompletely narrated history, news about Black women's fatal encounters with police does not travel widely or become familiar. The gendered contours of this history of anti-Black violence remain marginalized within our conventional narratives, not only about racism and sexism but also about law, justice, and democracy.

Undoing the silences of Black women's history is a project of recovery. Central to that recovery is articulating the contemporary significance of historical forms of anti-Black violence and reclaiming the gendered particularities within that body of abuses.[4] Performing the work of historical excavation with gender specificity is all the more important because contemporary struggles against anti-Black racism are inevitably steeped in the historical record of enslavement and its aftermath. Even now, the country's debt to its slave past is rarely acknowledged. And when such acknowledgment happens, it tends to take on the cast of old business—a begrudging (at best) recognition that present-day social arrangements continue to suffer a faint residue of racism. Yet there is nothing faint or residual about the still-thriving legacies of American slavery. From its inception, the practice of policing Black people has been grounded in the coercive enforcement of enslavement. As such, policing is an expression of a historical raced and classed order devoted to dehumanizing Black people via law and culture.

Yet these histories won't be fully recovered until we can also recognize the true proportions of state-sanctioned violence experienced by enslaved Black women—which also means laying bare the ugly ideological justifications of this brutality, then and now. Just as slaveholders felt total ownership of and license to invade Black women's homes and bodies, today's policing regimes go to enormous lengths to preserve and rationalize the same harshness and impunity. In police-led surveillance and behavioral crackdowns, Black women are denied basic rights to privacy and free will; in violent home invasions and other encounters with police, they can lose their lives. And in scores of other settings they can suffer the most intimate and violative brand of bodily usurpation in the form of sexual assault. The most recent example was the case of Daniel Holtzclaw, who sexually assaulted at least thirteen Black women on his regular patrol as a police officer in Oklahoma City from 2013–2014.[5] The continuities here are impossible to miss: Black women remain essential to the operation of our society, yet they continue to be treated as utterly expendable.

Contending with the foregoing history is a crucial part of the #SayHerName campaign. An overarching mission of #SayHerName is to emphasize the gender-specific debasement of Black womanhood as a foundational element of rationalizing the overall expendability of Black life in America. As the prior chapter discusses, Black women have lost their lives both in conditions that mirror the risks Black men face in their encounters with police and also in ways that reflect the particularly gendered dimension of their historic expendability.

The reason such continuities are difficult to see today is that their origins have been strategically erased from the standard narratives of our history. Black women's ongoing vulnerability to institutional violence and industrialized rape have not been clearly placed within the well-worn saga of the rise of the American nation from its hardscrabble colonial roots into a powerhouse of liberty, opportunity, ingenuity, and other lofty ideals. But once we know where to look, cultural traditions and stereotypes crafted to uphold and perpetuate the regimes of coercive control over Black women are obvious.

One crucial example is the racist folklore developed across centuries to rationalize the violent commodification of Black women's childbearing. This toxic tradition has focused on systemically treating Black women as a subspecies of women, hampered by a degraded capacity to mother, a pronounced sexual deviance, and a heightened tolerance for pain. These mythologized traits all add up to a key platform of white supremacist ideology: the profoundly compromised status of Black women to act as responsible agents in their own lives, and their biological suitability for physical exploitation.[6]

The formal abolition of slavery did not produce a corresponding suspension of this brutal ideological tradition. Instead, it evolved in concert with the postbellum regime of legally sanctioned racism—which is why Black women routinely experience state-sanctioned violence such as excessive force and sexual abuse by police in plain sight.

There is no way to make sense of this regime of state impunity—or to begin to rectify it at any structural level—without recourse to the gendered history of American slavery. Dorothy Roberts, currently professor at the University of Pennsylvania and a leading scholar in race, gender, bioethics, and the law, has written extensively on how the historical impact of white supremacy on Black women reverberates today. Roberts has documented our historic scripting of Black women's experience as a site of control, reproduction, and punishment in dozens of books and articles, but her 2019 appearance on the *Intersectionality Matters!* podcast gave lay audiences a rare opportunity to explore the relationship between the institution of slavery and instances of modern oppression against Black women.[7] In an episode that built out from Nikole Hannah-Jones's *1619 Project* in the *New York Times*,[8] titled "What Slavery Engendered: An Intersectional Look at 1619," Roberts showed that the routine and unchecked state punishment that Black women face today can be traced back to American slavery's earliest regimes of punishment and discipline. Roberts patiently laid out how the disregard for the family bonds of Black women paired with efforts to control their childbearing form a punitive matrix of anti-Black racism that has targeted Black women for centuries.

Roberts stressed a key point that has come up again and again in #SayHerName investigations: Slavery did not end the racist control of Black women's reproduction. Once Black women's reproduction no longer enhanced the wealth of slave owners, lawmakers developed new ways to control Black women's fertility. With the rise of the pseudoscience eugenics, more than half of the states in the Union authorized nonconsensual sterilization from the 1920s through the 1960s. The most notorious practice was known as the "Mississippi appendectomy." Roberts explained it as a routine procedure "when a Black woman goes to the doctor and thinks she's got her appendix taken out, and actually she's had her uterus removed."[9]

One Black woman brutalized by this procedure was the civil rights activist Fannie Lou Hamer. In the early 1960s, Hamer found a "knot in [her] stomach," which, according to historian Harriet A. Washington, was likely a benign fibroid tumor in her uterus. Hamer went to the hospital to have the growth removed and returned to her family's home on a nearby former plantation to recover.[10] Hamer eventually learned that the surgeon—a cousin of the plantation owner's wife—had removed her uterus, rendering her sterile. Asked afterward why she did not file a lawsuit against the doctor who sterilized her without her consent, Hamer replied, "At that time? Me? Getting a white lawyer against a white doctor? I would have been taking my hands and screwing tacks in my casket."[11]

As Roberts has shown, experiences of nonconsensual sterilization like Hamer's were widespread in the early and mid-twentieth century. The eugenics-driven war on Black reproduction has received scant attention within the white feminist movement for reproductive rights. (Indeed, white birth control pioneer Margaret Sanger was an early adherent of eugenics.) Moreover, while the saga of the crusade to control Black women's bodies and reproductive capacities should be front and center in today's debates over racial justice, it barely registers as noteworthy, even in the traditional centers of anti-racist Black activism. Hamer, for example, is celebrated for courageously giving voice and legitimacy to Black demands for political liberation. There's very little discussion, however, of the gendered racism that Hamer experienced—a particular form of state-sanctioned violence that remains stubbornly elusive to broader understanding, even in today's revived Black liberation struggle. In the face of this intersectional failure in the historical accounts of the lives of Black women activists like Hamer, it's fallen largely to Black feminist scholars and activists, such as Loretta Ross and Angela Davis, to recover and document this crucial history of state-sanctioned violence against nonwhite women and their reproductive autonomy.

African American family, circa 1898. PHOTO BY EDUCATION IMAGES/UNIVERSAL IMAGES GROUP/GETTY IMAGES

The reproductive war on Black women's bodies calls back to the twinned oppressions of enslaved women, exploited both for their field labor and their reproductive labor. Importantly, Hamer's story reminds us that Black women have neither been exempt from white supremacist violence nor absent in challenging it.

#SayHerName inherits the dual legacy of this buried history: the imperative to expand and deepen the narratives of anti-Black state violence so that it acknowledges the inhumane treatment that women also experienced, and the "women-targeted" expressions of violence that were uniquely gendered. The testimonies from the Mothers Network consistently reveal not only the ongoing salience of stereotypes of Black women as something other than women but also a studied indifference if not outright disdain for their familial bonds—their roles as mothers, the loving bonds with their children, and enduring commitments to their children's well-being. The heartbreaking stories of Valarie Carey and so many of the mothers and sisters of #SayHerName attest to the manner in which lives were taken and survivors were treated without regard to these family bonds.

Similar logics that justified the brutal violence of the slave patrols seem to hold forth today: the needs of securing the prevailing order—however minimal the supposed threat to that order might be—are more than enough to justify levels of violence against Black mothers that would otherwise prompt outraged media coverage and expressions of official regret. The permissiveness granted to officers is prophylactic, so that even shootings that endanger children can be written off as legitimate expressions of violence. And unlike the slave patrols in the past, where repressive violence that destroyed families and traumatized children were occasionally restrained by the economic interests of the owning class, today's constraints are mediated through the even more attenuated interests of taxpayers and municipal budgets.

The weak constraints on state homicide and the endangerment of Black children is perhaps the most profound expression of the diminished value afforded to Black motherhood that is deeply embedded in our post-slave culture. Slavery was built upon a transactional conception of Black mothers. It structuralized Black motherhood, including through acts of sexual violence, as a source of "property." This is not to say that Black motherhood was exhausted by that arrangement. The point is that within the legibility of Black motherhood in the context of slavery was transaction.

The transactional nature of Black motherhood under enslavement extended into the Jim Crow era. Under Jim Crow, Black mothers were "transacted" to be caregivers for white children under conditions that presupposed Black women had no children of their own or, equally troubling, that their children could be raised on what remained after white children were cared for. The racial and gendered dimensions of Jim Crow were predicated on the idea that Black women's domestic duties were the property of others, garnered through marketplace arrangements that left most Black women with few alternatives.

The contrast between the honorific entitlements of white motherhood during Black enslavement and Jim Crow and the transactionally commodified dimensions of Black motherhood shows how motherhood means entirely different things in the racialized poles of a white supremacist and patriarchal social order. Historically, white patriarchy devoted untold energy to the mythology of a motherhood that enshrined white women as producers of white citizens and keepers of the sacrosanct domestic sphere that relied on transactional Black motherhood. Under this regime, Black motherhood could not be afforded even the narrow and confining protections of the separate sphere. Under neither slavery nor Jim Crow did Black women have a separate sphere that the law was "bound to respect." Both their labor and their children were subject to market arrangements that elided and delegitimized Black women's kinship relationship to their children. Underwriting both slavery and Jim Crow was the idea that only white women's—not Black women's—attachment to their children should be nurtured and protected.

Part of what is insidious about the current construction of Black motherhood is that it positions Black mothers as embodying the very thing Black women have been forced to navigate: transactional motherhood. That is to say, at least since the 1980s, the assumption is that Black women have children purely for their own economic benefit, a perverse and vicious reprisal of the wealth-driven model of Black motherhood instituted alongside American slavery and carried over into Jim Crow. This vision of transactional Black motherhood saturates policy debates today, from the infamous findings of the 1965 Moynihan report on the Black family's waning patriarchal standing to the Reagan-era fabrication of the Black "welfare queen" to the Clinton administration's abolition of "welfare as we know it" in the Personal Responsibility and Work

Opportunity Act of 1996. The very concept of Black motherhood in most policy discussions is steeped in stereotypes and insults that reinforce and perpetuate the degraded status of Black mothering.

It was an all-too-predictable move for the defenders of white supremacy to disown the entirety of enslavement and Jim Crow, and to stigmatize Black mothers themselves for allegedly practicing a raw and opportunistic brand of the reproductive regime that the white supremacist state had itself mythologized. The slaveholder myth that Black mothers do not have a loving bond with their families survives in the ideological depiction of Black women as irresponsible, as perpetrators, and as unfit mothers. It is precisely that depiction that explains the complete disregard of the bonds between women killed by the police and their families. Rhanda Dormeus, whose daughter, Korryn Gaines, was killed by police in Baltimore, Maryland, in 2016, traces the brutal logic of this myth down through the horrors that her own family has endured:

> They don't believe that we have any connection or commitment to one another, to the point where we would be traumatized with the loss or traumatized with the separation. I don't even think they take those things into consideration, because I don't believe folks think that we're human, that we have that type of ability to have a bond. They've been ripping us apart from one another all these years. I guess they think we should be used to it. They don't feel like it was ever established from my perspective. If that's something that they're used to seeing because we had no choice but to scream and cry because our children were being snatched from us or our husbands were being sold or whatever the case. We weren't considered human.

In evoking those women who "had no choice but to scream and cry" because their children were being snatched from them, Rhanda draws a direct link both between her experience and that of other Black women today and to their enslaved ancestors. She too had her daughter, Korryn, snatched from her in spite of her cries to the authorities who were impervious to her pleading. The same unwillingness on the part of white police officers to recognize Rhanda's bond with Korryn is played out in the story that opens this chapter: a young mother, Miriam Carey, was killed by police who were indifferent to her bond with her young daughter who was sitting in her car as she died. In evoking this transgenerational memory of Black women's trauma, Rhanda and Valarie remind us of the terrible ongoing legacy of a white supremacist system, embodied, in this case, in their dehumanization.

And while this dehumanization of Black people extends across gender to Black men and boys, as Rhanda so chillingly reminds us, it takes a particular form in relation to Black mothers. For this reason, resisting anti-Black police violence requires us to more fully imbue our movement with the particularly gendered dimensions of our history, elevating the experiences and substantive vision of Black women that have yet to be fully incorporated into an anti-racist narrative. Anti-Black racism is a fully intersectional phenomenon, one that can be made more legible through a more robust incorporation of the experiences and leadership of Black women who have resisted. Where might our collective understanding

of reproductive freedom, violence against Black women, and the diminished valued of our family bonds be if the degradation of Black motherhood was as central in our thinking as the degradation of our vote?

The contributions of Black women to a robust understanding of the many faces of anti-Black racism run from Ida B. Wells's attempt to name and disown the horrors of lynching to Angela Davis's revolutionary effort to introduce the analysis of structural racism within the women's movement;[12] from Johnnie Tillmon's fight to center poverty as a women's issue[13] to Sandra Bundy, Mechelle Vinson, and Pamela Price's groundbreaking resistance to sexual harassment in the workplace.[14] We can reclaim and redeem their vision by revisiting Rosa Parks's early defense of Recy Taylor and Black women victims of sexual violence[15] prior to her stewardship of the Montgomery Bus Boycotts;[16] we can elevate the Combahee River Collective's analysis of identity politics and their demands for the dignity of Black women's lives.[17] We can and should look to Audre Lorde's prose and poetry on the interconnectedness of Black women's lives.[18] In all these settings, and countless more, Black women have laid out the ways that anti-racist struggle must continue to realize true and lasting progress by acknowledging the centrality of intersectional oppression in our history.

Attending to these oft-forgotten histories informs each and every step of the #SayHerName campaign and is consistent with the Black feminist project to challenge the multiple ways in which Black people are forced to live disposable lives.

India Kager

Chapter 3

Disposable Lives

"They left my baby on the concrete."
Gina Best, mother of India Kager
(June 9, 1988–September 5, 2015)

I am Gina Best. My daughter's India Kager. I call her Empress. India Jasmine Kager. Her middle name, Jasmine, means flower.

India was murdered by the Virginia Beach Police SWAT team. That lets you know that this was planned, because it was SWAT. She was murdered September 5, 2015, in a parking lot of a 7-Eleven with my four-month-old grandson, Roman Kager, in the backseat of the car.

One of the earliest thoughts I have of her emerging as an artist was when she was two years old writing on the wall with crayon, and my initial knee-jerk reaction was to be irritated. I have the memories of her childhood, the memories of her birth. She had a kind of deep voice. Unlike me, India was very soft-spoken, very gentle, very patient, very deliberate in everything she did.

India would be described hands-down as the wise sage. All of her friends would go to her for advice. She was an old soul, really. She was a musician and an artist. She covered everything with a group of friends who were also musically gifted, like she would play her violin. And then she had her friends who were more on the arts side of her visual arts. India was a tomboy, she was never really a girly girl, never really liked dressing up. But later on she was very expressive in all the ways she would do her makeup. She would get on me about perming my hair: "You need to stop frying your hair, Mom. Those are antennae, that's the energy. The antennae defy gravity."

She served four years in the navy, but hated it. India was going to be the peacemaker . . . I don't recall one argument in her entire life, ever. Not that she was a pushover by any stretch of the imagination. She was a joy creator. You never would see her on the front line on a picket or even protesting, she'd be over in the corner drawing the protest signs and sharing and expressing her art, or creating a song to lift up women in the movement for intersectionality.

India was a student of history as well, so she knew the struggle for civil rights, and we would have very deep conversations and talks about that. She didn't understand why there was such hatred for Blacks, for women. "Why is it that men relegate us to a lower position? That doesn't make sense to me." Audre Lorde, India loved her work, and Zora Neale Hurston's.

When her life was stolen from us, India was interviewing for a job at Google, and she was going to work there. She was a letter carrier, even carrying mail into the seventh and eighth month of her pregnancy with Roman. She had aspirations and dreams of continuing her art studies and artistic gifts by doing tattoos. She had a beautiful dragon tattoo down her back. Her energy would be very different in that she would have green lipstick one day, and she may have the Monroe piercing here, and then the septum piercing and maybe some strand of purple hair . . . this was India. She was very artistic, very, very bohemian.

She taught me so much spiritually that I know for a fact the portal was opened within me. She just wanted to be accepted for who and what she was: beautiful, Black, loving, artistically gifted, highly intellectual, highly articulate; a poet, a lyricist; and for writing her music; a woman who loved the male or female, if you want to even assign that gender—loving from the spirit. In this world, unfortunately, we look at labels before we really look at the love that people carry in their hearts.

It's very painful to think that in the last moments of her life on this realm, beyond any shadow of a doubt, she was thinking about her baby in the back of that car as the bullets pierced her flesh.

India being a loving young mother, wanted the father of her baby, Angelo Perry, to be around and familiar with his family. Angelo came to Maryland to meet baby Roman. That was the first time he met him. Roman was four months old. He came to meet the baby and wanted to take the baby back to meet the family. Beautiful Roman.

They went back to Virginia Beach to have the family reunion, and they went from house to house, introducing baby Roman to Angelo's family, at different locations. There was a text message on Angelo's phone that he was looking for a place for India and the baby to stay overnight. There were so many family members in town during the reunion, that there was really no place for India and Roman, and she didn't want to sleep on the floor. So, Angelo was looking for a hotel to place India and Roman, and that's what the text message says clearly. But unbeknownst to Angelo and India, the Virginia Beach police were pinging his cell phone as they traveled from Maryland back to Virginia. They were pinging his phone and following them. They tracked them because they said that they got a tip from a confidential informant, that he was "on his way to commit a crime."

That's the story. That's the narrative that the Virginia Beach police put out. This is Labor Day weekend. They assembled the entire highly trained Virginia Beach SWAT team and surveilled India as she went from house to house carrying baby Roman's car seat in and out of the houses. They had every opportunity, ample opportunity to de-escalate, had they chosen to do that and protect India and Roman's innocent lives. I'm not saying that Angelo was not innocent. He was entitled to due process of law. If they wanted to arrest Angelo Perry, just do a traffic stop.

They followed India. India was driving her car. Her 1990 Cadillac with Maryland tags. They ran her tag. They knew who she was. As they claim, they had an unidentified Black woman in the car but, of course, this is a SWAT team so you cannot in any way negate the training. They had all the intelligence they needed. They knew it was an innocent woman, and not one single officer made a lifesaving decision to stop this operation or wait until they had Angelo Perry by himself. They carried this out with full specificity and intention.

They had left the family members. She drove to the Shell gas station. We saw a video of India getting out of the car, going into the Shell gas station. She stayed in there for almost five minutes. They did not make an arrest at that time, although they could have. She was in the store, and they were separated. They could have arrested him, done a takedown if they wanted to. They chose not to. They waited until India got back in her car and drove to the 7-Eleven [with Angelo and her son Roman], and at that point, in an unmarked police SUV and panel van, they ran into the back of

India's car—ambushed her car—while simultaneously detonating flashbang grenades at her car. They launched the attack first. They wanted the element of surprise, which is why they ran into the back of her car with such force.

This came out in the wrongful death trial, that all of the officers that were in that van actually fell down and fell forward. That's the force. And you can see in the video, where the back of that old Cadillac was lifted up. You could see that impact, knowing the baby was in the car. At that moment, there was physical harm to an innocent four-month-old baby. Then they threw the flashbang grenades. In the video, you'll see four SWAT officers in full gear, helmets, all of that, with rifles, with the flashlights on the end of it—an entire lynch mob. They jumped out of the back of the van, and then they ran to the car and fired more than fifty-one rifle rounds into India's car.

And the Virginia Beach Police Chief, Jim Cervera, said that it was an accident, that they did not intend on killing India. What does that mean? They certainly did intend on throwing flashbang grenades. They certainly had no intention of de-escalating. They certainly had no intention of protecting her life. If they did, if her life mattered, she would be here today. And one thing is very clear. If she were white, it would not have played out in this way.

I learned that India did not die immediately. They pulled her body out of the car after they shot her. A white officer pulled my baby's body out of the car, after completely executing her. They left India's body there completely overnight. They waited to contact us as family, after they cleaned up the crime scene. They really did not notify us until after they cleaned up the crime scene. They left my baby on the concrete, and they had the baby taken away. And she died on the sidewalk. Her spirit left her body on the pavement in that 7-Eleven parking lot. And all I can imagine, if I were there, is just crowds surrounding her as her spirit left her body. And they were directly responsible. I wasn't even allowed to see the car, because the attorneys said that to give that to me now is a biohazard because of the blood. These are my daughter's belongings. I want them, even the car. They don't want to give me the car because it's a biohazard. They destroyed it and then sent me a bill from the city of Virginia Beach.

There's the complete and utter disregard, even for the dignity of our loved ones. The baby—for three days, they wouldn't even let me know where Roman was—my grandson. They did not answer the phone calls of where Roman was. He's in the hands of strangers, and they wouldn't even let me know. I was calling, even in my messed-up state, trying to find out where's my grandson. Where's my grandson? They refused to give me any information about where my grandbaby was. Refused. Three days. When I finally found him, he had cuts on his little legs from the shattered glass. He had blood on his clothes. He had human tissue in his hair.

India lived in College Park, Maryland. I live in Maryland as well. They sent a Maryland state trooper to College Park to deliver the news to India's father, Richard, and India's uncle, Roger, and her grandfather, the three of them. Roger told me that when he saw the trooper at the door, he knew something happened to India. Then they told him she had been killed by police. They released no more information other than that. That was it. That was it. Didn't even tell them where the baby was. Around seven, the phone rang and it was Richard. And he says, "Gina, India is not with us anymore." That's how he told me. "India is no longer with us anymore." He paused and I don't remember how I got out of my bed, but I found myself at the top of the stairs. I screamed and screamed and screamed, and my son and my daughter-in-law and then my youngest daughter came out and I was just screaming India's name. Apparently, I grabbed my purse and keys and ran barefoot out to the car to try and drive away from what I had just heard. Just trying to get away from that. Since then, there has been no acknowledgment by the police at all. At all.

People didn't know what to say to me when India was first killed. They offered words of what they intended to be comfort, you know, "God has his plan in this, she's in a better place." And I'm listening to that, and none of that is sitting with me or resonating at all. I'm not on that frequency, and I don't want to be. What do you think hurts worse, the silly statements people make, or the silence when they act like they are ignoring it? The stupid statements people make. "God had a reason for it." That's one of them. Or the silence when they ignore you altogether and they avoid you like the plague? It's their worst nightmare, and they are watching you live through it. And they literally don't know what to do. We haven't examined that enough and given ourselves space to speak what may be seen as wrong statements or hurtful statements or painful statements. We haven't been given that platform, and permission to use that. If we take it and express our rage, you know, you're an angry Black woman or a bitch.

Someone asked me, "Gina, are you always sad?" And I'm like, "Yeah." And when I say sad, let me explain what I mean by that. You see the triggers on social media. Are you reliving this all the time? I'm like, "I will never not live it." Never not live it. This is now a part of us. I hate the part of my life where I felt at one point that it wasn't—where I could not relate to someone having been killed by the police. For that, if anything has come out that I can hold onto, [is valuable], after the murder of my daughter . . . I can look at another human, another mother or father or child, and say, "You know what? I do see you. And no one has the right to take your life, because you're not in the right place. I don't believe any of our children were in the wrong place."

Roman's birthday was May 11. He is five now. He's got complete hearing loss in the left ear from the flashbang. He's disabled as well from the trauma. He's acting out, he's asking for me, he is really full of rage. He is waking up screaming in his sleep. He calls me MeMaw. "I want MeMaw, I want MeMaw." Our children are traumatized. For life. And once, while his brother Evan was in his bed, he said,"Grandma, I see angels all around." And I'm like, "Yes, you do." So how I keep them alive, how I keep India alive, is with chimes, wind chimes. One is a butterfly, because I call all my granddaughters butterflies. And there's another one just past the crystals, and there's one with crystals and just the sounds. I tell Evan every time he hears the chimes, that it's his mommy coming by. She's always there, and he loves that.

My mental health? I'm always walking the tightrope with that. I'm recognizing the stigma of needing mental health care, coupled with the stigma, if you want to call it that, of being a mother of a Black woman murdered by police. All of these are stigmas that we are forced to live through. I have to be very careful with how I present myself. If I'm seen as weak, I may not even get custody of my grandson because I can be viewed as unstable. But it's impossible to experience this loss and come through unscathed and stable. There's no way. You've heard me say that I walk around with an amputated heart. And that is literally the case. Here is a bleeding heart.

Let me just say this out front: You can never monetize the life of our children or our loved ones. Never. But [India's] attorneys, after getting on the phone and calling for no fewer than twenty-three times for her case, went in there and fought a good fight. It went from a $30 million wrongful death suit [to battery]. They could not even use the charge of murder or manslaughter. They had to distill it down to battery. Battery. In Virginia Beach, geopolitically, we know the environment. Let's just say it's very apparent. A $30 million lawsuit. They see both of my grandsons. And Roman, who was in the car when they murdered India, is now permanently disabled. And my other grandson, Evan, is on the autism spectrum, so we're dealing with two young boys. The jury filed past them, saw them playing in the hallway together, but the jury included only one Black gentleman, so you all can pretty much guess the outcome of that. The message was sent.

There were sixteen officers who killed my daughter, and I did not know that until the trial. Not one of them made a lifesaving decision to protect India's life. They did nothing, and I had to sit there and listen to each one of them admit this. It was a $30 million lawsuit to the jury. After two hours of deliberating they came back; they were deadlocked. It was almost a mistrial in that sense. The judge sent them back, and they returned a verdict. They held only two of the officers responsible. And again, none of us have had criminal charges against the murderers of our children. You have to go, unfortunately, to civil court. He held two of them responsible for India's death and assigned $400,000 to each officer. $30 million down to $800,000. Lawyer fees are deducted, and *both of my grandchildren now have only $200,000 in their estate with which to live for the rest of their lives. Every last one of the murderers of my daughter is home with their families, and we don't have our loved ones.*

Because of their badges, the police are seen as the vanguards and law keepers, law enforcers. But what do they really enforce? They enforce their will upon us. They enforce their lying, their vilifying, controlling the narrative, spinning that, sullying our daughters' names. These are police officers who have done this, so you have a group of people: "Well, the police did this, you know, they are trained to see this." No, they're not. They're human just like we are. But they also divorce themselves from their humanity while they shoot and murder our daughters. The attorneys would say "Don't say 'murder' on your social media page. They didn't murder India," and I'm thinking, you know, yes they did. They snuffed out her life, and permanently disabled an innocent baby and Angelo Perry even. No due process of law, none of that. None of that was afforded any of our children.

I envision that, when we say her name and we remember, we amplify our beautiful daughters and sisters and queens. I like to imagine India answering back. I like to imagine every last one of our babies, our loved ones, answering back. And I'll imagine a world where not only are we saying their names, but you all are doing it too, where we're not speaking against the silence. Tell someone. Speak their names. It emboldens us. It gives us strength and encouragement in those very lonely times, because there are no words to articulate the level of pain that we live with. It's off the spectrum. But we're here. We're here. We're gonna do something about this, sisters. It is starting with us. And we won't quit.

Gina Best

Not quitting is not just a personal choice we must make; it is a politics we must practice. Engaging in that practice is critical to exposing the disposability of Black lives, including the lives of Black women. For far too long, Black women have had to confront the hard truth that our lives are disposable. Pause and think about the ease with which the police not only killed India Kager but also treated and disposed of her body as if it were trash: "They left my baby on the concrete."

That the SWAT team that killed India considered her life to be disposable even before they opened fire is brutally illustrated by the fact that they chose not to pursue alternatives to shooting into her car in order to hit the man she was with—a man whose right to full and fair treatment under the law was also obliterated in that act. The Virginia Beach police chief claimed afterward that India's death had been an accident. Yet none of the sixteen members of the team involved in the attack did anything to prevent that "accident." Instead, they acted as if India and her young son Roman were acceptable casualties, guilty by association with the Black male suspect police were targeting.

Almost five years after India's death, the world would become familiar with another Black woman who lost her life to a police bullet because she had had a relationship with a man sought by the police. That woman's name was Breonna Taylor. Killed during a raid on her home during the very first days of the COVID-19 pandemic, and just three months before the murder of George Floyd, Breonna would become a household name. With hundreds of thousands of people saying her name, would Breonna's death shift the obscurity in which India and other Black women lose their lives to police violence? What kind of turning point would this be?[1]

In the early hours of the morning of March 13, 2020, Breonna and her boyfriend Kenneth Walker were awakened by an attack on their home in Louisville, Kentucky. Walker fired a single shot from his legally owned gun in self-defense. That choice to stand his ground prompted the plainclothes firing squad at their door to shoot at least thirty-two rounds, attempting to annihilate them both.[2] After she was struck by a fusillade of bullets, Breonna took her last breath as Walker begged her to stay with him.

Officers had forced their way into Kenneth and Breonna's home while executing a "no-knock" warrant—a judicial order that authorizes police to enter someone's home without warning and without identifying themselves.[3] They claimed to be searching for drugs and cash delivered to Taylor's home on behalf of her ex-boyfriend. After officers shot Taylor, Walker called 911 and reported: "I don't know what's happening. Someone kicked in the door and shot my girlfriend." He was subsequently arrested and charged with attempted murder of a police officer. "There were bullet holes everywhere. It was a war zone in there," Taylor's family attorney Sam Aguiar later explained.[4] In a wrongful death lawsuit filed by the family, attorneys contend that Taylor was shot at least eight times[5] and left to bleed out before she died.[6] She was twenty-six years old.

The police violence that killed Breonna did not end with the act of shooting. After the Louisville cops fired on her, they left her without medical attention for more than twenty minutes.[7] When Walker called Breonna's mother, he said their home had been broken into and her daughter had been shot, but at that moment he had no idea who had fired the weapons. Tamika Palmer lived only minutes from her daughter's apartment. She drove over immediately. But the authorities on the scene would not allow her inside. Instead, they directed her to a nearby hospital. When Tamika arrived, staff informed her that they had no patient named Breonna Taylor. After waiting two more hours in the hope that her daughter would be transported to the hospital, Palmer drove back to Breonna's apartment and waited for more than an hour outside. It was only then that an officer on the scene said to her, casually, "She's still in the apartment." *This* is how Tamika Palmer learned her daughter had been killed.[8]

The additional tragedy and outrage of Breonna's death is that her life was ended just as the country and the world were entering a period of unprecedented uncertainty at the start of the pandemic. During this time, there was a profound need for people to express both solidarity and mutual care. Many people did just that, including Breonna. In March 2020 she was a certified emergency medical technician working in at a hospital that was beginning to receive COVID-19 patients.[9] "She was a go-getter," said Jessica Jackson, a friend and coworker. Rukmini Callimachi recalls that Taylor would write out her "goals on every scrap of paper—junk mail, napkins, envelopes." Palmer confirmed this: "She would just make these bullet points. 'I want to have this done by this time.'"[10] She recalled:

> Breonna is like the family glue—even at twenty-six years old. She don't care what is happening, she is going to make sure we get together and have a game night or have a cookout or have something, because we all tend to get so busy and consumed with work and whatever. But she has a personal relationship with everybody, even all my little cousins. They don't call each other cousins. They all call each other sisters and brothers. All the kids, the younger kids, or even the kids her age, looked up to Breonna.[11]

Breonna dreamed of becoming a nurse. In her high school scrapbook, she wrote, "Graduating this year on time is so important to me because I will be the first in my family to accomplish this. . . . I want to be the one who finally breaks the cycle of my family's educational history. I want to be the one to finally make a difference."[12] In one tweet, she wondered what her life would be like if she had never moved from Michigan.[13]

In the days leading up to her death, Breonna had worked four overnight shifts in the emergency room at the University of Louisville Health's Jewish Hospital East.[14] There is a bitter but all-too-familiar irony here: A young Black woman who risked her life to help others lost hers because of the heightened risk posed to her very existence by racism and sexism. Breonna's lost life is a sobering embodiment of the twin pandemics that engulfed African Americans in 2020. The COVID-19 pandemic made it increasingly clear that the structural factors that make Black lives in the United States so precarious—poverty, limited access to health care, higher rates of life-threatening conditions such as diabetes—were also factors in making the COVID mortality rates among Black Americans significantly higher than they were for whites, especially in the early months of the pandemic.[15] Breonna's work in the very first days of the pandemic placed her in the eye of this storm, a key worker whose job put her at increased risk of contracting the virus, and a witness to an unfolding pandemic that would highlight underlying inequalities and racial injustice.[16]

Staying at home was one way to mitigate the risk of contracting the coronavirus, but that was an option that all too many African American women like Breonna either could not or did not exercise. The additional mortality risk that ultimately took her life—the danger of being killed by the police—could not be mitigated by shelter-at-home orders. When it comes to the pandemic of police violence, there is no safe harbor to be secured against state violence. The home cannot shelter us from individuals who are shielded and authorized by the state to take lives in pursuit of ill-conceived notions of public order.

The police killing of a healthcare worker on the front lines of the struggle against COVID-19 is integral to the wider history of state violence against Black women. Healthcare workers were heroes in the pandemic, often lauded—albeit more rhetorically than financially—for their sacrifice. Yet, for Breonna, no amount of sacrifice that she gave in valuing and protecting the lives of others would be extended to her in the execution of basic policing. Neither the exceptional circumstances of Covid nor her service to others in the face of it could halt the dynamics that heighten the risk of death at the hands of police.

There are many echoes in Breonna's story to the death of India Kager. Both women were treated as collateral damage, like casualties of a war against men suspected of engaging in criminal activity, instead of as people pursuing their own lives. In both cases police used warlike tactics, employing randomly lethal force with little restraint, and with the knowledge that there was a risk of innocent lives being lost. Both killings were effectively executions. After being shot, neither India nor Breonna was given the medical attention that could have saved her life. Each was left to lie and die. In the end, the police justified the deaths of these women as the cost of doing the business of "law enforcement." And like India's mother Gina, Tamika was treated with contempt both at the time of her daughter's death and afterward, with utter disregard for her love for Breonna and for what she, the rest of her family, and world lost with the loss of Breonna's life. Yet Tamika, like Gina, refused to remain silent in the face of this dismissal of her daughter's life, and her own grief and demand for justice.

Although Breonna was eventually spared the posthumous anonymity that awaited India and most other Black women killed by police, the details of her life and death are reflected in the determination of Tamika not to let her daughter's short life go unremembered. Many decades ago another mother, Mamie Till, chose to show the world what racism had done to her child. Her decision inspired an entire generation to rise up against a state of affairs that had held Black people under boot for generations. Breonna's story, and those of the many other Black women who have suffered a similar fate, could inspire a seismic shift in the struggle against anti-Black racism, one that turns on a fuller understanding of the gendered dimensions of anti-Black violence.

That Black people, and anti-racist organizers more generally, got behind Breonna Taylor's case was no guarantee that justice would be meted out. Breonna's case would have to reckon with the historical ways in which the legal system has sanctioned the killing of Black bodies. That reckoning began to unfold as early as September 23, 2020, when Kentucky attorney general Daniel Cameron delivered his much-anticipated decision on whether Breonna's killers would be prosecuted. Like so many other announcements in so many other cases like this, it proved to be a crushing disappointment for supporters of the cause of racial justice. The grand jury in the Taylor case, guided by Cameron's legal judgment, decided that none of the three officers involved in killing Breonna (Myles Cosgrove, Brett Hankison, and Jonathan Mattingly) would stand trial for her death. Only one officer, Hankison, was indicted on three counts of "wanton endangerment in the first degree."[17] Among the most shameful dimensions of this decision was the failure to even *mention Breonna's name* in the charges brought against Hankison. Instead, the complaint against Hankison related to the people who lived next door, "because the shots he fired had passed through Ms. Taylor's apartment walls into a neighboring apartment, endangering three people there."[18] Two years after Breonna's death, in March 2022, Hankinson was acquitted of all three counts of felony wanton endangerment.[19]

Attorney General Cameron's gut-wrenching announcement in September 2020 came on the sixty-fifth anniversary of another jury decision that absolved white men for a gruesome murder that transformed the nation. On September 23, 1955, twelve white jurors took under two hours to acquit two white men of torturing and killing a fourteen-year-old Black Chicago native named Emmett Till in Money, Mississippi.[20] The killers later confessed that they had abducted Till to avenge an alleged insult the boy had made against the pair's wife and sister-in-law. Later evidence suggested that several other unindicted men had been involved, and that the entire incident was spurred by a lie.[21] Till's mangled body, found tied to a cotton gin, was virtually unrecognizable.

Mamie Till rejected the advice of some to hold a closed-casket funeral in Chicago. Her decision to hold an open-casket service for her son in order to, in her words, "let the people see what they did to my boy," was a pivotal moment in awakening an entire generation of young Black Americans to take up anew the centuries-long struggle for Black freedom. Mamie's simple act demanded that the world *bear witness* to the profound savagery of white racism—and to reckon with the legal system that facilitated and legitimized its ongoing horrors.

The outrage over Till's murder was rooted in the undeniable realization that such a gruesome killing was essentially licensed by a legal system that would hold no one accountable. Similarly, the state's judgment that Breonna Taylor, dead from multiple gunshots in a police home invasion, amounted to a verdict that no legal or moral harm had occurred in the hail of bullets that took her life. The failure to so much as mention Breonna's name in the sole indictment for the inhumane assault in her home underscores a toxic equation in which the prosecution of a drug war reduces the value of stolen lives to unmentionable collateral damage. The judgment affirms once again how the lethal relationship between the police system and Black citizens is facilitated by law. Cameron's decision, like the Till verdict, allowed this toxic status quo to continue unnamed and unimpeded.

Breonna's death took place in very different circumstances to those of Till. But the failure of the legal system to prosecute the police responsible for killing her makes what happens to women in situations like Breonna's a gendered version of what happened to Till. In the years following her death, the question is whether her death and the failure to hold anyone accountable for it will bring the same shift in public consciousness as Till's. Breonna's death, like his, was not a singular event; other Black women have been killed, just as other Black men had been lynched. But a moment of profound injustice can sometimes spur a mass mobilization by making the intolerable dimensions of life lived under these circumstances particularly legible. Breonna's death may serve as a cornerstone for a generation of activism, as Till's did. If so, it will represent something new in the Black freedom struggle, something that the #SayHerName campaign has been fighting for since 2014: it will make Black women central to the continued struggle against anti-Black racism.

Some may seize on differences between the killing of Emmett Till and the killing of Breonna Taylor to discount the relevance of his death to hers. Till was tortured and killed by vigilantes enforcing southern codes of white supremacy, and his killers were acquitted after a full trial by an all-white jury. The trial's faux-murder-mystery framing belied the fact that jurors had every reason to know that the two accused assailants had conspired with others to kidnap and kill the fourteen-year-old.[22] Their hasty acquittal amounted to a brazen act of jury nullification.[23] Breonna, by contrast, was killed by sworn officers of the law who were executing a warrant. Her death was ultimately framed by a grand jury—in sealed proceedings headed by Kentucky's African American attorney general—as a permissible homicide, committed during the due course of law enforcement.

But the more relevant unifying factor here is this: in both Breonna's and Emmett's deaths, the prevailing codes blamed the victims for alleged behaviors triggering murderous responses from white men empowered to exercise their prerogative to kill. In Till's case, the savage murder was, for many, explained if not justified by his alleged breaking of the racial code of conduct governing interracial encounters between Black men and white women. The claim that Till crossed the line obscured both the fact that the line itself was a construct of racial power and that extralegal means of enforcing it essentially functioned as state policy. Breonna's death was similarly attributed to actions that placed her in a situation in which the three men who killed her were engaging in legitimate law enforcement activity. Breonna's blame was associational: her past involvement with a person targeted for arrest, and current involvement with a man who fired a weapon for which he held a license in order to defend them both, rendered her a legitimate victim of police homicide. This was the narrative uniting the claim that J. W. Milam and Roy Bryant had to kill Emmett Till *and* the assertion that Cosgrove, Hankison, and Mattingly really had no choice but to shoot into Taylor's home after they encountered one shot from an occupant who had the right to fire it. This eagerness to blame the victim for her own death is a common motif in the stories of the women whose lives and deaths we recount in this book.

The victim-blaming that links lynching victims and victims of police violence is tied together through a common trope of their alleged misbehavior that justifies lethal force. The historical patterns of media justifying lynchings and police killings has extended to contemporary media coverage that often focuses on rumors about drugs, or that misrepresents the victim as armed when in fact they were unarmed.[24] When the death happens after an alleged minor offense has taken place, as was the case with George Floyd, Eric Garner, or Shelly Frey, news stories often put more emphasis on the victim's alleged deed than the murder itself.[25] The gendered patterns of victim-blaming are particularly legible when the coverage trains its attention on, "Well, what did she do?" or "Who was she with?" In such cases, Black women's choice of company becomes yet another in a range of narratives used by our culture to effectively blame them for the violence committed against them, from rape to murder.

Consider the well-worn victim-blaming narrative that law enforcement and the press deployed to stigmatize Kayla Moore or Korryn Gaines or Michelle Cusseaux or India Kager for their own deaths at the hands of police—because they were gender-non-conforming, because they looked dangerous, because they were with the wrong man. These defamation campaigns—promoted by the police and spread by the mainstream media—are grounded in a rape culture that positions Black women outside the conventional protections from violence, including sexual violence. Gina Best, whose words open this chapter, underscores the fundamentally gendered and sexualized dimension of police violence against Black women powerfully and devastatingly as she reflects on the way in which her daughter India was presented to the public as culpable for her own death because she was riding in the same car with a man (the father of her son) who was being followed by the police:

> I believe that the underlying shame is that India got herself killed because she made a bad decision as a woman to be with an alleged criminal. So it was her. It's almost akin to, if you're in an abusive relationship or you're a transgender woman, that even being transgender, you brought that upon yourself. We're Black women,

NEWS

Woman killed in standoff with Baltimore County police was live-streaming

Posted: Aug 3, 2016 / 02:53 PM EDT
Updated: Aug 3, 2016 / 02:53 PM EDT

> we're same-gender-loving women, we're cis woman, I've learned that phrase. People don't even want to acknowledge the very identity that we've chosen for ourselves. They want to attach their definitions [to] what we are and how we're supposed to be. We're less than, so get in your place, sister, before I kick you back there; you made a bad decision, so you deserve that. Or, in India's case, you can't even introduce your baby to his father's family. We're gonna murder you, and somehow you are responsible for your own murder.

Gina situates the treatment of her daughter in death within a wider devaluation of Black women's bodies, Black women's different gender identities and sexualities, Black women's relationship choices. What Barbara Arnwine has called "racialized rape culture" legitimates different forms of attack against Black women, allowing them to become the specific targets of state violence—and enables their subsequent revictimization (in the media, in the courtroom) as marginalized others, criminal enablers, or criminals in the making.[26]

These gendered patterns of victim-blaming in the context of police femicide are also fully displayed in the aftermath of Breonna Taylor's murder. Her family's attorney, Sam Aguiar, said that after the case began to receive widespread publicity, the police department went to "great lengths . . . to dig up all of her past."[27] In fact, as documentary filmmaker Yoruba Richen explained on *Democracy Now!*, prosecutors offered Breonna's ex-boyfriend Jamarcus Glover leniency on drug charges if he would name Breonna as a member of an organized crime syndicate. Richen also noted that in the immediate aftermath of Taylor's killing, local news reports carried headlines such as "Drug Suspect Killed" or "Suspect Killed in Drug Probe . . . And Cop Was Shot."[28]

Even months after Breonna's death, media coverage continued to emphasize her relationship to Glover. These accounts claimed—again, without any firm proof—that through him she had been "entangled" in a world of crime and had had previous encounters with law enforcement, even though she personally was never suspected of any crime.[29] Taylor's mother recounted that when she first spoke to detectives at the scene of her daughter's killing, one asked her "if I knew anybody who would want to hurt Breonna, or Kenny, or if I thought they were involved in anything. . . . [and] if Breonna and Kenny had been having any problems or anything."[30]

This persistent search for any pretext to justify police action is a common preoccupation anytime that police kill. And the ready imputation that victims were "no angels," or otherwise deserved their fate on grounds of their allegedly defective moral character, harkens back to specifically gendered acts of violence and the general stigmatization of Black victims throughout the centuries-long struggle to protect Black lives.[31]

More than revealing the ease with which the legal system can render Black lives disposable, Breonna's death puts into sharp relief a particular law enforcement practice that has rendered Black people, including women and girls, vulnerable for far too long: the use of no-knock warrants.

Since 2003 a number of Black women and girls—including Aiyana Stanley-Jones, aged seven; Tarika Wilson, twenty-six; Kathryn Johnston, ninety-two; and Alberta Spruill, fifty-seven

—have been killed in botched no-knock raids.[32] All of them died in their own homes when police broke in without warning. Although we don't always hear about these home deaths because they take place away from the eyes of bystanders, this form of aggressive policing has a particularly severe impact on Black communities and families. For example, one American Civil Liberties Union study found that Black residents in Allentown, Pennsylvania, were "nearly twenty-four times more likely than white people to be impacted by" no-knock raids.[33]

On June 11, 2020, the Metro City Council of Louisville unanimously voted to pass an ordinance called "Breonna's Law," banning no-knock search warrants in the city. Soon after Breonna's Law was passed, the City of Louisville announced a $12 million settlement with Breonna's family.[34] The payment represented one of the largest and fastest settlements ever for a killing of a Black woman by police. Tamika told CNN that her daughter "would have been amazed to see the world changing" as a result of the law and the new wave of protests against police violence, racism, and injustice taking place across the world following her daughter's death and, shortly afterward, that of George Floyd.[35] Yet the law as well as the settlement still fell far short of what Taylor's family and supporters were seeking.

The pattern of paying out without addressing the wider structures that put Black women at particular risk of police violence reflects a pattern of using public resources to compensate citizens for police malpractice and corruption rather than changing institutional responses that lead to unwarranted violence and death. The United States spends close to $115 billion a year on policing, while systematically underinvesting in basic infrastructure, health care, education, affordable housing, and other vital programs.[36] These figures likely underestimate the money that states are willing to invest in sustaining the current model of policing.[37]

Viewed in this wider context, the $12 million paid to Breonna Taylor's family to compensate for the loss of her life is a drop in the ocean. It is merely a cost of doing business, a pay-to-slay arrangement that facilitates death dealing by occasionally compensating families for their losses. In October 2020, the *Wall Street Journal* reported, "The 20 U.S. cities and counties with the biggest police departments have paid over $2 billion since 2015 for alleged misconduct and civil rights violations. . . . The payments have settled allegations of excessive force, wrongful detention, and other abuses that sometimes stretch back decades and in extreme cases resulted in death or permanent injury."[38]

The overarching message here has forced every Black woman to confront a horrifying fact: "Breonna or India could easily be me." Like so many Black women, Breonna had curled up in the arms of a loved one after a long day of work to watch a movie as she drifted off to sleep. Those of us who have chanted "We are Breonna Taylor!" are saying that we can all too clearly imagine our lifeless bodies left in the hallways of our homes. We can imagine taking our son to visit his father's family and reaching to save our child in a hail of gunfire, then being left to die on the pavement as our infants cried out in pain. We can imagine being stepped over, written off as someone being in the wrong place with the wrong person, or with someone who dared to think that our life had value and warranted being protected. We can imagine our mothers not being told that we were dead or how we had been killed, and treating her loss of us like they would any other beast, unworthy of empathy or respect.

We can read the headlines that call us a "suspect," that throw up whatever they can to define us as people whose deaths do not prompt others to worry that the police power that has been unleashed will ever cross their doorstep. We can imagine ourselves exposed for hours while uniformed vultures pick through the remnants of our lives, seizing upon both the choices we made and those that were made for us.[39] And we can imagine these same officers exploiting our ransacked personal lives to quiet the qualms they might have harbored had we been another woman in a different body, in a different part of town, living a different life, with a different man trying to protect us.

We can witness in our mind's eye the belated but widespread saying of our names to insist that our cruelly truncated futures be made to count for *something.* We can feel the hope that with the gaze of the world finally upon us, the realization that we had done nothing wrong would make it wrong that we'd been reduced to nothing. And we can taste the tears that mark our bitter awareness that despite the countless demands to arrest the cops who killed us, our deaths would ultimately be dismissed as just *one of those things that happen*: a no-harm, no-foul misfortune counted among the acceptable costs of maintaining the anti-Black foundations of police and policing.

We can see it all. For some because it has already happened to those we love. For others because we know that until the power given to law enforcement to take life without significant fear of consequences is taken away, policing will operate in the same way that Till's killers were free to take his life. The law that exists above the letter will insulate killing done in concert with the imperatives of white security. Only a massive shift in the social narrative can change that—a shift that the Till generation was galvanized to enact. A shift that galvanized a new generation in the aftermath of George Floyd. And a shift that, with Breonna Taylor's death, might broaden enough to place the violation of Black women in their most intimate moments as a particularly gruesome *and* intolerable expression of racial power.

We can envision all of this because we know too well that the double loss of life that Black women experience—first at the hands of police, and then in the posthumous justification of their deaths—might have plunged another Black woman once more into anonymity. What made Breonna's case different is that this time the whole world witnessed its aftermath. We can see with unprecedented clarity the heinous truth beneath the surface of law-and-order rationales for lethal police impunity. Breonna, like Emmett, lost her life under the false, fatalistic view that this is just the way things have to be. This brand of institutional resignation is a lie built around a contingent set of practices upholding a historic pattern of racist and misogynistic police power.

Gina Best calls these practices “kill culture,” a parallel to rape culture:

> They brought it upon themselves. These people aren’t even worth standing up for. These people aren’t even worth writing new legislation for, so that there’s equality. These people aren’t even worth—but you’re a woman too?
>
> You’re a woman who happened to be killed by police. Oh, and by the way, you’re in a car, you’re in a home. How dare you have a gun like Korryn protecting your son? “We’re there to serve a warrant.” “We’re law enforcement here to do our job.” But she can’t do her heartfelt job as a mother and protect her son?
>
> India can’t do what she felt in her heart, to go and introduce the baby, hopeful that there’s going to be a surrounding of this child with blood relatives, family? So that this child is growing up in a proverbial village?
>
> You can’t get help when you’re in the middle of a mental health crisis, like Michelle Cusseaux, and just trust and hope that when they arrive on the scene, they’re going to help you versus then murder you?
>
> Our mothers, our sisters, our daughters are dying in fear.

Gina Best—like Mamie Till sixty-five years ago for her son, and like Tamika Palmer, Fran Garrett, Rhanda Dormeus, Michelle Shirley, and Sharon Wilkerson today—is fighting to show the world what the law did to her daughter. The efforts of all these mothers are crucial not only to building a movement, #SayHerName, but to building community.

Korryn Gaines

Chapter 4

Building Community

"We went to sleep one set of people, and after our tragic event or the murders from the terrorists in blue suits, we'll never be the same."
Rhanda Dormeus, mother of Korryn Gaines
(August 24, 1992–August 1, 2016)

My name is Rhanda Dormeus. Korryn was my twenty-three-year-old baby. She was a very, very feisty young lady from toddlerhood. Very outspoken, kind of bossy at times. She was just matter-of-fact. She knew what she wanted, and she sought out to get what she wanted. Growing up, she did very well in school and excelled in all her classes.

Elementary school and middle school were uneventful. When she got to high school, she branched out and did things like marching band. She played the clarinet. She had to have a blue clarinet. Everybody had a black clarinet, but her favorite color was royal blue, so I had to buy her a royal blue clarinet. It worked out, because I could always spot her on the field when she was performing. That was her freshman year. During her sophomore year, she was on the debate team. She went to a college prep high school called Baltimore City College High School, and she was interested in political science. She also did swimming, which I was opposed to because she was an asthmatic. And so, her doctor said, "Look, let her do it. It'll expand her lungs." And she wound up being an exceptionally good swimmer.

During her senior year, she lost interest in political science because there were so many things going on in society that contradicted what she was being taught. I think that was the beginning of her starting to reach out and learn more about the government outside of what was made available through the media. She wanted to go behind the scenes and do her own research. She was an avid reader. Oh my God, I could buy this girl ten books in a week, and she would go through them. She read urban novels, but she also read books about Marcus Garvey and other informative things.

As she read and learned different things, she applied them to her everyday life. She saw some of the struggles from these books that these characters depicted and correlated them to what she was dealing with or what everyone was dealing with. She graduated on time and she chose to go to Morgan State University. She only stayed two semesters. We were local, but she wanted to have the experience of campus life so she stayed on campus. Then she found out she was going to have Kodi, so I started looking at different colleges that would allow young mothers to have their children because I wanted her to stay in school. But then she was like, "Mom, you know, that's going to be too much."

So she directed her attention to her other passion: hair and makeup. She got a cosmetology license and started doing hair and makeup, and she enjoyed it. She bought two homes as rental properties that she used for income. She bought her own vehicle. She was independent. Even though she was young, once she found [out] that she was going to have a child, she knew that she had to take responsibility as her own adult. So, once she left college, she never came back home. She was on her own.

With Kodi and her cosmetology license, she went off on her own. And again, she started really, really delving deep into the government and following different stories that the media would put out, but she wanted to go behind and under to get a sense of the backstories. We come from a law-enforcement family, but the evolution of police has gotten so much worse. It just happened that she came into consciousness about problems in policing at a time [when] they were peaking. It was out in the open more. It was more obvious. And she was saying, "What are they trying to tell us? Our eyes are lying to us?" That would infuriate her.

After Michael Brown, there was a whole snowball effect of police murders. Freddie Gray was a neighbor of ours. I didn't personally know him, but I knew him from the neighborhood, and it was literally a few blocks away. Everything that unfolded was literally around the corner from where she grew up. That was our community, and our community had been robbed. She was an activist role model. She wanted to teach because she was self-taught. She just wanted to enlighten the masses about things that were going on around her. She has a few spoken-word poems that are out. She would always do her little rants on Facebook or Instagram about things that were going on in the world. She just wanted to uplift. She shot straight from the hip. Korryn was much like myself in a way, and maybe even more; she took every opportunity as a teachable moment. That's what I saw her do with her children, every chance she could get, even about Santa Claus: "There ain't no white man coming down my chimney." She would tell you, "Don't tell my kids nothing about no damn Santa Claus, because I buy this stuff." She taught them about the positive and the negative. I know she would've taken her babies down to the Museum of Black History [National Museum of African American History and Culture]. I know they would've gone more than once. I think she would just be involved with anything that would defeat racism or be making an attempt to defeat racism.

That Friday before she was murdered, we were FaceTiming, and she wanted to share with me that [Korryn's daughter] Karsyn called her Mum, and not Mom. She was so tickled that she was calling her Mum but just had to add the British twang to it. She was excited to share things about her children with me.

Two weeks before she was killed, she stood in my dining room with my fiancé and me and told me, "Mom, they're going to kill me." She says, "I'm making too much noise." There were a whole bunch of things that had happened prior to August 1, and even March 10, that indicated that she was being monitored. I asked her two weeks before she was killed, "Basically, what is the importance of what you're doing?" And she just said that people need to know "I'm never going to stop talking until they silence me." And I asked her, "Are you prepared to become a martyr?" And she said, "Yes. If it affects change."

Korryn was 5'2", 105 pounds. She was really, really tiny but she had been extremely outspoken on the police terror that had been going on because of Freddie Gray. It had overwhelmed everybody nationwide, but can you imagine people who knew him? She was already speaking out against the violence and just the whole oppression idea. She spoke out about it, and I think sometimes people come to their breaking point, like "You're not going to just do anything to me."

That was something about Sandra Bland's documentary that really moved me. She was going to cuss, and she was going to vent, and she was going to make a stance. That was Korryn. When she felt like she was being wronged, she would unleash. She would say, "Look, you're not doing this shit to me. Who do you think you are?" You know? People compared her to Sandra Bland because they were both activists in that way. They both wanted to let people know how we, as African American people, feel about the way we are treated by law enforcement, and she wanted to awaken us to the real world. White people aren't always good people to deal with, especially in law enforcement. You know what I mean? It's unfortunate but true.

What resonated to me about Korryn's case in comparison to Sandra Bland was that they both spoke their minds, and they were opposed to what was being done to them. Ultimately it caused their demise. In Korryn's case the traffic stop—which I guess was the basis or the premise for her untimely death—was in March of 2016. I think it was in February when Korryn contacted me saying that her tags had been removed from her vehicle. And I remember her calling me, and she was actually on her way to my house, and she said, "Well I can't come now." And I said, "What's the matter?" And she said, "Well, my tags are gone." And she showed me through Messenger the card that she had found under the windshield wiper.

And so, again, in March of 2016, that's when she got stopped for those tags. Of course, there was a verbal back and forth. She was asking them for their delegation of rights and different things that are legal documents that a lot of regular officers don't know about. Any form of documentation saying that you have the right to arrest me. And so it was back and forth. There was a struggle. They ripped her out of her car because she didn't want them to touch her children. She said, "Don't touch my children!"

Korryn wasn't a fan of law enforcement because she felt like most or all of them were corrupt in some way or somehow. So they had a verbal altercation, and things got escalated. A struggle ensued. And she was taken into custody, she was taken to the hospital because she was pregnant with twins. And when they took her to the hospital they worked her up, patched up her little scratches.

When she was released from the hospital, they stuck her in an isolation cell by herself. Which means she's out of view and you could barely hear her. They never gave her a reason, but I'm sure it was because they didn't like her mouth. It was very similar to how they treated Sandra Bland. And let me tell you something, this isolation stuff is not by accident. When you isolate somebody, especially when they're upset, confused, or their emotions are heightened, it puts them in a vulnerable situation. The goal is to break their spirit—to bring them down a notch, for lack of a better term.

The cops holding her in isolation didn't give her any food or water. I still have the labs to prove it. When they rushed her back to the hospital after hours and hours of her begging and crying and pleading, her HCG count had dropped, which was indicative of her losing the babies.[1] *Within a twenty-four-hour period things went from normal to devastating. I believe it was intentional, to break her mentally. I would hate to think that they were intentionally trying to make her lose the children. But the process that led to her losing her twins started there, and not long after she was released she miscarried.*

When she was finally released, the paperwork that they gave her didn't have any of the information that was pertinent to her court date. She went to the station and actually requested the documents. The officer, at first, did not recognize her, and then she gave him her name, and he recognized her and said, "Well, the supervisor that would have that document or be able to access it isn't available." Because of this, she missed her court appointment. So it was a snowball effect. They sent an arrest warrant because she missed her court appointment—for a traffic violation. She wasn't killed during the traffic stop, but the outcome was the same.

On August 1, I got a call from Korryn at about eight, eight thirty in the morning. I missed it. So then I texted her, and she said, "Ma, they're here." And I said, "Who?" She said, "The police." I said, "Well, what are you going to do?" She said, "I'm not, they're not taking me. They're not going to take me and hurt me again." I said, "Where're the children?" and she said, "They're here." And I think I said, "Don't do anything crazy." And if I'm not mistaken, that was like the last interaction that I had with my daughter.

When the officers knocked on the door and heard children, they went to the rental office to get a key. They decided that the children could be in danger. Korryn's perception of it was, "Everybody who needs a key and has a key is in here, so who would be coming in my door with a key?" She sat and waited in the middle of her living room floor with her shotgun, which was a legally owned shotgun. She sat in the room. I guess when they finally gained entry they saw her sitting there and they pulled back. She asked, "What are you doing here?" Then, I guess they shared with her why they were there, although during the whole situation, the officers kept saying, "We aren't here for you. We aren't here for you." I'm like, "How are they connecting the traffic ticket if they're not there for her? Why did they send out a warrant to arrest her and now you're saying you're not there for her?" It was a lot of manipulation from law enforcement.

So about twenty minutes later I get a call from Karsyn's dad, who was hysterical. And he said, "Ma, they're gonna kill her." I knew they were. I knew they were. I knew because of her mentality that they weren't going to negotiate with her. It would have been just too much for them. Not worth it to negotiate with her. And I said, "I'm on my way." He was already detained. And the officer didn't know he had his phone. So the officer snatched his phone in the process of him talking to me. And I heard him say, "Who is this?" And I said, "This is Korryn's mom." And I said, "I'm on my way." I said, "Let me get there to my baby." He says, "Oh no, it's past that now." And I said, "What do you mean? You're just going to go kill her?" And I said, "Who is your supervisor?" So I didn't get that guy's name, but I'll never forget the name of the supervisor, Officer Terry. I said, "Look, I'm on my way. I'm in the city, she's in the county, about thirty minutes away. Let me get there. And let me talk to her." He says, "Oh no, it's beyond that now." I said, "So do you mean to tell me, y'all just going to go in there and kill my child? You're not going to give me the option to come and try to negotiate?" He said, "That's not protocol." He told me it was not protocol to have the family try to negotiate.

So I called my best friend: "Retta? They're going to kill my baby." I got on the phone and started calling family members. We had at least ten family members show up to that scene. They held us in a daycare center in a nearby church. They moved us into this room, and they guarded us. We had people monitoring us while we went to the bathroom. They wouldn't give any of us access to her. They took my phone and communicated with my baby as though they were me. She knew that it wasn't me. She knew it wasn't because we communicated differently. Family started calling and texting my phone almost immediately because the officers told the media it was a hostile situation. The cops were texting my family, although they later lied and said that they didn't. I didn't sign a release for my phone until two days later.

I begged everyone I saw for answers. They said, "You have to wait until the lieutenant comes." When the lieutenant finally came back, I ran up to him and asked, "Did you kill my baby?" He says, "Yes, she's gone."

Royce Ruby killed my child. At the deposition, he said that he felt his life was in danger and also feared that Korryn might kill Kodi. After instructing Facebook to cut Korryn's live feed, Officer Ruby shot her. She was making Kodi a peanut butter and jelly sandwich. When Royce Ruby killed her, she was standing at the counter making Kodi a sandwich. He couldn't even see her; he shot her through a wall. He also shot Kodi twice. The one that hit him in his face, thank god it was a ricochet, but the one that hit him in the elbow, it tore his whole elbow out. He'll never be able to do push-ups. His elbow had to be rebuilt. One of the bullets went through her and hit him.

It wasn't until the story hit the news that they came and told me. I wanted to know where my grandbaby was, but they had already taken him to the hospital. By this time, I had fifty to seventy-five family members assembled there, and we were all just screaming.

When I get to the hospital to see my grandson, they won't let me see him. They have two officers and a social worker questioning him. This five-year-old child [who] just saw his mother get murdered by the police, and now they have police surrounding his hospital bed. They wouldn't let any of the family members in to see him, to comfort him. He was so scared.

I've heard all kinds of evil things, mean things, said about my daughter. She was crazy. She was [a] "suicide by cop." She was putting her child in danger. All kinds of things were said. People have a right to their own perspective. I guess it's up to myself and the family to clear her name. She just wanted to teach. She just wanted people to understand.

It's a nightmare that we will never wake up from. We have grandchildren that won't know how wonderful she was, and family that will forever be broken because of someone else's split-second decision. It's life-altering, shattering. I know all of the moms feel like this. I don't know whether I'm coming or going sometimes, and I just gotta get a grip, because I have responsibilities. I've been so messed up that I've almost forgotten to pick Karsyn from school. I was lost in the moment, and then I realized, I've got to go get my baby. I'm here grieving over her mother and forgetting about her.

How will I ever be able to explain or show or teach my grandchildren how wonderful their mother was. Even with all the footage and pictures, they'll never be able to feel her embrace. Her hugs were different than my hugs, her kisses were different than my kisses. I can never ever give them a sense of what they are missing. Karsyn was still nursing when Korryn was killed. That bonding, and then nothing. That's going to be traumatizing for a two-year-old. She was traumatized.

It's almost like you want to cease to live because the pain in your heart is so much.

Justice for Korryn, what does it look like? It looks like an officer shouldn't be allowed to make lateral moves within the department if they've had other issues. This was not Royce Ruby's first shooting. Justice for me is getting officers better training, making sure that they adhere to policy, and not create new ones as they go along.

The officer [who shot Korryn] was found not guilty because of the statutes of such and such, and such of the police code or this and that. They chose not to indict the officers.

In September 2016 an internal police investigation concluded that Officer Ruby, who had previously been involved in a fatal shooting, was justified in shooting Korryn Gaines and would not be charged. He was subsequently promoted.

We went to civil trial. It was February 2, 2018. It was four white jurors, two Black jurors, who came up with their own settlement amount of $37 million. They came up with that money based on the information that was presented from evidence. The county appealed, and on February 15, 2019, the day before the anniversary of the settlement, the judge decided to overturn it based on qualified immunity, which had been on the table three *times before the trial even started. He did that because he never expected us to win. He never argued for us to have qualified immunity, because he didn't expect us to win based on the circumstances around the case. Once the jury heard all of the evidence, they came back with $37 million. The jurors. So that says a lot.*

Needless to say, we're going to appeal. It's not about the money—we have to get the truth out there. When they decided to decline criminal charges, they thought we were going to go away. They want us to go away.

[In July 2020 a jury reinstated the original amount of $38 million awarded Korryn Gaines's family in the 2018 civil suit.][2]

I just want everybody to know that the fight continues. There's no dollar amount that can remotely replace what we've lost. I can do without the dollar[s]. I want accountability. I want the people involved to be held accountable. I'm going to go out on a limb and speak for all of us and say: I want them to pay. I want them to feel our pain. They need to know. They need to come from behind the wall of protection and be held accountable. That's what I want.

Korryn felt like she was in a fight by herself, so she would be so happy that I am continuing her fight. In her last hours, she felt like she was alone, because that's the way the stage was set, for her to feel alone. And I'm going to continue battling for her because she had a message to get out. It wasn't received by everyone in the way that she wanted to present it, but I'm going to clear it up for her. I'm going to clear it up for her. I'm going to deliver it the way I know she would want it to be delivered.

Rhanda Dormeus

Public denunciation and social mobilization have long been tools to demand justice—yet when we fail to listen to and elevate some narratives of loss, we allow episodes of lethal violence to escape scrutiny. This marginalization thwarts any hope of recognition and accountability. As I have already argued and want to emphasize again here, so long as Black women's vulnerability to police violence remains an afterthought, it remains a near-perfect crime. The loss is not registered as yet another episode of anti-Black violence, and the actions of killer cops are subject to virtually no denunciation, much less legal consequences. This cycle of erasure can perennially renew itself, and the pathologies of lethal policing and social amnesia will continue uncontested, politically, legally, and morally.

This publicly orchestrated double loss is an added injury to the families of Black women who have been killed by the police, driving home a message that their grief and anger is literally unspeakable. Rituals of remembrance reverse this conspiracy of silence. They build community by recovering the lives that should have been and rededicating us all toward more inclusive demands for justice.

From the earliest moments of #SayHerName, the African American Policy Forum (AAPF) has prioritized the need to create a space that grants recognition and support to the families of Black women whose lives the police "just came and snatched away from us like nothing." This crucial space is one where surviving family members grieve with those who understand the depth of their losses, find new ways of living, and collectivize their demands for justice. #SayHer Name gatherings have birthed rituals that enact a core imperative of the campaign: to bear witness to the lives lived, the lives lost, and the lives that could have been.

The very refrain "Say Her Name" carries within it a community-centered ritual: through repeating the names and the stories of those whose lives were stolen, we work collectively to make present what has been absent. The collective chanting breaks through conspiracies of silence, creating a communal space where losses that have gone unmarked become visible and audible. As the writer Nicole Young describes:

> When we march we chant. Chanting is the drumbeat of sound that helps carry us past cops with billy clubs in their hands. It's the sonic reminder as we trudge through hot, humid, rainy days that we are here for a purpose, one bigger than ourselves. A chant is a call to those who may be watching, an invitation to join us as we fight for a brighter, freer world. We chant so many things. "No justice, no peace, no racist police" and "This is what democracy looks like!" But the chant that always jangles my soul and forces even my most tired

> voice into a frenzied scream is "Say her name!" . . . We shout HER name as we continue to protest, because her name has power. Power that one day will bring an end to a system intent on our destruction.[3]

Within the world of #SayHerName, Black women do not need to contest whether their lives and their grief matter. Relieved of the need to assert their simple humanity and to force hostile institutions and social actors to acknowledge the devastating pain that attends the loss of a daughter, sister, mother, niece, or aunt, these women can begin the difficult and indispensable work of healing, remembering, and agitating for accountability and justice. #SayHerName rituals focus on creating a safe space curated by and for Black women, where families are able to mourn, to rage, to hope, and to imagine otherwise.

These gatherings bring Black women and girls into community with each other, their families, and the larger movement for Black liberation in ways that reconnect the material and immaterial, the body and spirit, the mind and soul, and the realm of what Toni Morrison describes as "discredited knowledge" with the struggle for remembrance and justice.[4] Our work mobilizes language from various sources—from collective memories of the civil rights movement, from traditional spiritual beliefs in things not yet seen, and from more ancient inspirations in African history and culture. Looking to our past to fashion something unique, we seek to empower Black women and to disrupt the taken-for-granted dimensions of the material world that have worked to marginalize our pain, our resilience, and our experience writ large. And by combining those different ritualistic elements we intend to create something unique, powerful enough to empower Black women and disruptive enough to challenge the technologies of power in our time.

The rituals of #SayHerName are about giving inspiration and purpose to continue the fight, and they are about clearing minds, hearts, and souls with the practices of witnessing. Such powerful acts also inevitably work to strengthen us as a community, as women holding space for other women, while inspiring us anew to claim our own spiritual peace and social power in a minefield of intersectional oppressions. They are rituals of re-membrance, recovery, and rededication. In the words of the actress Thandiwe Newton, "When I see the erasure of Black women victims and survivors, I see a narrative in need of a new script! We can 'flip the script' on our erasure in countless ways. If Black and Brown women the world over are provided a stage, or a silver screen, to tell our stories, we will show that the beauty and bounty of our lives can save this precious world."[5]

Performing arts director and AAPF colleague Awoye Timpo outlines the importance of ritual remembering to different African traditions:

> From an African lens, giving someone a name has cosmological implications, and the importance of naming can never be underrated. Names identify our being. They have power. They transcend time.
>
> [T]hese 197 names we know of [women] who have been killed [mean] that 197 communities have been transformed, but communities and names cannot be buried. They are a dimension of the immortal self. By calling someone by their name, we call their energy. By calling their names, we are reminding ourselves that they are still with us, and, above all, we are not

condoning the injustices done to them with a culture of silence.

Each element of each ceremony—from singing and chanting to planting and watering, from libations to the call-and-response—is ritualistically meaningful and has a unique purpose: to bring forth a cultural memory. Each exists not only in the specific time and place of the ritual but also draws on past rituals and pushes forward to the future. Here we offer some words and images from one ritual, held on the fifth anniversary of #SayHerName on a Saturday in December 2019 at Columbia Law School. We invite you to take those elements that work for you and make this ritual your own.

Columbia Law School is hardly the setting one would imagine for a healing. It is a space typically reserved for the sterile business of an Ivy League institution that primarily trains corporate lawyers, not a domain to stage a confrontation with the various ways in which the law has fostered a particularly lethal relationship between Black people and the police.

One day prior, the convening room where the Remembrance Ceremony would take place had been awash in white, with only a clock and portraits of two ancient white male professors adorning its walls. The room—sleek, impeccably clean, blanched of anything that might make an impression on the senses—was not one in which the lives and stories of Black women were welcome with open arms. Nor was that room welcoming of the spirituality and reflection the remembrance ceremony contemplated.

But on December 14, 2019, the room was transformed. The stale air was filled with the aromas of ginger and turmeric, the white walls were strung with soft, twinkling lights, and the stiff concrete columns to the back of the room were adorned with the faces of Black women killed by the police. As the ceremony began, the sunset cast warm hues of golden light onto dozens of glass jars decorated with strips of kente cloth. As the sun moved slowly across the western sky, the light in the room gradually shifted from vibrant and bright to serene and gentle.

Amid the images of the woman along the walls were roses, a reminder both that we are roses that have pushed up through concrete and that none of us should have to. And at the far west side of the room, the decorated jars were sitting atop a white cloth, waiting to be filled with tulip bulbs in recognition of the Black women to be honored that evening. Although the common denominator holding these women together was death by agents of the state, we were there to celebrate something else: their lives before that fatal moment, and the lives that should have been in the absence of it. In this remembrance, we were there to build community.

Since the inception of #SayHerName, we've struggled to change the lexicon around Black women's fatal encounters with the police. Contrary to what headlines would have you believe, these women did not simply leave the material world due to unavoidable circumstances; they were violently ripped from it.

With this planting ceremony, we endeavored to embed the memories of these women in fertile soil—a garden lovingly tended by the community that together constitutes #SayHerName. The fruits we hoped to harvest were the possibilities of a future in which their names will always be on our lips, in a world bequeathed to us in which each and every Black woman can live free of the risk that they might be taken by those who are sworn to protect and serve.

In the frontmost chairs of the room were Gina Best and Rhanda Dormeus, the mothers of India Kager and Korryn Gaines. They were dressed completely in white, with white headwraps. And at the place where the windows converged in the southwest corner of the room stood a podium, where I welcomed the mothers and opened the ritual.

Kimberlé Crenshaw: Thank you all for coming out to this ceremony of remembrance. Today is December 14, 2019, the five-year anniversary of #SayHerName. Five years ago today, there was a massive protest in New York City. It was a protest to bring attention to police brutality, and in particular to demand justice after the New York grand jury refused to indict the officer that killed Eric Garner. Many of you were at that protest marching and demanding justice. And we were saying the names of many of the African American men and boys who had recently been killed: Eric Garner, Tamir Rice, Michael Brown. We changed those names, we demanded justice for brothers, fathers, and sons taken too soon. And we also said the names of Michelle Cusseaux, Kayla Moore, and Tanisha Anderson, also African Americans who were killed by the police, but they were women. They were also people whose names were not on every tongue, people whose lost lives were not known by the masses demanding justice and police accountability. We came to that march with an intention to hold space for all African Americans who were killed by the police, including the women whose names were not known. Now, an interesting thing happened at that moment. What happened was some people who were aware of these names were grateful that we brought them into the march, and they paused with us, with our banner, to hold space for these people who lost their lives. Others were shocked. They had no idea that Black women and girls are also killed by the police. How would they, when there isn't much news coverage of what happens when women and girls, when their lives are taken.

To our knowledge, there had not been a massive march like this for any woman or girl who was killed by the police. So, we knew that there was work to be done. It also told us that that work wasn't going to be easy. There was a third group, and that group was not happy that we were inserting women into a space that they saw as exclusively a problem that impacted men. So some of them said, "Where are the men's names?" We said, "The men's names are on all of the other posters. The men's names are on everyone else's tongues. We're saying them as well. What's happening here is that you are not saying the women's names. That's what we are here to do." So #SayHerName was born when we insisted that the names on our banner be said side-by-side with the names of the men. #SayHerName is more than a hashtag; it is an imperative.

So that was five years ago. Since then we have met with many of the mothers of women whose pictures you see around the room here. Two of our wonderful mothers are here today, Rhanda Dormeus and Gina Best.

They're here representing their daughters and their many sisters who have also lost daughters to police violence. Today is our ceremony of remembrance. We believe that rituals are important in social justice work to hold an image of a world that ought to be, to take back what was taken from us. Lives were taken, their stories were taken, their futures were stolen, with an epitaph that reads, "Your death was 'justifiable, a nonissue, an unfortunate thing that just happened.' While we can't reverse the theft of our sisters' lives, we can do something about the snuffing out of her story. We can reverse her erasure, we can repair the muting of her name."

So that's what we're here today to do, to lift her up, to nurture her memory, and, in her name, set our intention to live in a future in which no Black woman loses her life to police violence. What you see before you here is a representation of every African American woman who we've come to know as a woman who has lost her life to police violence. You see their photos in our memory gallery, and you see their representations in many of the pieces that we have here around the room. At a certain point this evening we're going to ask you to join us in this ceremony by holding and carrying a name of one of the women who has been stolen from us. We're going to ask you to come forward and plant a perennial in her memory.

And then, as we step forward to water these perennials, we will conclude by saying all their names. We want this to be so cacophonous, so loud that they hear us, they feel us, and know we are here with them. Is that alright with everyone?

Crowd: Yes!

Together we call out the names of the women who should be here, who we are here to honor and remember: Kayla Moore, India Beaty, Korryn Gaines, India Kager, Shelly Frey, Michelle Cusseaux, Rekia Boyd.

After we say these names and others together as a group in person, we open the space up, remembering the many other acts of remembrance and protest over the past few years, actions that have brought us together with others in the struggle for racial and gender justice. Together the participants and attendees watch the music video for Baby Got Back Talk's "When They Go Low, We Go Six Feet Under," which is dedicated to the #SayHer-Name campaign.

Black women comprise less than 10% of the population, yet 33% of women and girls killed by police are Black.

The video opens with a chilling reminder of the disproportionate impact of police violence on Black women: "Black women constitute less than 10% of the population, yet 33% of the women and girls killed by police are Black." In the background we hear some of their names called out: *Danette Daniels, Alberta Spruill, Yvette Smith, Margaret Laverne Mitchell, Latoya James, Gabriella Nevarez, Shelly Frey.* As the song opens, the camera pans the faces of Kayla and other Black women smiling out at us from posters with their names. The scene then cuts to a series of television images of white officials speaking into microphones, trying to justify the unjustifiable, their voices silenced in a symbolic gesture of reversal. As the song plays on, we see scene upon scene of groups of friends, family members, allies, carrying posters with photos of murdered women, bearing their names, shouting or standing silently, some with hand-painted placards lovingly displaying their names, demanding that police stop shooting and killing Black women, demanding justice for Black lives. Demanding simply: Stop Killing our Friends.

Then we hear from the mothers:

Sharon Wilkerson: *They need to feel what we're feeling! Cause it hurts!*

Gina Best: *We will not stop.*

Fran Garrett: *Justice to me would be for us to come together and stand, not justice for Michelle but for all of us.*

Cassandra Johnson: *And once you become pissed you don't cry a lot anymore. You get busy. You get to workin'.*

Afterward Rhanda and Gina share a few words.

Rhanda: First of all, thank you everyone for coming out and supporting. It's a very emotional night because #SayHerName has been the pillar of our support. They reached out to me—no one had reached out to me before when I lost my daughter and . . .

Everyone associated with #SayHerName keeps me motivated. They give me a reason to keep moving forward because they constantly uplift our girls, and that's what the mothers need. We just battle emotionally, internally. I just wanna say thank you, Dr. Kim, AAPF, and #SayHerName for everything that you do.

Rhanda passes the mic to Gina.

Gina: You see how, when Rhanda was speaking, it becomes overwhelming, and you have to stop for a moment. That's every day for us, every single day for us. We are arrested with the overwhelming, crushing grief, living a life of duality where our hearts are amputated, but we have to still find a way to keep moving forward. It's comforting that our babies are not forgotten, but, by the same token, it is not comforting to know that it's going to be someone else's mother or child unless something is done [*She pauses, steadies herself before continuing.*]

We do wonder what our daughters would be doing if they were here. We do wonder as their children get older, what are you going to say when they ask questions? How are they going to feel when they see police, or see other children with their mommies, and their mommy is not there? What do you say? We are here today to say her name, and we are going to do that. Thank you all, and please, continue the utterance of their names, so it is not a curse but an affirmation. We are here for our daughters, and we are not going anywhere.

Kimberlé thanks Rhanda and Gina for sharing the precious lives of their daughters and invites them to join all the guests in saying their names. Abby Dobson, a sonic conceptual performing artist and composer and AAPF artist in residence, begins humming the opening bars of her song "Say Her Name":[6]

Say her name

Say her name

Say her name

Say her name

Say their names

For all of the names I cannot say

Say their names

For all of the names I'll never know

Say their names

Black girls matter

Say their names

Black women matter

Sing a song full of the faith that the dark past has taught us

Sing a song full of the hope that the present has brought us

Facing the rising sun of our new day begun

Let us march on 'til victory is won

Say her name

Say her name

Say her name

Say her name

Say her name

Say her name

Say her name

Say her name

As Abby sings, members of the audience are handed cards, each containing the name of a Black woman who has lost her life to police violence. The audience then forms a line around the perimeter of the room. One by one, each person steps up to the microphone at the front and says the name printed on their card. The room then repeats the name three times.

Eleanor Bumpurs

Say her name!

India Beaty

Say her name!

Natasha McKenna

Say her name!

As each person steps from the mic they approach Rhanda and Gina, who stand behind a table filled with tulip bulbs in a wide bowl. The mothers holding and passing the bulbs are symbolic of their role as givers of life, and now they pass out the seeds so that we may all participate in their renewal. Each person plants a seed in a jar along with their woman's name card. This ritual continues until all the names are read, and the ceremony continues with the watering of the newly planted blubs. The participants receive the ladle from Rhanda or Gina as a symbol of their willingness to nurture the remembrance of the daughters and sisters of #SayHerName. Planting the bulb symbolizes the sustained life force of the woman taken and the water a collective commitment to keeping their memory alive.

The responsibility for planting and nurturing this symbol of their daughters now rests with the community. After the final watering, the audience sits in silent reflection for several minutes. The silence is finally broken with two musical selections from Abby Dobson. When the applause subsides, the mistress of ceremony approaches the podium to close out the evening.

Kimberlé Crenshaw: So we've done this together, and we now will go our separate ways, bonded in collective commitment to hold these women in our hearts. Tonight, we make a pact with our sisters, their mothers, their families, and to each other.

I am deeply moved and indebted to the efforts that so many people put into making this happen. And I want to take this moment before we call Abby for one final song to thank everyone. First and foremost, I have to thank Gina and Rhanda for their trust.

I want to thank the team at AAPF: Julia, G'Ra, Emmett, and Michael, my cofounder Luke Harris and our board member Ann Thomas. Thank you so much for your trust as well. Unending gratitude goes to our minister of music, Abby Dobson, and also give our deepest thanks to Awoye Timpo, who cocreated this ceremony, and Brittany Bradford and Yu-Hsuan Chen, who transformed this space tonight. This is a law school; look around to see how art transformed this space.

And thank you to all our artists and musicians: Margaret Odette, Fedna Jacquet, Karen Chilton, Jasmine Rush, Rihanna Hernandez, Jake Lazaroff, Nate Harris, and Wes Mingus. And, of course, thank you all of you for coming out on a Saturday to participate in this ritual.

Abby Dobson closes the event by singing Nina Simone's "I Wish I Knew How It Would Feel to Be Free."

Our annual rituals of remembrance draw on the vision of the mothers. They present new spaces into which the artivism of #SayHerName can be. In this spirit, our next ceremony took place online in December 2020, in the throes of what was then called the twin pandemic of COVID and anti-Black police violence. There was in this particularly vexed moment an opening—a door to greater awareness of the risks of police violence and the fact that Black women like Breonna Taylor could function as representative figures of just how pervasive and violent state power could be. The challenge, however, was that few people knew the names of Black women killed by the police, and thus their names could not easily be employed as a galvanizing force. To navigate this space between challenge and opportunity, the mothers and families of #SayHerName came together with AAPF and our supporters to hold an online Ritual of Remembrance and Rededication for the daughters and sisters lost to police violence.

We were deeply moved and honored to be joined in that effort by Melania Brown, sister of Layleen Polanco; Debra Shirley, mother of Michelle Shirley; Katrina Johnson, cousin of Charleena Lyles; Ashley Carr, sister of Atatiana Jefferson; Yolanda McNair, mother of Adaisha Miller; and Valarie Carey, sister of Miriam Carey. Our cohosts were Gina; Sharon Wilkerson, mother of Shelly Frey; Rhanda; Fran, mother of Michelle Cusseaux; and Maria Moore, sister of Kayla Moore.

The mistress of ceremony for the evening was Awoye, who introduced the performance artist Gina Loring to open the virtual event with a piece she had written for the *Chime for Change Zine* dedicated to #SayHerName:

#SayHerName

Her heart beats in realms you can not see
these fleshy, fragile suits are but vessels
you can't box up the sun or hold the milky way hostage
can't capture the wind, chain something as illusive as sound
her name is written in the ridges of your palm
hidden beneath your first waking breath
she is in the sky, in sunsets golden violets and blues
in the clouds, in the waves, her name is written there too.

Her womb, the cradle of civilization
Akashic Records trace it back, everyone is Black.
Do you not hear the wind testify?
We made you possible.
And what have you become?
What have you done?
Strayed so far from your own humanity, you can't see ours.
What God do you pray to?
What laws do you live by?
Are you not ashamed to breathe
having stolen so much breath?
Karmic debt
almost beyond repair
who dares such barbarity?
Violence as generational practice, as tradition.
Such sins are cancerous to the collective soul
and we are all connected to the whole.
You violate the most sacred
carriers of light
divine feminine
we are the moon
we are life.
What upside down world did you create to take
the sanctity of our bodies and make it a thing?
The blessing of our skin, and make it wrong when all along
we are built by divine design.
You are haunted by your own doing
some sick sibling rivalry
you hate us, but want to be us.
No booty lift, lip injection, tanning salon can give you soul
no redemption, no ascension can be bought with silver or gold.

Just say her name, the constellations spell it out.
Say her name, it's your passport to freedom, your only route
repent, confess.
Stole our bodies, our culture
the shoulders we stand on, but the ancestors' spirits are not for sale.
Our regality and resilience are not for your taking.
Every peak and valley, her name is shaking
it echoes out from that core
she is both after and before
the very earth you walk on
the air in your lungs
the rhythm of your breath.
Say her name, it's all that will be left
when you are called to judgment
stripped to ash and bone
say her name, that's your only way home.[7]

Although we missed being in each others' physical presence, by performing our annual ritual of remembrance online we were able to invite more people from around the country into the space, to share the mothers' grief and lighten some of the burden on them.

Sharon told us of the importance of continuing to hold these rituals, even in times such as these, of the enduring power of the Mothers Network, the Sisterhood of Sorrow:

> In the natural realm, I don't have any sisters. But in the spiritual realm I have sisters. We need each other. You know what's so hard right now? I can't touch my sisters. I can't hug my sisters. We cannot show love to

> each other. But one thing we do know: we have each other's backs. We love each other.

We were also blessed to have two mothers and one sister share with us, via video, some of the personal everyday rituals they perform to remember and honor their lost loved ones. One by one Maria, Fran, and Gina invited us into their homes and showed us the beautiful memorials they have constructed in their daughters' and sister's honor: the photographs and visuals, paintings, words, poems, furniture, clothing, and other treasured and sacred objects they have gathered together in their most intimate spaces in order to keep their loved ones close to them and central to their lives. These are profoundly personal and powerfully political memorials, forms of commemoration that grow, evolve, and change as the years pass, at the same time that the memories and the pain and the loss do not in any way diminish.

For Fran, these are rituals that "get me through the day, keep me focused and centered."

For Maria, they are "projects of love."

For Gina:

> This helps me deal with the grief, and when I'm in tears, which is every day, and I think every mother can attest to that, we don't move forward, it's hard to move forward without trying to ascend above. It helps to center myself and ground myself because I am in a constant state of rage. We want to gather their essence, we want to gather everything around us to help us to cope with the daily grief that's inescapable. There's that undercurrent of rage at the injustice that was done to our daughters. And that we

still, no matter what, are forced, on this realm, to live through.

Following these presentations from the mothers, Awoye led us all into a collective ritual:

> We invite the element of water into the space and pour a libation. A libation is a ritual pouring of a liquid as an offering to a god or spirit or in memory of those who are no longer with us. Pouring libation is practiced in numerous cultures and traditions around the world. We offer libation for those who were connected to us physically or spiritually, to the energies of the universe and to those who came before. We choose water for our libation because it has no enemy. It cannot be overcome. This water is for rejuvenation and to offer a blessing.

And as we moved through the ritual, Abby guided us with her voice, humming as Awoye invited everyone to join in a collective breath, our feet placed firmly on the ground, joining our energies, united in the present moment wherever we were in the world. She then asked those of us who could to stand and take our bowls of water, to join in offering a libation to honor the lives we've lost and acknowledge the work that lies ahead. With this ritual, we also remembered all the ancestors we've lost. In the words of an Akan saying:

> When we call one ancestor's name we are calling/begging all to come.

Each time Awoye said "Say her name," the rest of us repeated a name and poured a small amount of water into a plant, a bowl, or onto the floor, each in our own space.

Following this libation, together we called out the names of Black women killed by the police. We wanted our voices to be so loud that they knew we were there with them. We wanted their spirits to be here with us.

The call and response evoked a rhythm. Abby continued singing and humming "Say her name" throughout the ritual. The name of each woman was said once and repeated several times, until all the names had been spoken aloud.

After the final name, Breonna Taylor, was spoken and repeated, we said as many of these names as we could together all at once. We built a wall of sound. We shook the earth Saying Her Name. We concocted a cacophony of sound with the names of murdered women and girls.

At the same time, we all held up signs, each with the name of a woman we've lost.

Even as we held this anniversary in a digital space, we honored the traditions and rituals that have made the Mothers Network a place for healing and reflection over these past six years. There is power when we channel our ancestors through ritual, there is power when we come together to honor what has been lost, and there is power when we Say! Her! Name!

Before we said goodbye, Abby again lifted us and sent us off with a vibrant rendition of "I Wish I Knew How It Would Feel to Be Free." That song, and the entire Say Her Name ritual that preceded it—including the expressions of love and rage and hope and despair—held the lives of Black women killed by the police in memoriam.

Tanisha Anderson

Chapter 5

In Memoriam

"I have to walk past it every time I leave my house, a constant reminder of the worst day of my life, of seeing my daughter murdered right in front of my eyes."

Cassandra Johnson, mother of Tanisha Anderson
(January 22, 1977–November 13, 2014)

My name is Cassandra Johnson. Tanisha is my daughter. There's a lot to tell about Tanisha. She was a loving daughter and a wonderful mother and a wonderful sister. She just has one daughter, and her name is Mauvion. She was involved in every aspect of her daughter's life, making a difference. I'm raising her daughter now. She's a wonderful granddaughter.

Tanisha as a little girl was just the most wonderful, loving little girl any mother could ever ask for. She loved people. She loved making everybody happy. She loved laughing. She just giggled at everything. Her dream was to be a journalist, a reporter. She loved the news. She went to school for that, she was studying for that. And she was a darn good actress too, when she wanted to be.

Tanisha loved people. She loved the world. She loved just making people happy. Her favorite holidays were Mother's Day, Easter, Christmas, all of them. She'd get psyched about the holidays for the kids. She'd always buy candy and give it to all of her nieces and nephews, and host an Easter egg hunt. Her favorite color was blue. She loved basketball, was a huge Cavs fan. Never forgave LeBron. She played too. She was tall.

Once we got Tanisha balanced, you wouldn't have known she was bipolar. She had days that she wasn't feeling very well. But the really bad, bad part of it Tanisha didn't experience because we kept her very balanced. As long as she was on her medication, you wouldn't know. She was on her way to becoming who she wanted to be, until her illness came and that was put on hold. But as far as her as a person, you couldn't ask for a better daughter. To have her taken so early from us was a very traumatic thing, and our family is still trying to move through it. Trying to turn it around, to make her death meaningful to the world.

I remember that day like it was yesterday. But it's something I don't like to talk about very much.

Cassandra's daughter Jennifer recounts what she remembers of the night Tanisha was killed:

From what I was told, my sister started doing the five things [she did to care for herself]. And my mother felt like, "Okay, well we need to get her to the hospital." Instead of them calling me, they called the ambulance.

[Tanisha was] sitting at the table smoking a cigarette. That's what she was doing. She was sitting at the table, smoking a cigarette at that time. The reason that the ambulance was called is because she needed to go to the hospital. She was leaving the house

and coming back in. We didn't want her to wander off somewhere and not knowing, seeing where she was. We know that we have to get her in so they can adjust her medication. Anytime they adjusted the medication, she was back to her— You know what I'm saying? Her normal self. That's all she needed, was just an adjustment of the meds.

The ambulance did not show up. Actually, the police officers did. They wasn't very nice with her. They handled her pretty roughly, because she did not want to get in a police car due to the fact that my sister was claustrophobic.

Still to this day, I don't know why they sent the police instead of the ambulance, because the 911 call specifically said "Ambulance." Even if the officers came on scene and they didn't know what the call was for, once they got there and it was explained that she's having a mental crisis, they should have known how to handle things a little differently. But then, we come to find out that the officers never had the training on how to handle a person [who's] going through a mental crisis. But common sense, and you being a human, you should know that you treat things a little bit differently when it comes to a certain situation and you know they're not being hostile towards you. Sit down and talk to them, calm them. Sit down and talk to them. Calm them, ask them, What's their favorite foods. What's your favorite color? What do you like to do? Well, what are you into? To make them feel that they're in safe hands.

[Instead, they said] "Get up!" You know, from the table. You know, "We need to take you to the hospital." But not asking any questions, and it was just done wrong. It was just done completely wrong. All of their common sense just went out the window. It was just like, "Come on, hurry up. Let's put you in the car so we can go

to whatever next thing that's going to come up." That's just how I felt like it went.

The backseat of a police car was very small, and it scared her. And I don't understand why they couldn't recognize this is a crisis right now. You have to handle a person that's going through a crisis with care. Especially if they're not violent. They just want to do things on their own. You have to make them feel comfortable, that you're not a threat to them. And since she didn't want to cooperate during the time that they wanted her to get in the car, they did a takedown move on her.

When Tanisha tried to call for help, my mom and my niece, son, and brother, were on the steps and they tried to come to her, to assist. The other officer drew [his] gun on them and told [them] that they had to stay where they were. And that was the hardest thing that my mom had to keep in her mind, is that she couldn't help her child. And her child was calling for her help, to help. "Help me, Mom!" And she tried, and she couldn't, because at that time you have a gun drawn on you. And you're trying to go forth to try to help your child, you don't know if you are going to get harm too.

Cassandra has a similar memory of the family desperately trying to get to Tanisha while the police had her in their hands:

The police officer wouldn't let [my son, Joell] come down and help her, and [he had to] see her go through that, while she said "Mommy, help me, Mommy, help me, help me." I sat at the dining room table, because [the people from] my church would not let me come outside and see that. They didn't want me to see that. They were going to kill her that day, but they wouldn't let my son come down. They wouldn't let him come down to help her. They had their guns drawn. If he'd have stepped one foot off of that porch, they'd have shot him.

Tanisha had her house dress on, and probably her little sandal shoes. Yeah, that was another thing. When the officer did the takedown move on my sister, her bottom half was exposed. They didn't bother to even [pull] her house dress down. So she wouldn't be showing her bottom half. It's like, they just let her lay there. And I know, normally, in the back of a police cruiser that they do have blankets, you know what I'm saying? To put over a person, and they didn't. So, her dignity was thrown out the window.

One officer put his foot in . . . excuse me, not his foot, his knee in her back and laid on it. The other officers, the officer that was there, actually was holding our family members back. As far as my brother, my mom, my son, Jacob, and Mauvion, tell him that they couldn't come forward. And he had his gun drawn.

So the police, in order to get Tanisha down, stayed in the prone position on her too long, and that's what killed her. Because she didn't want to get in the police car. She wasn't under arrest.

Or we didn't know what the next thing was going to be. If they had tried to come forward. So my brother, after a moment, noticed that my sister wasn't moving, but he does remember her quoting the Lord's prayer before she actually died. And he asked the officer, "Why she ain't moving?" And he said, "She went to sleep."

So, I guess during that time that he actually noticed that something was wrong, that she was asleep, and that she wasn't breathing. So he called for just the lieutenant to come out, [when] she arrived, and she felt like nothing was wrong because she didn't take the situation seriously. Until you started checking, like,

"Okay, we need to call the ambulance." She laid on the ground for fourteen minutes before the lieutenant called for an ambulance.

They picked her up and put her on a gurney. When she was in the back of the ambulance, we was told that she had a faint pulse at the time, but on arrival, going to Cleveland Clinic, she ended up dying. They were still trying to work on her to bring her back. But it was . . . It didn't happen. If they had responded . . . Well, if the officer had noticed that something was wrong instead of saying that she was asleep, and called for an ambulance, then it possibly would've been a chance that she would be here.

My mom had a ride to the hospital, and my grandparents had a ride, and it was maybe twenty minutes. Our doctor comes through the opposite door that we actually came in and he said, "I'm sorry." He said, "We have been working on Ms. Anderson for a while, but we were unable to get a pulse. Your loved one has passed away."

Mauvion was a teenager at the time. She's just holding her ears because she couldn't believe what came out of the doctor's mouth.

There was a cabinet between a chair and a wall. My mom just ran to that cabinet and she squeezed herself in between the cabinet [and] the chairs and just fell down on the floor.

They knew what happened. They knew what happened. That's why they ruled it a homicide, not one coroner but two . . . I thought they were just making me wait to make me wait. Being mean, to make me wait. Homicide, okay, this is really an open-and-shut case. They're going to have to say that they did it, because the coroner says they did.

❦

In February 2018, a grand jury declined to indict the officers who killed Tanisha. Later that year, the Cleveland Police disciplined the officers; Officer Scott Aldridge received a ten-day suspension while Officer Bryan Myers was given a written warning. On the day of Tanisha's death, Aldridge was Myers's training officer. As of the time of the murder of George Floyd in May 2020, the Cleveland police force had not banned the restraining techniques that killed both George and Tanisha.

Shortly after that decision, Cassandra was reunited with the Mothers Network and told the other mothers about the impact of this decision:

I saw on television that the grand jury chose not to convict the officers who killed Tanisha. They didn't even bother to call and tell me themselves. They gave one of the officers ten days off, and the other, a written reprimand.

I've been waiting four years for that decision.

Two separate coroners ruled her death a homicide, but the police say in court that she died of a heart condition. My daughter didn't have no heart condition.

I was on my way back to me. Four years later, I was finally starting to climb back up, finally coming out of the darkness, knowing her death was ruled a homicide, knowing those cops were gonna go to prison. I was going to be a happy soul.

Police can kill someone you love and not spend a day in jail. Still work on the force, still get paid. This officer got a ten-day leave. Ten days. I guess I was supposed to be joyful he even got that.

I'm just so angry. I'm so angry I'm about to bust. So I'm going, "Lord, what do I do now? What do you want me to do? Which way should I go now? I'm completely dependent on you. Which way should I go now?"

I never gave up on God. I never stopped believing. Never stopped going to church. I didn't even start drinking. I didn't smoke no weed. I didn't turn to drugs. I did none of it. None of it. Now I'm saying, "Lord, what do you want me to do?" Most women in a situation like this, you find them on dope. They're trying to cope. You find them on crack. They're trying to cope. They become alcoholics. They're trying to cope. Who are we to judge? Who are we to judge?

So, what I need from you all is to keep me in your prayers. When I fall on your mind, say, "God, help her. Help her to stay strong." Because now I want to get some drinks. Now I want to have something to get high with. I never wanted that in my life.

Sometimes I just sit at home for days looking out the window at the spot Tanisha died. I have to walk past it every time I leave my house, a constant reminder of the worst day of my life, of seeing my daughter murdered right in front of my eyes. I walk out my front door and I'm right back there—watching them kill my baby, desperate to go and save her, but having a gun held on me.

I cannot forget the sound of her calling to me "Momma! Momma!"

My baby. My baby.

You might not believe it, but I used to be an energetic person. I was always moving, always on the go. Now I can't hardly do anything. God tells us that hurting ourselves is wrong, but what if God doesn't know right from wrong himself? Because this is so, so wrong. My son says, "Momma, if you don't stop, you're going to die. You gotta stop, Mom, you gotta let it go." But it's easier for him to say.

But I've got to start living. I got grandkids, I have a son, I have a daughter. I gotta start living, but how? What do I do? God's gonna take care of it. God's gonna do it, God's gonna do it. Did you ever get tired of hearing that?

But if you believe, you don't question.

The thing is, I never wanted bad things to happen to the officers. All I wanted was justice. I didn't want to see him die, I just wanted the right thing to be done. I wanted our system to do the right thing, and I have found out so much about our system. They're just as crooked as the day is long.

That's it. You just want the truth, but life don't work like that. Life don't work like that. Sometimes I ask myself, how could you have been so green to the world? How could you not know this? You're more than fifty years old, how could you have not known certain things?

Her life didn't mean anything to them. Basically, she was just another number. And then they move on to the next case. She still had things to do, she still had a child to raise, still had a life to live. There's a lot more things that she wanted to do, and she didn't get a chance to do them.

So now I got a harder fight. That was supposed to close the door. It's kinda coming out of darkness and beginning to find me again. It has changed me so much. The Cassie—everybody calls me Cassie—that I used to know, is no longer there.

Justice for me has many colors. Once you get over being angry, you begin to think, "What can I do to change things?" To get justice for just one person wouldn't help the rest—we need justice for all of these women. It takes time to get things done, but if you keep pushing at it, you can wake up the people's minds. It's time to stop it. It's time to wake the people up.

Because they're not coming back. Your daughter or son is not coming back. So what can you do? You help someone else get justice. You petition for the police to get more proper training like we have in Cleveland. Because of Tanisha Anderson, that is in effect now. They must get mental health training.

Because if they have the proper training, they'll already know when they get to the house, "I'm going to address a mentally ill crisis," or "I'm going to a domestic crisis."

I've heard the word "de-escalate" so much, it's stuck in my head. De-escalate. De-escalate. Talk to them. Ask them what color they like, what kind of food they like, what's their name. If you go in aggressive just like them, then it's going to blow. But if you can talk them down, you might save their life. They're not just anybody to just be pushed under the rug. They're someone somebody loves. They belong to families, and they have children, and they have a life. As they say, they matter too. When people's lives are unfairly taken from them, it should be strongly addressed. There should be strong repercussions. It doesn't matter if you're police. It doesn't matter if you're a pedestrian. It doesn't matter who you are. If you take a life, that should be addressed. That should be properly addressed.

Sometimes you think you're about to climb up out of this, and then you get knocked right back again. I thought the system would do the right thing, and they didn't. It's hard to accept.

That badge is its own dark magic. A special evil that leaves us without justice, without our babies. A special evil that would make a murderer a hero. A special evil that would hold us at gunpoint while her life slips away.

Cassandra Johnson and Jennifer

Beginning in 2014, the African American Policy Forum (AAPF) has tracked police killings and other forms of state violence against Black women. The statistics are alarming. Over the past ten years alone, more than one hundred Black women have been killed by law enforcement officers or died while in state custody. Extending back to 1975, our research uncovered an additional two hundred Black women whose lives had been stolen in these ways. They are listed at the end of this chapter and make up our "#SayHerName in Memoriam."

Yet the list is woefully incomplete. Too often, the historical record is silent with respect to the names and stories of Black women killed at the hands of the state. The #SayHerName memorial is an attempt to preserve the names and stories of these Black women, so as to break the pathological conspiracy of public silence that has erased the deaths of those who came before them.

The first name on the #SayHerName memorial is that of Denise Hawkins, an eighteen-year-old woman who was fleeing her abusive boyfriend in November 1975 when police officers shot and killed her in Rochester, New York. Hawkins was not, of course, the first Black woman to be killed at the hands of the American state. State-sanctioned violence against Black women has existed since 1619, when enslaved Africans first arrived in what is now the United States. Sometimes the state carried out the violence directly. For example, in 1669, Virginia's colonial legislature enacted a law providing for the execution of enslaved persons who resisted their "master, mistris, or overseer."[1] In other instances, the state ignored violence by private actors. Southern slave patrols, a forerunner of modern police forces, subjected enslaved and free Black people to violence, reenslavement, and

lynching with impunity.[2] Despite evidence that the state tolerated widespread violence against Black people, historical records often obscure the true extent of this lethal predation. In 1997 Saidiya Hartman discussed how official legal bodies rarely reported or documented instances of rape against Black women because raping a Black woman was not considered a crime.[3] Piecing together the historical experiences of Black women often means relying on "what can be extrapolated from an analysis of the ledger or borrowed from the world of [their] captors and masters."[4] If those creating the records considered violence against Black women unremarkable, it went undocumented.

Some of the names of the women in the memorial were brought to our attention by their families. Others were gathered from local media accounts, death records, court filings, and databases that track police violence. When their stories are told, captured through local news sources, they have often parroted the police narratives. These media records, therefore, are at best unreliable, and at worst malevolent. Indeed, a consistent theme in the buried and distorted record of state violence against Black women is the complicity of the press in perpetuating this long-standing conspiracy of victim blaming and silence.

#SayHerName challenges this complicity head on and in order to model a more responsible brand of public storytelling aimed at justice and healing—one that collects extensive narratives from the mothers and families of murdered Black women. This act of reclamation and recovery is an ongoing challenge and necessarily a work in continual progress. Our in memoriam list is thus the first draft of a restorative sort of history, keenly focused on excavating the names and stories deliberately excised from the standard, consensus histories of race and state violence in the United States.

While the #SayHerName memorial primarily seeks to reclaim stories concerning Black women killed in direct encounters with police, this agonizingly familiar sort of police encounter isn't the only setting in which agents of the state have robbed Black women of their lives. Accordingly, we have also included the names of thirty-three Black women who died while in custody, while confined in a prison, jail, detention center, or hospital. This is only a fraction of those who have died in custody. As we researched these stories, we came to understand that conditions of acute confinement—involving isolation, racist and sexist power relations, and lack of access to adequate physical and emotional care—often replicate the conditions that lead Black women to encounters with police in the first place. Details of the women who died in custody are particularly hard to track. The names of several such women—for example, Sandra Bland and Layleen Polanco—are well known, but we tend to know less about their underlying stories than we do about Black women killed in direct police encounters—in no small part because conditions of custodial isolation permit police and legal authorities greater control over public narratives than public confrontations with the police generally do.

There is no state-level or national database of post-arrest deaths in custody. By contrast, prearrest deaths and deaths during arrest are tracked by Fatal Encounters, the *Washington Post* Fatal Force Database, and Mapping Police Violence, among other projects[5]—although these databases have only launched recently and operate on incomplete stores of government information.[6]

Even if there were a national network to track deaths of Black women in custody, it would run quickly into a major obstacle: individual prisons and jails are often unwilling to release the names of incarcerated people who die while in their custody.

Until recently, they were not legally obligated to do so. In 2000 Congress unanimously passed the Death in Custody Reporting Act (DCRA), which required states to release information regarding the death of "any person who is in the process of arrest, is en route to be incarcerated, or is incarcerated at a municipal or county jail, State prison, or other local or State correctional facility."[7] The law required individual states to provide this information to the US attorney general on a quarterly basis and to include, at a minimum, the name, gender, race, ethnicity, and age of the deceased, as well as a brief description of the circumstances of their death.

But even as state and federal prisons have technically observed the letter of the law, they haven't delivered the critical context that can produce a compelling account of how and why Black women are killed in custody. The Bureau of Justice Statistics (BJS) has released only national- and state-level data, which is not disaggregated by gender and race. This undifferentiated block of data has made it impossible to know with any certainty the number of Black women who have died while in custody. And it's harder still to come by any detailed accounts of the relevant causes of death—or even to learn the names of the prisons and other custodial settings in which Black women have had their lives cut short. Reporting delays compounded the problem. As of October 2020, the most recent deaths-in-custody data released by the BJS is from 2016.[8]

What's more, even this sketchy body of official statistics likely marks a drastic undercount of deaths in custody. This has been the broad pattern when such inquiries depend on reports from government agencies. A review of the BJS data on arrest-related deaths showed that it only included about half of law enforcement homicides. In response, independent investigators launched a pilot study that relies on open-source information to complement reported data.[9]

In 2014 Congress passed a new DCRA that was intended to fix some of the issues with the 2000 law. The new legislation included penalties for states that failed to report the required data in an adequate and timely way. But when President Donald J. Trump took office in early 2017, the Department of Justice (DOJ) scrapped the Obama administration's 2016 plan for implementing the DCRA. The Trump administration did not release its own proposal to update reporting protocols until 2018. Not surprisingly, the Trump DOJ loosened, rather than tightened, existing protocols. The 2018 plan eliminated open-source verification of reported data—a method that's crucial for improving accurate counts of deaths in custody and identifying unreported deaths.

The Trump proposal also reduced the more detailed requirements for reporting on deaths in custody drafted under the 2016 compliance plan. That plan had required states to report the reasons for law enforcement's contact with the decedent, behavior by the decedent and law enforcement during the incident, and the manner of death.[10] But these important requirements were omitted from the 2018 plan; in their place was a mandate to supply a brief description of the manner of death.[11] A 2018 report by the DOJ Office of the Inspector General (OIG) noted that state data collection had not begun and would not begin before fiscal year 2020. The OIG report bluntly concluded that "[w]ithout complete information about deaths in custody, the Department will be unable to achieve DCRA's primary purpose."[12] The DOJ had been collecting information about deaths in custody through its Mortality in Correctional Institutions program—but as the OIG noted, this threadbare record failed to cover all types of data that the DCRA reauthorization called for. Nor could this haphazard model of data collection support any effective penalties against states that did not comply with the DCRA.[13]

This sort of bureaucratic inertia dogs the effort to document and contest the grim roll call of Black women killed while in state custody—it is, in fact, the state-authored initiative to distort and erase the state's own complicity in such deaths. It's also the principal reason the #SayHerName memorial includes the names of only a small portion of the total number of women who have died while in custody.

Since then, the Biden administration has issued an executive order requiring the attorney general to issue a public report "on the steps the DOJ has taken and plans to take to fully implement the DCRA." In response to the publication of figures in the most recent report, lawmakers have highlighted some of the problems in the ways that the DOJ collates information together with a "lack of transparency" on the part of the DOJ that are likely to continue to hamper the potential effectiveness of DCRA. Senator Jon Ossoff from Georgia, recently called the DOJ to task for these problems. Working with the Government Accountability Office, his Senate subcommittee conducted a review of death in custody in the fiscal year 2021 that highlighted a DOJ undercount of at least 990 deaths. Their report went on to note that 70 percent of the DOJ's data was incomplete. According to its own estimates of its errors, the DOJ captures no more than 82 percent of deaths in state prisons, 61 percent of deaths in local jails, and as few as 29 percent of arrest-related deaths.[14]

Still, #SayHerName's data collection efforts have unearthed some valuable findings. We have focused on Black women whose in-custody deaths involved allegations of misconduct, malfeasance, or negligence. Their names were gathered from court records, news stories, and the accounts of family members. As with the list of Black women killed by police, we know there are more—many more. Many of our stolen sisters' names may be lost to history, but others are recoverable—through oral histories, local newspapers, and other records. The list below is just a beginning, one we offer as a foundation to at last say and honor the names we can recover—while continuing the struggle to uncover those that have so far eluded us.[15]

#SayHerName

In Memoriam

#SayHerName

Homicides: 1975–2022

Total: 177 women

Denise Hawkins
Rochester, NY • November 11, 1975 • 18

Eulia Mae Love
Los Angeles, CA • January 3, 1979 • 39

Sherry Singleton
New Orleans, LA • November 13, 1980 • 26

Eleanor Bumpurs
New York, NY • October 29, 1984 • 66

Rhonda Harris Ward Africa
Philadelphia, PA • May 13, 1985 • 30

Theresa Brooks Africa
Philadelphia, PA • May 13, 1985 • 26

Netta Africa
Philadelphia, PA • May 13, 1985 • 11

Delisha Africa
Philadelphia, PA • May 13, 1985 • 9

Rebecca Garnett
Gaithersburg, MD • May 23, 1991 • 20

Sonji Taylor
Los Angeles, CA • December 16, 1993 • 27

Kim Groves
New Orleans, LA • October 13, 1994 • 32

Carolyn Adams
New Brunswick, NJ • September 10, 1996 • 39

Frankie Ann Perkins
Chicago, IL • March 22, 1997 • 37

Dannette Daniels
Newark, NJ • June 8, 1997 • 31

Cora Bell Jones
Detroit, MI • August 13, 1998 • 79

Tyisha Miller
Riverside, CA • December 28, 1998 • 19

Margaret LaVerne Mitchell
Los Angeles, CA • May 21, 1999 • 55

LaTanya Haggerty
Chicago, IL • June 4, 1999 • 26

Andrea Hall
Orlando, FL • July 25, 2000 • 40

Annette Green
Wellston, MO • February 6, 2001 • 37

Andrena Kitt
Pensacola, FL • February 26, 2001 • 21

Andrea Nicole Reedy
Hampton, VA • July 27, 2001 • 32

Melanie Jones
Newport News, VA • December 21, 2001 • 21

Marcella Byrd
Long Beach, CA • January 19, 2002 • 57

Sophia King
Austin, TX • June 11, 2002 • 23

LaVeta Jackson
Boston, MA • July 2, 2002 • 36

Martha Donald
Minneapolis, MN • August 1, 2002 • 60

Tessa Hardeman
Atlanta, GA • August 5, 2002 • 35

Nizah Morris
Philadelphia, PA • December 24, 2002 • 47

Charquisa Johnson
Washington, D.C. • April 26, 2003 • 23

Kendra James
Portland, OR • May 5, 2003 • 21

Alberta Spruill
New York, NY • May 16, 2003 • 57

Denise Michelle Washington
Aurora, CO • August 5, 2003 • 30

Tereshea Tasha Daniel
Tulsa, OK • October 15, 2003 • 20

Adebusola Tairu
Culver City, CA • October 22, 2003 • 26

Annie Holiday
Cherokee, AL • March 12, 2004 • 78

Andrea Umphrey
Monroeville, PA • April 18, 2004 • 35

Summer Marie Lane
Riverside, CA • December 6, 2004 • UNKNOWN

Carolyn Jean Daniels
Fort Worth, TX • June 24, 2005 • 35

Patricia Thompson
Rochester, NY • March 3, 2006 • 54

Emily Marie Delafield
Green Cove Springs, FL • April 24, 2006 • 56

Erika Tyrone
Houston, TX • June 19, 2006 • 28

Rekha Kalawattie Budhai
Dekalb County, GA • November 13, 2006 • 34

Kathryn Johnston
Atlanta, GA • November 21, 2006 • 92

Clara Morris
Plainview, TX • January 25, 2007 • 54

Linda Joyce Friday
Kansas City, MO • February 12, 2007 • 55

Marnell Robertson Villarreal
Houston, TX • May 6, 2007 • 42

Dougressa Elaine Crawford
Corpus Christi, TX • May 7, 2007 • 27

Milisha Thompson
Oklahoma City, OK • May 19, 2007 • 35

Denise Nicole Glasco
Las Vegas, NV • June 12, 2007 • 24

Dorothy Williams-Johnson
Chicago, IL • July 15, 2007 • 50

Reora Askew
Philadelphia, PA • September 8, 2007 • 38

Elaine Coleman
Hawthorne, CA • September 9, 2007 • 21

Tarika Wilson
Lima, OH • January 4, 2008 • 26

Anita Gay
Berkeley, CA • February 16, 2008 • 51

LaToya Grier
Jacksonville, FL • April 1, 2008 • 22

Lori Jean Ellis
Cassatt, SC • April 21, 2008 • 52

Tameika Jordan
Norfolk, VA • August 9, 2008 • 17

Duanna Johnson
Memphis, TN • November 10, 2008 • 43

Barbara Stewart
Biddeford, ME • March 24, 2009 • 47

Brenda Williams
Scranton, PA • May 28, 2009 • 52

Yvette Williams
Rock Hill, SC • June 4, 2009 • 15

Tiraneka Jenkins
Charleston, SC • July 14, 2009 • 26

Amanda Anderson
Jersey City, NJ • July 16, 2009 • 22

Martina Brown
Jersey City, NJ • July 21, 2009 • 58

Katherine Hysaw
Phoenix, AZ • September 9, 2009 • 32

Sarah Riggins
Albany, GA • October 23, 2009 • 49

Linda Hicks
Toledo, OH • December 14, 2009 • 62

Sukeba Jackson-Olawunmi
Atlanta, GA • May 15, 2010 • 40

Aiyana Mo'Nay Stanley-Jones
Detroit, MI • May 16, 2010 • 7

Arika Hainesworth
Pittsburgh, PA • July 11, 2010 • 24

Letha Coretta Adams
Muskogee, OK • October 1, 2010 • 38

Ciara Lee
Houston, TX • December 16, 2010 • 20

Gwendolyn Killings
San Leandro, CA • December 29, 2010 • 39

Carolyn Moran-Hernandez
Lakewood, WA • February 14, 2011 • 46

Derrinesha Clay
Lansing, MI • March 14, 2011 • 17

Brenda Williams
Watts, CA • April 27, 2011 • 57

Armetta Foster
Bradley County, TN • May 21, 2011 • 30

Catawaba Howard
Miami-Dade, FL • August 12, 2011 • 32

Denise Gay
New York City, NY • September 5, 2011 • 56

Yvonne McNeal
New York City, NY • October 1, 2011 • 57

Jameela Barnette
Marietta, GA • December 25, 2011 • 53

Shereese Francis
Queens, NY • March 15, 2012 • 30

Rekia Boyd
Chicago, IL • March 21, 2012 • 22

Sharmel Edwards
Las Vegas, NV • April 21, 2012 • 49

Shantel Davis
New York, NY • June 14, 2012 • 23

Alesia Thomas
Los Angeles, CA • July 22, 2012 • 35

Erica Collins
Cincinnati, OH • October 13, 2012 • 26

Malissa Williams
Cleveland, OH • November 29, 2012 • 30

Darnesha Harris
Breaux Bridge, LA • December 2, 2012 • 17

Shelly Frey
Houston, TX • December 6, 2012 • 27

Yolanda Thomas
Westwood Lakes, FL • January 4, 2013 • 34

Linda Sue Davis
Tamarac, FL • January 9, 2013 • 60

Barbara Lassere
LaPlace, LA • January 24, 2013 • 60

Kayla Moore
Berkeley, CA • February 12, 2013 • 41

Kendra Diggs
Baltimore, MD • May 7, 2013 • 37

Kourtney Hahn
Clintonville, OH • May 15, 2013 • 21

Miriam Carey
Washington, DC • October 3, 2013 • 34

Angelique Styles
Chicago, IL • October 24, 2013 • 60

Sharon Rebecca McDowell
Anderson, SC • December 20, 2013 • 49

Ariel Levy
Hayward, CA • February 4, 2014 • 62

Yvette Smith
Anderson, TX • February 16, 2014 • 47

Gabriella Nevarez
Citrus Heights, CA • March 2, 2014 • 22

Pearlie Golden
Hearne, TX • May 6, 2014 • 93

Angela Beatrice Randolph
Glen Burnie, MD • June 7, 2014 • 38

Michelle Cusseaux
Phoenix, AZ • August 14, 2014 • 50

Tracy Ann Oglesby Wade
Louisville, KY • October 1, 2014 • 39

Aura Rosser
Ann Arbor, MI • November 9, 2014 • 40

Tanisha Anderson
Cleveland, OH • November 13, 2014 • 37

Yuvette Henderson
Oakland, CA • February 3, 2015 • 38

Janisha Fonville
Charlotte, NC • February 18, 2015 • 20

Monique Jenee Deckard
Anaheim, CA • March 8, 2015 • 43

Meagan Hockaday
Oxnard, CA • March 28, 2015 • 26

Mya Hall
Fort Meade, MD • March 30, 2015 • 27

Alexia Christian
Atlanta, GA • April 30, 2015 • 26

Redel Jones
Baldwin Hills, CA • August 12, 2015 • 30

India Kager
Virginia Beach, VA • September 5, 2015 • 28

Marquesha McMillan
Washington, D.C. • October 26, 2015 • 21

Bettie Jones
Chicago, IL • December 26, 2015 • 55

Janet Wilson
Dearborn, MI • January 27, 2016 • 31

Sahlah Ridgeway
Syracuse, NY • February 12, 2016 • 32

Kisha Michael
Inglewood, CA • February 21, 2016 • 31

India M. Beaty
Norfolk, VA • March 19, 2016 • 25

Laronda Sweatt
Gallatin, TN • April 6, 2016 • 40

Kisha Arrone
Dayton, OH • April 17, 2016 • 35

Deresha Armstrong
Orlando, FL • May 5, 2016 • 26

Jessica Nelson-Williams
San Francisco, CA • May 19, 2016 • 29

Korryn Gaines
Baltimore, MD • August 1, 2016 • 23

Deborah Danner
Bronx, NY • October 18, 2016 • 66

Michelle Lee Shirley
Torrance, CA • October 31, 2016 • 39

Morgan London Rankins
Austin, TX • February 22, 2017 • 30

Elena "Ebbie" Mondragon
Hayward, CA • March 14, 2017 • 16

Alteria Woods
Gifford, FL • March 19, 2017 • 21

Robin White
St. Louis, MO • May 10, 2017 • 50

Jonie Block
Phoenix, AZ • May 15, 2017 • 27

Charleena Lyles
Seattle, WA • June 18, 2017 • 30

India N. Nelson
Norfolk, VA • July 17, 2017 • 25

Kiwi Herring
St. Louis, MO • August 22, 2017 • 30

Sandy Guardiola
Canandaigua, NY • October 4, 2017 • 48

Cariann Hithon
Miami, FL • October 8, 2017 • 22

Geraldine Townsend
Bartlesville, OK • January 17, 2018 • 72

Crystalline Barnes
Jackson, MS • January 27, 2018 • 21

Alkeeta Allena Walker
Tarpon Springs, FL • March 9, 2018 • 33

DeCynthia Clements
Elgin, Illinois • March 12, 2018 • 34

Shukri Ali Said
John Creeks, GA • April 28, 2018 • 36

LaShanda Anderson
Deptford, NJ • June 9, 2018 • 36

Dereshia Blackwell
Missouri City, TX • September 9, 2018 • 39

LaJuana Phillips
Victorville, CA • October 2, 2018 • 36

Tameka LaShay Simpson
Calhoun, GA • December 11, 2018 • 27

April Webster
Darlington County, SC • December 16, 2018 • 47

Angel Viola Decarlo
Hopewell, VA • December 18, 2018 • 31

Eleanor Northington
Indianapolis, IN • February 8, 2019 • 43

Latasha Nicole Walton
Miami, FL • March 12, 2019 • 32

Nina Adams
Greensburg, PA • March 13, 2019 • 47

Pamela Shantay Turner
Baytown, TX • May 13, 2019 • 45

Crystal Danielle Ragland
Huntsville, AL • May 30, 2019 • 32

Atatiana Jefferson
Fort Worth, TX • October 12, 2019 • 28

Tina Davis
Spring Valley, NY • January 4, 2020 • 53

Breonna Taylor
Louisville, KY • March 13, 2020 • 26

Helen Jones
Phoenix, AZ • December 28, 2020 • 47

Ma'Khai Bryant
Columbus, OH • April 20, 2021 • 16

Latoya James
Woodbine, GA • May 4, 2021 • 37

Briana Sykes
Flint, MI • June 19, 2021 • 19

Alexis C. Wilson
Dolton, IL • July 27, 2021 • 19

Fanta Bility
Sharon Hill, PA • August 27, 2021 • 8

Faubricia Virtaux Gainer
Sterling, VA • March 18, 2022 • 36

Erica Graham
Washington, DC • April 23, 2022 • 42

DEATHS IN CUSTODY, 2003–2022

Total: 33 women

Desseria Whitmore
Seattle, WA • October 25, 2003 • 52

Jameela Yasmeen Arshad
Kenner, LA • January 10, 2005 • 52

Shirley Andrews
Cincinnati, OH • March 3, 2005 • 38

Mytia Groomes
Newark, NJ • July 30, 2005 • 34

Mary Malone Jeffries
Holly Springs, MS • October 1, 2005 • 53

Kendra L. Williams
College Station, TX • December 17, 2005 • 29

Shatica Fuller
Greenwood, SC • June 8, 2006 • 23

Uywanda Peterson
Baltimore, MD • April 24, 2007 • 43

Ahjah Dixon
Corsicana, TX • March 4, 2010 • 23

Talia Barnes
Erie, PA • July 3, 2011 • 29

Anna Brown
Richmond Heights, MO • September 21, 2011 • 29

Kyam Livingston
Brooklyn, NY • July 21, 2013 • 37

Nimali Henry
Chalmette, LA • April 1, 2014 • 19

Latandra Ellington
Ocala, FL • October 1, 2014 • 36

Iretha Lilly
McLennan County, TX • October 6, 2014 • 37

Sheneque Proctor
Bessemer, AL • November 2, 2014 • 18

Natasha McKenna
Fairfax, VA • February 8, 2015 • 37

Sandra Bland
Hempstead, TX • July 13, 2015 • 28

Kindra Chapman
Homewood, AL • July 14, 2015 • 18

Joyce Curnell
Charleston, SC • July 22, 2015 • 50

Ralkina Jones
Cleveland Heights, OH • July 26, 2015 • 37

Raynette Turner
Mount Vernon, NY • July 27, 2015 • 42

Barbara Dawson
Blountstown, FL • December 21, 2015 • 57

Gynnya McMillen
Shelbyville, KY • January 11, 2016 • 16

Wakiesha Wilson
Los Angeles, CA • March 27, 2016 • 36

Symone Marshall
Huntsville, TX • May 10, 2016 • 22

Kim Doreen Chase
Baltimore, MD • April 20, 2017 • 52

Aleah Mariah Jenkins
San Diego, CA • December 6, 2018 • 24

Janice Dotson-Stephens
Bexar County, TX • December 14, 2018 • 61

Layleen Polanco
New York, NY • June 7, 2019 • 27

Tiffany Alexis Eubanks
Yakima, WA • June 3, 2020 • 33

Priscilla Slater
Harper Woods, MI • June 10, 2020 • 38

Ta'Neasha Chappell
Huntsville, TX • July 16, 2021 • 23

No moment of silence is easy to end. That is certainly true of this one. I have read the preceding lists many times. Each time I do, I experience not only the weight of the loss the names represent, but also the weight of knowing that their stories—and the stories of other Black women killed by state violence—need to be told.

There are, of course, many ways to tell those stories and honor the lives they capture. That is why the storytelling that #SayHerName has engaged in transcends the boundaries of any particular modality. Which is to say, our storytelling efforts have included the utilization of town halls, community organizing, public policy advocacy, litigation, and various media formats. But we have also endeavored to rework Black women's stories of state violence in the form of art activism.

Kayla Moore

Chapter 6

Art Activism

My Outer Skin

The time of day,
where I like to stay,
can open and release my shell.
But the hurt within
can start and begin
my outer skin. You can tell
The lies and uncomfort I gave
myself. It's myself I'm starting
to ask.

My lies turned into clay. It hardened
that day, and now I'm wearing a mask.
One day will come.
The hurt will run.
The mask will peel off again.
My life, I'll face
and give if a base.
I'll shed my outer skin.

—Kayla Moore

Maria Moore, sister of Kayla Moore
(April 17, 1971–February 13, 2013)

My name is Maria Moore. Kayla and I were born and raised in Berkeley, California, and we lived with our father. We lived on a wonderful street. Our grandparents were right across the street from us, and we really had our two homes that we fluctuated back and forth between. Our dad's, our grandparents'. It was actually a really good upbringing, a good childhood.

At a very young age, Kayla was just different. She didn't do the typical things that five-year-old boys wanted to do. She wanted to dress up. She wanted to wear Grandma's shoes. You kind of see it as a curiosity, and then as time goes on you realize that's what she preferred. There were so many times I would get mad because I would get this cute outfit and I couldn't find it. I was like, "Where did my outfit go?" And, of course, Kayla had it in her room, and she would be wearing it. I was like, "Why's she always taking my clothes?" I have a picture of Kayla. She's not only wearing my skirt, but the shirt and the belt that went with it. And she looked good, I can't deny that. She knew how to work it. At the moment I was so mad, but I look at it now and she was just being her true, authentic self. This was not a phase. This was not something she would outgrow. This is who she was. And she was a girl.

As time went on, she learned that even though she had a family that accepted her, society didn't accept her. She did not stay in school very long. She would end up getting into fights because she didn't back down. She was tough. She knew at a young age she would have to continue to fight to not be disrespected. That was hard for her. When she got to be a little older, in her teens, she met a group of kids that were like her. And that's really what she needed because they made her feel normal. And she was, but she needed that affirmation from other kids around her. My dad put Kayla into an art school, and that's where she really thrived because she was around people who had a different mind-set and had an artistic mind about them. She loved to sing. She loved to dance. She was a poet. She was a writer. And she got to explore all that in this alternative school. And she did well. She was a published poet at age sixteen. She really was just a hidden genius. But people couldn't see past the outside of her.

At some point, she went to live in San Francisco so she could be around people like her, so she could fit in. And in San Francisco she fit in. In that area, there was more of a community for her, and she loved that. She was part of it.

Kayla was an activist herself. I remember she'd talk about her landlord: how the housing units were horrible, how they weren't fixing anything. She'd stage protests and get all her people involved: her girls, the gay community, the lesbian community, everyone. She was just a fighter, and she didn't take no for an answer, but she was also very educated and proper in her tone. She knew how to play that role—let's put it that way. She could live in one world, and she could live in another world. But she was just so intelligent and analytical in her thinking that she knew how to get people to help her do things to get the things that she needed. I think that speaks to her genius and her hustling abilities, too.

I think her mouth was her best trait—she could talk her way in and out of everything. And she was kind. She was also a really good cook. She loved to cook southern food, to make new things, and was just very creative that way. If she were still here today, I definitely see her being a social worker because she loved to help people, and she knew all the resources. She knew where the food bank was, where you could get clothes, housing assistance, all that. I think she would have been a really good social worker for people.

Kayla was also diagnosed as schizophrenic when she was in her thirties, but she dealt with that as well. She managed it. Kayla would be sitting there talking to people who weren't there, but it was just the way she was, and we got used to it. When she'd come over to visit, she'd be on the couch, and my daughter would be right next to her on her computer, and Kayla would just be talking to whoever. And that was normal for us. That was normal for my daughter [Kayla's niece]. That didn't scare her. You realized, it's just kind of how she was. As a family, it didn't bother us. But to other people, when they think of schizophrenia, it brings up violent images. That wasn't her.

Kayla had a strong spiritual side. She was always giving blessings; that was her way of giving love. Whenever Kayla was having a hard time, she'd say, "I'm just gonna put blessings out there and see what comes back." And it would come back! I'd be like, "How did you do that?" She'd be down on her luck, and suddenly someone is offering her an apartment. Or she'd be out of money, and a check would come in the mail.

Eight years ago, I received a phone call at work that changed my family's life. As I rushed home to my dad, all I could think was, "My sister is dead, my sister is dead, my sister is dead." That mantra

ran through my frantic mind as I tried to navigate the traffic and absorb the reality that I would never see her alive again. I never got a chance to return her phone call from two days before. I never got a chance to update her on the latest family gossip. And I never got a chance to keep her safe.

Kayla was killed on February 13, 2013, just around the early days of the Black Lives Matter movement. She didn't attack anyone; she locked her roommate out of the apartment because he was probably being an ass. But the police put Kayla on their radar when she moved back to Berkeley and into Section 8 housing. She stood out, and I don't feel as though she was truly accepted back the way she should have been. Unfortunately, when she moved to Berkeley, which used to be all-inclusive, diverse Berkeley, it was a different type of Berkeley. It was, "Why are you in our neighborhood? You're in an apartment that's right by the university. That's way too good for you." You're in the city where you grew up, but it is so different now. You stand out.

The police know about you so they're going to do drive-bys, and they're going to watch you. So, when someone makes a complaint about these two roommates fighting, your name is going to pop up, and they're going to know who you are. Unfortunately, that's what happens. She was on their radar. So, when she was killed, half of those officers in that room knew her. And they saw her as a nuisance.

The year prior, my dad and I had to make what's called a 5150 call because Kayla was off her medication.[1] *She wasn't violent, but she was talking to people. You couldn't get through to her, and Dad was just worried. That time, Mobile Crisis showed up instead of the police.*[2] *Mobile Crisis is a group of trained professionals. They understand the population of people they're working with.*

The night Kayla was killed, her roommate placed a similar 5150 call because he felt that she was off her medication. Kayla had committed no crime, nor was she a danger to herself or others. There was no Mobile Crisis Team this time. Instead, a group of police officers showed up, four of whom had previously interacted with Kayla. They knew exactly who she was when they got the call.

One of the officers who had interacted with Kayla before was Officer Gwendolyn Brown. In my mind, I think she had had enough. She's like, "Here we go again." She ran a warrant on Kayla and found an old warrant with Kayla's birth name, but it was a different date of birth. It was an invalid warrant. We found out at the deposition that the officers knew the warrant was not valid. But they put it in their back pocket just in case an incident like this happened. So they were looking for a reason to get rid of her, and when they saw an opportunity they pulled out this bogus warrant.

They told Kayla, "We're not here to arrest your roommate. We're here to arrest you. We have a warrant." And she was like, "No you don't. That warrant's not for me." After speaking with the officers for four or five minutes, Kayla turned to make a phone call. That's when the officer grabs her arms and the struggle ensues. After maybe thirty seconds, the officer calls into the other room for backup, and seven more officers come in. They pile on top of Kayla, intending to put her in what's called a wrap device, which is basically just a cruel way of constricting someone. They basically hog-tied her.

So Kayla's on her stomach. And she's a big girl—355 pounds at that time. And they have her on her stomach, facedown. Once she was subdued, they checked on each other to make sure they were okay. Afterwards, when they looked down to check on her, they realized that she had stopped breathing. They turned her over, and they gave her the chest compressions, which is not what you're supposed to do. As a first responder, you're supposed to do mouth-to-mouth to get oxygen to the brain. But they didn't. You know why? Because that officer did not want to put her mouth on Kayla. End of story.

When someone is killed in police custody and it's not a shooting, the district attorney will not investigate. No charges were ever filed against these police officers for what they did to my sister. Kayla was in her own home, cooking dinner for her roommates. They entered her home and tried to arrest her on an invalid warrant that wasn't even for her because they thought that by taking her to jail, they could get her to mental health services. What kind of backwards bullshit is that? That's not how you treat someone who is in crisis.

The families go through so much pain. You try to get information, and you're lied to. They withhold things. You have to beg to find out what happened to your loved one. It took us three months to get the police report. Three months to get the coroner's report. They had it done within forty-eight hours of her death, but they held out because they didn't want it to get to the press. But what the police didn't know was that Kayla had a family. They didn't know that Kayla had a community that would fight for her. Kayla was a daughter, a sister, and an auntie. She was loved by her friends and family, and she did not deserve to die that night.

When Kayla died, we didn't know what to do at first. So that's why it is so important that there's information out there for families now—so they can know, well, these are the resources. The first thing you have to do in terms of the paperwork is getting information to the coroner's report, to the police report, all these little bureaucratic details that you don't care about in the moment because you're grieving. But it's important, because you need to get as much information as you can, because they will not tell you the truth.

When we finally got that police report, about three or four hundred pages, I spent the weekend reading every page. And I said, "This is absolute bullshit." Everything that you're hearing from them, everything that you see in the paper—nothing was correct. You look at the police report and you see everything that they did wrong. Excessive use of force, the invalid warrants—it's like, what crime did she commit? Someone, tell me. What crime did she commit? She didn't commit any crime.

We had to go to the city council meeting and shut it down just to get them to hand over the paperwork. They make it so hard for the families to get any type of details, and no one wants to talk to you. So you have these reporters calling who get their information from the police, and they're telling you these horrible things that your loved one did. And the narrative that I heard was that Kayla was violent, she was struggling, she was high on drugs, she wasn't listening. The media is controlled by law enforcement. They are basically fed this information, and then they regurgitate it out to the world. We have to put out our own versions of the stories.

A lot of the stuff that we were doing, especially in the very beginning with the people's investigation, is showing this is what the officers did, but if only these policies were in place this could have been a totally different outcome. And it's just little things, like if the roommate hadn't called 911. What if he was able to call a mental crisis line instead? So we've been thinking what are the alternatives that could have saved her life. If she had made a phone call. My dad was six minutes away. What if they didn't act on that warrant that wasn't for her? There's just so many what-ifs and certain alternatives that could have changed the outcome. She would have called me the next day and been like, "Girl, guess what happened." It would have been like, "My stupid roommate this." And it would have been just another story she had to tell. The first thing I'd say is, "Hey, girl. What's up?" And then she'd ask about [my daughter] Isabella. I'd go, "She's fine." And she was like, "Well, you're never going to guess what happened to me last night." And I'm like, "Okay, what happened?"

Being a Black person with mental health issues is extremely challenging. When the police respond to someone like Kayla, they don't know how to handle her. Police shouldn't be involved in these calls, period. Other states have done this successfully. We need to get on board with this and make it a national issue. Mental health services need to be a priority, period.

For Black women who have mental health challenges, the constant dehumanization is debilitating. Mental health problems are seen as crime problems, which invokes violence through restraint and punishment. Kayla was obese, she was on drugs, she was poor, she was Black, she was schizophrenic, and she was killed because these characteristics were all that the cops saw.

Kayla always wore muumuus, and during the struggle her muumuu came undone. Instead of covering her up and being humane about what they had done, they said, "Well, what is it? Is it a man or a woman?" And that's exactly how they saw her. She wasn't a person; she was an "it." And they continued to dehumanize her like that through the whole investigation. She did not deserve to die on that floor, exposed and uncovered.

We went to court a few times but never made it to trial. The judge dismissed the case in April 2018. A week after it was dismissed, our lawyer filed an appeal. That process can take a while, but we do have a much better chance of being successful in appellate court, so I'm hopeful.

The City of Berkeley has had seven years to implement change, and they have yet to get it right. The police continue to be called as first responders to mental health emergencies. Even though I feel contempt in my heart, my mind is focused on preventing the next death. The fight is not over because I'm not just fighting for Kayla—there are so many other families that need that support and that could benefit from knowing what we know. They need to know how to request police records and personnel records. We want to share this information with others, so that if it does happen in their city, they'll know exactly who to go to, how to respond, and what resources exist.

As a movement, we don't focus enough on women who have been abused and murdered by cops. We don't focus on what it means to be a Black woman—how we're perceived, and what we have to face. And that's my fear for my daughter, too.

We fight through the pain that greets us every single day so that no other Black woman, girl, or femme loses her dreams—so that Black women's lives don't turn on a dime on the whims of untrained and relentlessly unconstrained cops. This whole experience has been a crushing, draining, uplifting, and empowering exercise in patience. I pray that something positive comes out of it, that we're able to help others. That we're able to give voice and humanity to the Black, transgender, mentally disabled woman named Kayla Moore.

Kayla would say, "Go, bitch! You're standing up for me, and you're advocating for me, and you're fighting for me." And that's what I'm going to continue to do. It's not over 'til it's over. And even then, it's not over.

Maria Moore

From the start, the #SayHerName campaign has invoked the arts—music, visual expression, theater, poetry—to enrich our community, hold us together, and resist degradation. Our cultural traditions and their creative legacies empower us to produce and perform our politics as a practice we call "artivism." The singular achievement of artivist work is to bring about an organic fusion of artistry and social change. This union of art and politics echoes throughout all facets of the #SayHerName project: in how we share stories, histories, rituals, and re-create the world with one another. When we make and circulate art that confronts ugly and unsettling truths, we affirm one another. This is a profound dimension of the movement's healing agenda: by seeing the ugliness that surrounded the beautiful lives lost, we reject the false collective comfort that erases our pain and enacts the loss of our loss.

Art has the power to release trauma and open possibility. For example, in our new creative commons, we call out and retire the orthodox rites of mass forgetting and set our intentions to produce something radical and new. Mainstream detractors of political art dismiss the creative impetus to dream up a more just world as unreasonable, utopian indulgences. But as James Baldwin writes in *The Fire Next Time*, there is nothing more indispensable than the utopian imagination: "the impossible is the least that [we] can demand."[3] Art, in its freedom to make such demands, can disrupt the passive acceptance of the status quo that rationalizes violence and injustice. Art and storytelling are, in short, critical resources in helping those who too often have not been given a public platform to assert their voices and renew the struggle against illegitimate power.

An example of this power within our movement is the work of Abby Dobson, who uses her incredible gifts to counter the long-standing silences that enveloped the experiences of Black women and girls within our justice movements. Abby has created a sobering, haunting soundtrack for #SayHerName, capturing both the depths of despair and our ever-present quest for lives freed from the shadow of violence. She explains the role she and other artists play in our political struggles:

> As artists, we hold up a mirror to society to reflect its beauty, flaws and deepest wounds. My mission includes creating music-based cultural works that serve as both salve and shield in turbulent times, and help to reimagine and build a just world. As a Black woman who sings and writes to help us all get free, I am interested in more than just symbolic notions of freedom, equality, protection, and justice. My responsibility to my communities, particularly Black women and girls, is my call to action as an artist, scholar, activist, and global citizen. My cultural work is undergirded by the sensibilities and practices of Black feminists, who help us imagine Black futures where our whole selves and humanity are resoundingly recognized, supported, and protected.
>
> "Say Her Name" sounds the basic truth that Black women and girls are human beings deserving of dignity, empathy, justice, and care, in life and in death. It is a sonic quilt stitched together with fabric made of memories, cries and names, to shelter us all from veils of ignorance that would hamper our ability to achieve intersectional racial justice.[4]

#SayHerName takes form in many different spaces. And though the movement has evolved into new venues and communities since its inception in 2015, its most steadfast home is in its birthplace in protest. City streets, like so many public spaces, too often serve as the backdrop of Black deaths. In the wake of these lethal assaults, we must make our outrage and demands for justice just as visible and public as those public deaths. We keep faith with the victims of police violence through these acts of public witness and ensure that the core injustice that has cost them or their loved ones their well-being will not be shunted out of view or dismissed as everyday collateral damage in the war on Black self-determination.

We embrace the centuries-old Black cultural tradition of bearing public witness in our singing, drumming, and chanting to protest the police killings of Black women. When we do so, we think of Margaret LaVerne Mitchell, a fifty-four-year-old homeless woman; an Los Angeles Police Department officer stole her life by shooting her in the back. Her alleged crime was the theft of a shopping cart. We also think of Frankie Ann Perkins,

a thirty-seven-year-old mother of three; Chicago police officers strangled her to death after they accused her of swallowing drugs. We think as well of Duanna Johnson, a forty-three-year-old transgender woman; she was shot to death by still unidentified assailants as she was preparing to sue the City of Memphis for the horrific beating by Memphis police officers she endured just months prior. When we march, we honor the memory of these and hundreds of other women, some of whose lives and circumstances of death the prior chapters spotlight.

We're unaccustomed to thinking of marches and rallies as art because of the narrow ways in which western cultures define and police the boundaries and purposes of art. But our own traditions recognize and celebrate protest as vital and creative self-expression—what theater director and activist Augusto Boal calls theater: "two human beings, a passion, and a platform."[5] Protests are unmistakably the act of expressing a passion as they serve a powerful means of dramatizing and redressing group trauma. Scholar and activist Aidan Ricketts notes that this understanding of theater is intended to encapsulate a whole range of psychological devices associated with protest that can be intricately woven into the fabric of the experience. "Devices such as imagination, ritual, ceremony, romance, and symbolism, when combined with bold physical acts of protest, disobedience, and defiance produce a powerful medium for asserting dissent."[6]

Protests also produce indelible images of dissent through the textile tradition of banner- and flag-making, the chanting of powerful slogans at rallies, and the choreography of marches. Abby echoes this sentiment, recounting how her song "Say Her Name" grew out of collective protest:

I want to tell you a story about the birth of a sonic intervention. On Martin Luther King Jr. Day in January 2015, I was one of many who rallied in Harlem and marched to the United Nations to protest police brutality of Black and Brown bodies. During the final stretch of the march, tears rushed forward, as "Glory" by John Legend and Common, boomed from speakers. The song helped reenergize us. But something was missing. I also wanted to hear a contemporary song that spoke to the specific experiences of Black women and girls and our longing for true inclusion, equality, justice, and freedom.

As a New Yorker, I began to reflect on stories of Black women and girls who had been killed or otherwise brutalized by the New York Police Department, women like Eleanor Bumpurs and Rosann Miller. I began to wonder: What can we all do in the face of practices and systems that make life so challenging for Black women and girls? As an artist, one pathway forward is to create art in response to pain, erasure, and brutality. We create to insist on truth-telling and radical societal transformations. We create to resist.

In May 2015, at the #SayHerName vigil in Union Square, I listened as loved ones and concerned citizens told stories of Black women and girls who had been killed by police officers. I resolved to craft a song that could be a soundtrack to the #SayHerName movement for intersectional racial justice, a song thick with weight and rooted in history to privilege our experiences, knowledge, memories, and demands.

Sonic narratives move and propel us to soar beyond limiting forms of life. As observed by Dr. Bernice Johnson Reagon, founder of Sweet Honey in the Rock, when we sing, we announce our existence. We sing ourselves into view. I created the song "Say Her Name" to be a sonic expression of our unique positionality and precarity as Black women and girls, and specifically with respect to policing. I hope to transport the listener to a space where s/he[/they] can feel and understand why the stakes are so high.

Black women have historically used art to render ourselves visible and to transform hostile realities. Just listen to the catalogs of Bessie Smith, Nina Simone,

Aretha Franklin, Sweet Honey in the Rock, and Tracy Chapman, who offer examples of this vital practice. The singing of Black women constitutes sonic remembrances of melodies and blood memories uncovered and handed down to those of us fortunate enough to sound the canary's cry or the lullaby of the caged bird who sings of freedom.

Composing the melody and lyrics to "Say Her Name" was emotional for me. In songwriting, simplicity is king. I posed some questions to myself and then tried to answer them through song. How do you remind people that Black women who mourn their daughters killed by cops deserve our recognition, empathy, and support? How to give voice to a mother's undying ache compounded by community silence and erasure of their loved one's lives? They deserve to hear us acknowledge their daughters by name.

As a cappella composition, "Say Her Name" is a lullaby and lament that brings our ancestors into the space with every hum and every wail. The sonic citation of "Lift Ev'ry Voice and Sing" is intended to extend the Black national anthem to explicitly reference the particular experience of Black women on this ongoing march toward freedom.

"Say Her Name" is a modern-day spiritual that cavorts with breath, silence, and memory to name the devalued and disappeared to declare that we, as Black women and girls, matter. It calls us to place this erasure on a continuum of violence connecting Black women victimized since the Middle Passage. It is an embodied sonic petition reinforcing today's

> progressive social justice movements rooted in a Black feminist ethic.
>
> Who could have predicted that in 2020 the nation would rise up to support the Black Lives Matter and Say Her Name movements? "Say Her Name" sounds that Black women and girls are human beings deserving of dignity, empathy, justice and care, in life and in death. It is a sonic quilt stitched together with fabric made of memories, cries and names, to shelter us all from veils of ignorance that would hamper our ability to achieve intersectional racial justice.[7]

To prevent the tragic drumbeat of women's deaths from echoing any further into the future, we need to continue engaging and reenergizing our movement's legacy of artivism. We must ensure that we loudly and insistently speak the names of our lost sisters—and that we tell the stories of our pain, loss, and communal resilience to do the essential work of activism: to inform, to galvanize, to insist, and to demand. #SayHerName centers this artivist agenda in all of our efforts, whether we're convening our community in traditional art spaces, street protests, or legal spaces like Columbia Law School. In the process, we continually stay connected to our grassroots and activist origins.

In November 2016 AAPF expanded its artivism when we brought ten mothers and sisters of women killed by the police to New York City for the first annual #SayHerName Family Weekend. Though the event was necessarily a space of collective mourning, it also furnished abundant healing and joy for the participants. Buoyed by their shared experience, the women developed a profound connection, giving themselves and one another permission to laugh, sing, and experience joy. For some of them, it was the first release of these healing emotions they had permitted themselves in years. Though tears were never far away, the family weekend touched off these smiles and laughter, between karaoke performances, birthday dinners, backstage Broadway tours, and informal storytelling and group solidarity sessions.

The trip culminated with a sold-out #SayHerName artivism event at the legendary Nuyorican Poets Cafe on New York City's Lower East Side. Featuring a wide selection of talented artists, from spoken word poet Kai Davis to Tony Award–winning actor Tonya Pinkins, the night's performances elevated the lives of Black women and girls killed by the police. In a powerful act of witnessing, each of the family members in attendance shared memories of their loved ones and what they believed justice would mean for their families. Cassandra Johnson, mother of Tanisha Anderson, offered a testimony that conveyed her anger, pain, laughter, defiance, and faith. She delivered her speech slowly, deliberately—her passion heating the room.

Cassandra: The Lord enabled all of us to be here today. God works through each one of us. We cannot get anything done without each other. I didn't wake you up this morning. You didn't wake me up. There's a higher power that done that. So I give honor to God, most of all, for this opportunity.

This opportunity that has been given to us through Ms. Kimberlé has been the greatest experience of my life. I have not laughed in two years, since my daughter's death. Really laughed. This time around I did laugh.

Justice for me, for Tanisha Anderson, is to simply have the officer pay for what he done. And if that doesn't happen on earth, his ass gonna burn in hell. (*Crowd assents*)

So either way, either way, he gonna pay. He gonna pay.

Crowd: He gonna pay.

Cassandra: There will be justice. And it don't stop here. It does not stop here. It's like a fad, a pair of tennis shoes. It catches on. Somebody else looks at them and says, "Hmmm! I like them." Then somebody else looks at them and says, "Man, where you get them from?" So it's like that. This is how it catches on like wildfire. Because see, I am you, and you are me. Start listening, paying attention, for we gonna need one another.

Crowd: Yes. Yes.

Cassandra: I'm not so sad anymore. I have my moments, I have my times each and every day. But I'm pissed off now. See, you become pissed after a while. And once you become pissed you don't cry a lot anymore.

You get busy. You get to workin'. To change laws. That's my mission. I'm reaching for a Tanisha Law. The mentally ill, they are human beings too.

Crowd: Yeah! Yeah! (*clapping*)

Cassandra: See, I can go on and on. When the opportunity comes for me to really speak up you will see me. Remember my face. Cause I'm gonna be on every talk show there is. Anywhere they will let me speak out about what's going on with police brutality, with the mentally ill, you will see my face. Because we have to open the doors. See, it don't stop with just us. Yes. We're in pain. We hurt. And we have to live in the world too. We have children. Grandchildren.

We want them to be treated like human beings. So, it don't stop here.

I'm so thrilled. I am so happy. I am so thankful. For this privilege to be here. To be among the women that know your pain. Some people say, "I know this pain." No, you don't.

Crowd: No, you don't!

Cassandra: You don't understand. It hasn't hit your door. And you don't want it to hit your door. Cause it's a place that takes you, and you have to bounce back yourself. And some of us don't bounce back. So we need to help each other. We need to have this kinda thing going on everywhere. And we thank God for the people, the vessels, that you God used to do this. We thank God for them.

Crowd: Yes, we do.

Cassandra: Where do you think this all came from? Us? No. It took something to plant the seed into their mind. I thank God for them, for all of them, and for this opportunity. Pray my strength in the Lord.

Crowd: Say her name!

Although we didn't know it at the time, this moment would mark the beginning of a new chapter for AAPF and the #SayHerName mothers. In all our performances, events, and protests since, we've relied on art to help alchemize individual grief into collective action. Thus, all #SayHerName performance and events now feature participatory elements: chanting, planting, dancing, drumming, singing, and testifying. The radical possibilities of artistic expression come to the fore when performances

and events move beyond the conventional understanding of artworks as objects for passive consumption and into the realm of galvanizing collective experience.

#SayHerName's distinctive embrace of participatory, multimedia experiences also shapes our "Her Dream Deferred: A Week on the Status of Black Women" project, which dates back to a March 2017 event at Los Angeles's Hammer Museum. On the second day of our residency at the Hammer, we produced a live event called #SayHerName: An Evening of Arts and Action. Curated in collaboration with our artist-in-residence Abby Dobson, the event elevated the voices and stories of Black women through musical and dramatic performance, spoken word poetry, and video art.

To open the event, we designed an interactive sound and video installation in partnership with Los Angeles theater-makers and artists Darcie Crager, Vaneh Assadourian, Afia Walking Tree, and Dina Joseph. The installation produced an instant immersive effect by conducting the audience through a black box entryway, which in turn opened onto an ensemble of images, sounds, and videos. These documents all represented various campaign events and protests, including personal footage of the #SayHerName women and the voices of their mothers demanding justice.

Unbeknown to the #SayHerName mothers in attendance, a group of distinguished Black, female actors including Kelly McCreary, LisaGay Hamilton, and L. Scott Caldwell had been rehearsing the testimony the mothers had given earlier that year at the Nuyorican. They were preparing a performance dedicated to their struggles and activist commitment. As Abby sang the opening bars of "Say Her Name," each actor emerged from behind a curtain wearing a black #SayHerName T-shirt and holding a photo of the woman whose mother she was portraying. One by one, they delivered impassioned renditions of the mothers' own words, elevating their call for justice and demanding action from the audience. Hearing the strength and power of their testimonies given back to them, the #SayHerName mothers were moved beyond words.

By dramatizing these speeches and putting the words of the #SayHerName mothers into the mouths of actors, we hoped to take the burden off the mothers to be the sole voices telling their stories and advancing their urgent cries for justice. After years of shouldering that burden on behalf of their daughters—of rehashing their most traumatic memory over and over again—they had at last arrived at the point where they could both see themselves as the powerful conduits they were and pass the word to others. To us, this was the conjuring that art and movement made possible.

After this breakthrough installation, #SayHerName has gone on to sponsor and curate a series of even more dynamic and participatory gatherings. At AAPF's Twentieth Anniversary Gala in June 2017 and later at the National Museum of African American History and Culture in March 2018, attendees encountered several innovative installation pieces. At one station of the installation, participants reached into a basket and pulled out a card containing the photo and name of a Black woman killed by the police. They then went on to identify the name on their card on a four-by-six-foot banner. Once they located their assigned name, they circled it in permanent marker and mounted their card on a treelike sculpture, displaying wooden branches connected to one another by a network of string. As they fastened their card to the string, participants said the name on their card three times, joining in real time an audio recording of people chanting the full list of names played on a loop. By the end of the event, participants had placed photos of all the women along the string like flowers on branches, representing rebirth and continuity within our communal traditions.

The art that has documented the #SayHerName mothers' and sisters' grief, joy, victories, and setbacks as milestones for the movement—captured, recorded, and given back to them in various forms—culminated a year after the 2017 Hammer event in our greatest experiment thus far: a full-length play, *Say Her Name: The Lives That Should Have Been.*

Say Her Name: The Lives That Should Have Been sought to answer the call that Ntozake Shange sounded in her landmark play *For Colored Girls Who Have Considered Suicide/When the Rainbow Is Enuf*, pleading for "somebody/anybody" to "sing a black girl's song."[8] We set out to provide in it an intersectional counter-history to explore this largely untrodden narrative terrain. The plot weaves the stories of six female victims of police violence—Tanisha Anderson, Michelle Cusseaux, Shelly Frey, Korryn Gaines, India Kager, and Kayla Moore—together with the struggles and testimonies of their mothers and sisters. The resulting multivoiced narrative serves as a tapestry of intergenerational loss, grief, resistance, and rebirth.

To create the script, we combed through hundreds of pages of transcripts from Mothers Network interviews and focus groups dating back to 2015 and conducted a series of new interviews to direct our work on the play. In one exercise, we asked each mother to project how the lives of their lost loved one might have played out had it not been stolen. What might she be doing now? Where would she be living? What would a normal day look like for her?

The mothers also engaged in improvisational exercises in which they played the role of their loved one in different scenarios, imitating her cadence, vernacular, and overall energy. The resulting script bears the imprint of asymptotic recovery: a process of real-life data collection that spans the chasm between the reality of Black women's experiences and the dominant narratives that circumscribe their lives.

As we drafted the play, we did our best to construct complex, three-dimensional characters that did justice to their individual essences and personalities. We also wanted to ensure that we foregrounded their lives beyond their deaths. We sought to balance the heaviness of the play's subject matter with moments of levity and joy that brought the women to life; to clearly and powerfully communicate the truth of what happened to them, and to provide a window into the lives of their survivors. The goal throughout our effort was to present a rich and lifelike image of an alternative universe in which their lives might have continued on, together.

The play constructs many encounters between the women that #SayHerName memorialized, each one elevating aspects of their character and life plans as shared with us by their survivors. In this scene, Michelle approaches India Kager, who has been sitting in the corner of a train terminal drawing various passengers that she sees, including Michelle.

MICHELLE: (*In accusatory tone*) So, I couldn't help but notice—that drawing looks a lot like me.

INDIA: Oh my god, I'm so sorry. I sometimes come here and draw people, but it's just for me. I wasn't planning on showing it to anyone—

MICHELLE: Sis, I'm just kidding! I love it.

INDIA: Really?

MICHELLE: Yeah! I don't think anyone's ever drawn me before. I like how you did my hair. Do I really make that face, though?

INDIA: (*Laughs*) I guess!

MICHELLE: I need to work on that. Hey, I'm Michelle.

INDIA: India.

MICHELLE: You're really talented, India. Are you a professional artist?

INDIA: (*Laughs*) You're kind, but no. I do love it, though. I'm actually thinking of going back to school for it.

MICHELLE: For real?

INDIA: Yeah! I've had the idea in the back of my mind forever, but now feels like the right time. It's funny, I thought having kids would pull me further from my art and music and closer to practicality, but it's actually been the opposite. I feel more responsible for pursuing my passions than ever before, to model that for them.

MICHELLE: Wow, that's great. I don't have any kids, but my nieces and nephews sometimes feel like mine. Hey, sorry if this is weird, but would you be willing to sell the drawing to me? My girlfriend's birthday is coming up, and I think it'd be hilarious to give her a drawing of myself.

INDIA: Oh my god, of course! You can honestly just have it.

MICHELLE: No way. From this point forward, you're a professional artist, and professional artists don't give away their talent for free. Here. Consider this a small contribution to your first semester's tuition.

(MICHELLE *hands* INDIA *money*)

INDIA: Are you sure? Thank you so much—I really, really appreciate it.

MICHELLE: No, I appreciate it. It's so rare to be able to catch a glimpse of how someone else sees you. I mean, I'm used to being stared at, but actually being seen? Can't say it happens often.

INDIA: Totally. You know how the brain only processes the first and last letters of a word, and then just kinda fills in the rest? I feel like we do the same thing with people. Categorize, file away, move on.

MICHELLE: That's a beautiful way of putting it. Thank you for seeing me, India.

INDIA: My pleasure. Thank you for seeing me, Michelle.

The play was first performed as a staged reading in March 2019 at the Hammer Museum, as part of our #HerDreamDeferred Fifth Anniversary programming. Local actors read for a packed audience that included the Mothers Network.

After the reading, we held a talkback onstage with five of the mothers who shared their thoughts on the play. Their reactions were a moving testimony of the power of artivism. They spoke to the emotional impact the play had on them: "I felt a sense of relief

and comfort in seeing the girls together, all of the young women whose lives had been taken at the hands of the police. I just felt comforted seeing them together and comforting each other," said Fran Garrett. She went on to suggest that, after the event, she felt like her daughter was "not gone; like she's still here." In Fran's mind, the daughters were "laughing and talking and taking care of each other . . . [and] doing what they love." It was "comforting" to Fran to believe that her daughter was "not suffering, she's free."

Gina Best's reactions were similarly moving and profound. "For a moment I imagined I was able to embrace my daughter again. . . . We had a chance to hold our babies again." That experience "was so wonderful. I haven't been able to hug India, but to hear and see this young lady who's portraying my baby, India, to hold her in that space . . ." Gina further described *imagining* "their spirits beaming down all their love on us. And I whispered in her ear, and she said, 'I got you, Mom.' And when she said, 'I got you, Mom,' I could hear my India saying it." Particularly compelling to Gina was the sense that the play created space in which "this ocean of people, the sea of people" were "finally paying attention."

To put Gina's point another way, this ocean of people, the sea of people, was finally bearing witness.

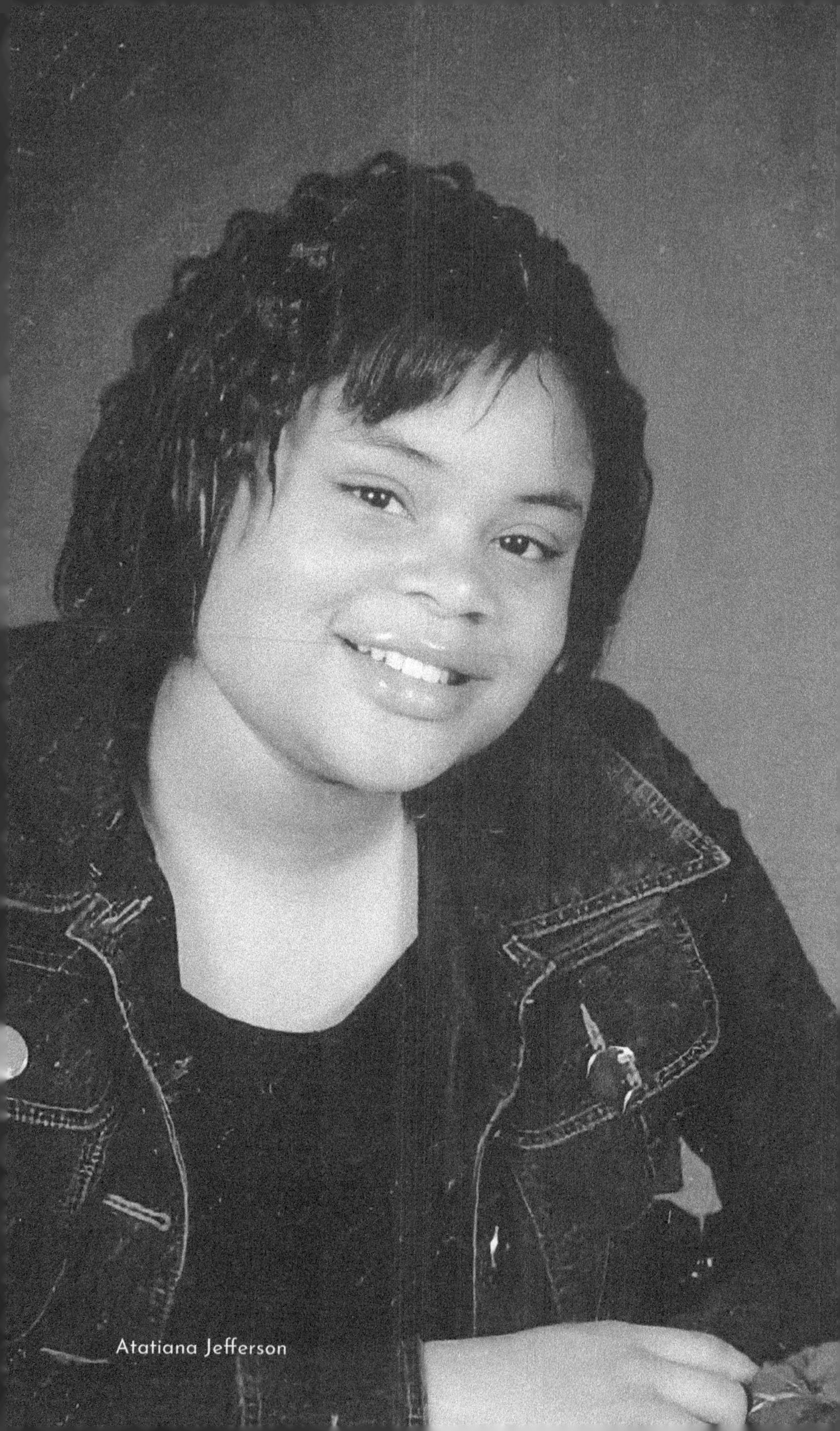
Atatiana Jefferson

CONCLUSION

Bearing Witness

"What we learned is that laws matter."
Ashley and Amber Carr, sisters of Atatiana Jefferson
(November 28, 1990–October 12, 2019)

Hi, my name is Ashley Carr. I'm a sister of a Atatiana, and I'm a part of the Say Her Name Mothers Network.

I'm Amber Carr. I'm Atatiana's sister, and I'm a part of the Say Her Name Mothers Network

Amber: *I'm a cofounder of the Atatiana Project. I'm here for Atatiana Jefferson, who was shot and killed by police in Fort Worth, Texas. She's my baby sister. From my perspective, she was a tomboy in a skirt because that's how we were raised, in skirts and dresses. She was into sports, science, video-gaming for sure. She was a comedian. A really dry comedian. Only certain people could catch on.*

Ashley: *Intellectual people could catch it.*

Amber: *She was really cool. She was like a rainbow. And you can tell because her friends were rainbows. She had friends from all over and all types of friends. So growing up in the house, she was a tomboy, so her typical hairstyle was a ponytail. So my greatest* *memory will be that time she actually started to allow me to do her hair. You know, when she got older and she started to become a little bit more feminine and she would get her hair pressed, would curl it, you know. I would ask [her] like, "Where are you going?" And it would shock me sometimes when she would say, "I'm going to the club." But yeah. So that's my greatest memory, of bonding, you know, by her allowing me to do her hair.*

Ashley: *We connected a lot on the, I guess, academia level. She was extremely smart, extremely smart. Sometimes it was kind of scary. So for her to have just a wealth of knowledge and it always wasn't all about schoolwork. She knew about different life hacks. A memory I always go back to is, Atatiana and I, she came down to Houston to go to a Beyoncé concert with me. I had called her, and I was like, "You wanna go to a Beyoncé concert with me?" And she was like, "Yeah. I'm part of the Beyhive." And I was like, "What?" Because my sister, she was in the band in high school, she was in the choir at Xavier. She graduated from Xavier University in four years. So she had a musical ear. She loved all genres of music and things. I just did not think she was a [Beyhive]! She was part of the [Beyhive]. But she came down. She brought her dog with her because she didn't have any children. But her dog was her life. I had a dog then too. So we left the dogs at the house, and we went to the concert, and she was just like really into it. And I was like, "Oh wow! Well now I know you like to go to concerts, you got to be my new concert buddy!" That was the plan. That was literally the plan. But due to tragedy, that was the only concert that we ever got to go to together. Because, you know, we didn't come from a family with money. Our village was building itself. So that was the only* *opportunity we got to do that. I love that she was evolving into this beautiful butterfly. Well, she was already, I guess they say, she was a beautiful caterpillar.*

Amber: *And to piggyback off of Ashley, when it comes to music, I remember when we tried out for band. They lined up all the different instruments. And she and I both wanted to originally do the flute. But someone, one of the instructors, said our lips were too big. Ah! We were like, "What??" But so that's why we ended up doing the clarinet.*

Ashley: *Although she was the youngest—*

Amber: *—she was the problem solver.*

Ashley: *She was. She was the person that we both called on.*

Amber: *And now we don't have her to fix everything. We have to go to each other. She was the middle person. And now we don't have that.*

Ashley: *There's definitely some stuff we have to learn, to communicate without her. If Amber and I had a disagreement—*

Amber: *Cause we're so much alike.*

Ashley: *Yeah, and I would call Tay, and I would be like, "Tay! Get your sister! Let me tell you what your sister did." And she was like, "Well. I'm gonna go over there and check on her." And she would just show up over there, just to make sure that we were okay. She was also a protector.*

Amber: *Always.*

Ashley: *She was extremely headstrong. She knew what she wanted in life, and she knew what she didn't want.*

Amber: *I envied that.*

Ashley: *When she went to Xavier, everybody kept saying, "Why you going all the way to Louisiana?" But she just knew, "That's where I'm going." And she did. She executed that with grace and made it look easy. She knew what she wanted. She knew that she just didn't want to go to any medical school. In her head she was like, "I want to go to a top-line medical school." She didn't want to struggle like she did in undergrad. Her goal was, "Let me save my money, so that I can be fully invested into my medical program." And all of us understood that. We were all on that play, that Tay's gonna save her money, and were all gonna help her get to her next destination.*

Amber: *She gave me a lot of confidence. Really she did.*

Ashley: *I would say this: my mom named us the A-Team because she wanted us to understand that regardless of where we're at in life, where we're living or anything like that, any type of struggle, we are a team. We are a team. So then when we lost part of that team, it was hard to figure out. How does this team move? So we're literally learning each other without a member of the team.*

Amber: *As adults. Without a mum.*

Ashley: *In August 2019, Amber had her second open-heart surgery. At this time, my mother is in another hospital.*

Amber: *All the way on the other side of town.*

Ashley: *I am having to be the voice for both of them. Also while trying to figure out what my mother's conditions are. Amber had to go to two rehabs. She had to go to a rehab just for the trach. Then she had to learn how to walk. How to talk. All over again. This was the sixty days, literally sixty days, before our sister was killed. Amber got out of the hospital Wednesday night, Wednesday, Thursday. And this is how she gets out of rehab. Atatiana was murdered that Friday.*

Amber: *Two days later.*

Ashley: *So we have been running since before the murder.*

Amber: *It's crazy because that last weekend when I was in the rehab, Atatiana was at my mom's house. She had already moved in, to save money, so she was watching Zion. At the time he was eight. Her nephew, my son. And she came and saw me at the hospital that weekend. She brought me a cell phone. We talked, we laughed. She was telling me they were planning to take the boys to the fair. They had all these plans; 2019 was crazy.*

Ashley: *While she was in the hospital, her youngest child, Zayden, had a birthday. She couldn't do it because she's in there fighting for her life. So me and Tay took the boys to Sissy's Pizza, and they loved that. And then we went to an indoor play area. I'm the aunt that pays for things and watch[es]. Tay was the aunt that actually got in and played with them. That's the type of person she was. All of this was happening, and that night, October 12—*

Amber: *The first thing that I remember was my mom calling me. And she was just really sad. She was like, "I need for you to go and* *pick Zion up from a facility somewhere here in Fort Worth." And that's it. "A facility?" "Yes, something happened at the house. An incident happened at the house." And the first thing I thought was, well, where is Tay? She goes, "Well the—" What is it, "deputy"? "Chief"? . . .*

Ashley: *The chief of police.*

Amber: *. . . was in her hospital room. In her hospital room telling her about the incident. And when I say "Well, where is Tay?" I'm thinking she said "altercation." And I'm like, "So what? Is she in jail?" "Listen," she said, "No, they're saying she's not here." I said, "What you mean, not here?" She said, "My baby. They're saying she's gone." You know, I was so weak. I wasn't really taking showers then. I was taking sponge baths. But for some reason, I had a burst of energy. It was just like, my adrenaline. I ran into my aunt's room, because I was staying with her for awhile until I got better. And I said, "Hey. Something's happened, and Mum says Tay's gone, and Zion is at a facility." That's all I knew. Until I got to the facility. And when I got to the facility, they're questioning me like I'm a criminal. You know, I'm the boy's mom. They're questioning me. It was crazy. But then I woke Zion up, and he's so happy to see us. And he looked up from when he woke up, and he said, "The police shot Aunt Tay." That's the first thing he said. He's like, "The police shot Aunt Tay." It was like, 'verything just stopped. My aunt was there, and she was just like, "What?! What are you saying to us?" So that was it. And once we talked to my mom again, she asked us to go by her house. So that's what we did. And the neighbor came out and talked to us. And, you know, of course, there were people walking up trying to interview us right then and there,* *like, just so inconsiderate. And while we were sitting in the car, with the windows down, talking to the neighbor, I had a cousin that was in the driver's seat. And for some reason he found the body cam footage on YouTube. I don't know what made him think to go there and look. So I'm watching it, and, you know how body cams are. They're leading up to the house. They're passing up the doors. They're not announcing themselves. They're going in the backyard. He made that command, but within that command, he didn't give her time to respond. And when I heard the gunshot, it's like' I freaked out because it became real. It's like, "Oh, this really did happen! This is crazy." But I think before we got Zion, I called you, right?*

Ashley: *So our aunt called. And I was teaching my Saturday class. I had just got a job at the community college, cause my sister needs help. She hasn't worked for two months. How is she gonna survive? My mechanism is, "I'm gonna go out and work, get a second job, give this month to Amber so her and the boys can survive." I did not want her to work. I wanted her to rest her heart. And my aunt called. Like, why is she calling me? It's eight-something in the morning. So I answered the second time, and she says, "You need to get here. You need to get here. Something is happening at the house. You need to come home now." I'm like, "Something happened at the house?" So I'm like, I know Amber's with her, so the first thing I do, I call Tay. She's not answering her phone. That's not like Tay. She always answers my phone calls. I call Zion, cause he also answers all the time. So I'm like, "Okay. What is going on?" I call my mother, and she says, "I want you to listen to the chief of police." And so they start trying to explain what happened. And I'm still confused because I'm thinking,*

"Did my sister—?" Cause I know my sister has a concealed handgun permit.

I was like, "Did she shoot somebody? What did happen?"

And they was like, "No, she didn't do anything wrong. She was, you know, she was killed there."

And I was like, "What?"

Then my mom's side is screaming, "They killed my baby!"

It was like a chill. I didn't know what to do. I didn't know what to do. I literally froze. And remember all this conversation is happening in front of my Saturday class, 'cause I didn't step out of the room or anything. I'm literally standing in front of the class getting all this information. It was crazy. It was extremely crazy. It was so surreal. And it was, like, soon after that I was like, "Okay, I will go home." And everything started happening. People started calling. People, like Amber said, people started sending us the body cam footage. There really wasn't no code on what we were experiencing. We were pushed into something.

I had to call my brother. And I had to tell my brother that our sister was killed. He's in active military. He's out serving our country. Doing that since the age of nineteen. And he had to literally leave to come home. And we get to Mom's hospital room, it's so surreal. It's so many people in there. People we don't know. There was no shield on us.

Amber: *And I just cannot believe the nurses was allowing it. So we finally told them, "None of this, and no TV." She had no TV. Because anywhere you went, even when you drove down the street and you see bars with televisions, that's all you saw because it was local. So that's all you saw. Everywhere you turn, it's all yourself.*

Ashley: *And, you know, she was in the hospital room. She felt helpless that she couldn't get [up] and fight for her baby.*

Ashley: *On the morning of October 12, 2019, the across-the-street neighbor called 311, which is a nonemergency number, and said that my mother's house doors were open. He knew that my mom had been sick and wanted to know if somebody would just check on it. I don't know what happened in between, but it was sent out as an open structure. The police did not park on the street, didn't do any lighting on the street in front of the house or anything. What they did do is they parked a'ound the corner and approached the house as in, I'll say, a Call of Duty way. Guns were already out. You go to my mother's house, you see that all the exterior doors are in the front of the house. So if you're in the back of the house, you can't get out. He passed up both doors. The screen doors were closed, but the exterior doors were open. All lights were on in the house. Never rung the doorbell on both doors. Instead, he passed them up, and flashed lights through the windows and things of that nature. Gets to the back of my mom's house to the gate. The gate is hard to open. So you have to jiggle at it to open it. But the catch of that is Atatiana's bedroom is literally on the other side of that gate. So that night, her and Zion was up playing video games, as they always do on a Friday night till the wee hours, till the sun comes up. That's Tay. She goes to sleep when the sun comes up. And he came in the backyard, and I guess she looked out the window and in the same breath it was like everything was literally, simultaneously with each other. And he said, "Show me your hands." And in that breath of saying "Show me your hands," he shot through the window. There was never any time to comply. There was never any time to figure* *out, "Who is this in my backyard?" Oh, at this moment, we don't know what happened after. We can only speculate. We're currently waiting for trial. So he was charged, but he was charged with murder. I guess that [at] grand jury he was charged. She [the district attorney (DA)] got an indictment. And now we're waiting for trial.*

Amber: *And he was arrested. But then he was bailed out by the police union. So he didn't really spend any time there.*

Ashley: *Spent no time there.*

Amber: *Got in and got out.*

Ashley: *And he got presidential treatment.*

Amber: *He got out, and he's been out, and he's still out. And he's trying to continue to be out. To this day.*

Ashley: *Yeah, they're trying to figure out what ways and law. What stall tactics can be done. And they have pulled every card.*

Amber: *And [they've] been granted.*

Ashley: *Yes. The trial was supposed to be in November [2020], then it got moved to November of 2021. Then it got moved to January 2022 to then from January got moved to May 2022. In May it got moved to June 2022. And every time this happens you're trying to anticipate. Our anxiety is up. Trying to figure out, you know. Life at that moment is up. People say, "How can you live?" We're at this moment where we just stuck. We're literally stuck at this moment.*[1]

Ashley: *So, you know, what we learned is that laws matter. And we're also learning that local elections extremely matter. So we definitely push voter registration. We definitely push local elections and making sure that the people we know are in the know, when it is, and who's running. Because we had to learn that the DA is our attorney. We don't get to pick who gets to fight for Atatiana. The city has chosen that person. And so this fight is crazy. We had to fight for our own sister's funeral. It was so much drama. People forging documents and lying to the courts. About who they were. And because we didn't know that their courts granted those things. And we had to go and mediate with people about a funeral. They weren't even a part of her life. I'm being honest. That was hard. And my momma was not there.*

Amber: *The whole time. She couldn't go to the funeral.*

Ashley: *She could not go. That was so hard. That was the hard part for me. I begged those administrators at the hospital, "Please, can I just have her for one day. If something happens to her, I won't sue or anything." But my mom needed to be there and . . . couldn't because she was so weak. And I have to be strong through all this. I gotta be her legs. I gotta be her arms. I gotta be her voice through all of this. As Amber says, it was an adrenaline rush. People say, "You know, you're strong." But I wasn't here. The flesh was here. But being honest, that wasn't me.*

Amber: *It's like the Energizer [bunny] running. It just keeps going and going and going and going and going. So when it comes to justice, we held Black Voters Matter.*

Ashley: *We did a children's protest. We taught the children how to protest.*

Amber: *And it was the best protest I've ever been to.*

Ashley: *We can't do protesting. Because what we've learned is that everything that we do will be used against us in a court of law.*

Amber: *So you asked us, what have we done for justice. And everything that we have done was brought up in court.*

Ashley: *Everything we've done, because we have a gag order on our case. So we can't really talk about it. But we don't know nothing. We only know what everybody else knows. So our goal was we wanted to uplift Atatiana.*

Amber: *Memorialize her.*

Ashley: *Talk about her legacy, how wonderful she was, how much of an impact she was to the community, to our family. So we done parades, community outreach, we started a nonprofit in her name called the Atatiana Project, where we bring STEAM [Science, Technology, Engeneering, Arts, and Math] exposure to urban youth. We're about to do our second year of summer camp where the kids will be building computers on their own and learning about coding. This year we're getting some robots so they can learn about coding with robots. Our goal is to do what Tay was doing the night she was murdered; exposing youth to STEAM.*

So we took that moment, and we just want to expand on the greatness of Atatiana. We want to do an Atatiana book scholarship because that was one thing that we like talking to people who went to school with her, is that Atatiana had issues getting books when she was in college. One of her college friends told us that they had a fire drill in the dorms and everybody's out. And Tay is not out of the building. No. And they were like trying to figure out, "Where is she? Where is she? Tay comes downstairs." She got all her books with her and she said, "Well, it's drill. So I was trying to see how long it's going to take me to get all my books if it was a real fire," she said. "Because I can't, you know, I got to have my books."

I love her. I miss her. So, so, so much.

Amber: *We've had a street renaming, so the whole block where my mom's house is, [is] memorialized. So it's a Atatiana Jefferson Parkway. My mom's house now is officially the Atatiana Project headquarters.*

Ashley: *We lost two people in that house. When my mom finally got out of the hospital, she went home.*

Amber: *A week later . . .*

Ashley: *Not even a week. She was gone. And every day she would just go and stand in that room. And I tried my best because I didn't want her to see the blood on the floor, and I wanted her to see none of that. Oh, because the crazy thing about it, I didn't even know these things. I didn't know that, if you leave that too long, it can get into your foundation, of your house. And then you have to do extremely detailed cleaning that costs an arm and a leg that nobody's paying for. They told us that for the state to pay for it, first we have to file a claim on our insurance. We didn't do anything! They didn't change the window. We had to do everything. My mother died, and that January [2021] we didn't even get to go to our loved one's things, because my mom's house, while everybody else was on quarantine, our mom's house was being ransacked.*

Amber: *Somebody started living in there.*

Ashley: *They stole everything. They ransacked that house. Destroyed my mom's house. That was the pride of my mother's; she finally got a home built where her kids had a place to go to feel safe. And to know that the place you built for your children to feel safe is the same place your child got killed. That's hard. That's extremely hard. How do you live through that? I was mad at my mother. She left. She had three other children left. But to lose your child in your house? That's a lot. That's a lot to deal with. So I can't even be mad at her.*

Amber: *You know, when she died, she actually had on an Atatiana's shirt with her face on it. So when we came in and the first thing I see is her on the floor, I guess after they tried everything that they could do, I'm just, like, oh, my gosh, you know, I went crazy. I laid on the ground weeping on the floor with it. They wanted me to get out of there, but I couldn't. Her body was still warm. To me, she wasn't dead. She was just sleeping.*

We have a lot of plans for the Atatiana Project and to live out Atatiana's legacy. This is a lifelong [project]. Because once we're gone, we want Zion and Zayden and all the people we've brought together, we want this to keep going as long as it can.

Ashley: *Some people will say, death penalty, things like that. Personally, I feel like that's the easier way. I want you to suffer. 'Cause I've been suffering since it happened. We should both be in the suffering mode.*

Amber: *He should not be allowed to do the things that he does on the weekends. The community, community talk[s], they always come back and tell us, "We saw him at his favorite brunch spot on*

Saturday." And I'm like, that is awful. We don't have a place to meet up for our holidays anymore. Holidays are not the same.

Amber: *We would go to my mom's house, that we already knew. You didn't have those worries. And now the matriarch is gone.*

Amber: *I feel like #SayHerName doesn't get enough publicity. You guys helped us, helped us in so many ways that people wouldn't even understand.*

Ashley: *We've never gotten help without an agenda with this situation. That's what we've learned. We were extremely green. We're thinking, "You felt our hurt as well. You want to come and support." But all the while they were just using us to better their platform. But that didn't happen here. To me it's a relief, to know that I literally have people who didn't grow up with me. But they still want to be there for us and genuinely do it.*

Amber: *And you want to be modest because you don't want to really say what you need help with. But then, they already know. Cause you don't like asking.*

Ashley: *I don't like to ask because, we were brought up, you don't go walking around asking people for stuff. That shows that you're in a back mode. But we do need to ask.*

Amber: *We need help.*

Ashley: *We can't do it all by ourselves. That's the theme of my life. I cannot do it all by myself.*

Ashley Carr and Amber Carr

I cannot do it all by myself.

In December 2022 former police officer Aaron Dean was sentenced to twelve years for manslaughter for the death of Atatiana Jefferson. Just one month later, in January 2023, Atatiana's sister Amber died, leaving behind two young sons as well as Atatiana's two surviving siblings.

The survivors of police violence against Black women cannot—must not—do it all by themselves. By coming together with the family members of Black women killed by the police, #SayHerName actively supports them in their quests for justice for their daughters and sisters, join them in their struggle to hold the police to account, and bear witness to the lives that should have been, the lives that have been lost, and to our ongoing struggle to end police violence. These acts of coming together not only bring us closer as a community of Black women fighting racism and sexism. They also connect us to a wider and national struggle that views police violence as a structural phenomenon, rather than as a problem that derives from a few "bad apple" cops.

On Wednesday, June 17, 2020, just a month after the murder of George Floyd, the African American Policy Forum and the Center for Intersectionality and Social Policy Studies hosted a two-hour virtual event to foreground stories of African Americans killed by police. Together we bore witness to the individual and institutional contours of anti-Black police violence, and we challenged the conventional framing of the policing crisis as a matter of a few bad apples.

Our forum was one of myriad groups across the country challenging the regime of racialized policing and its lethal impact on the African American community. Millions of people rushed to the streets in righteous outrage to demonstrate against Floyd's murder and the broader culture of impunity surrounding racialized police violence. The centuries-long vulnerability of Black people to lethal, state-sanctioned violence had, for a brief moment, become the focal point of national concern and international condemnation. And the casual violence that Derek Chauvin executed in front of the world revealed the wide-ranging, almost unregulated, power of police to take lives without fear of significant consequences. George Floyd's death presented a spectacle of abject dehumanization, which in turn raised the curtain on tens of thousands of other deaths at the hands of police. In the explosive moments of civil unrest that continued throughout the summer of 2020, the country seemed ready to move beyond the complacent acceptance of racialized police murder in the punitive carceral state. At this charged moment, Americans were more primed than ever to confront the historic and structural nature of lethal force against populations of people of color, particularly Black people.

As we began to work through these issues with our virtual audience that night in June, a whole host of related questions about over-policing and structural inequality emerged. We recounted stories that tracked the intersecting and lethal consequences of the war on drugs, racial profiling, paramilitary policing, implicit and explicit biases, police-sourced solutions to mental health crises, and other problems. Family members of victims killed in police encounters recalled how their loved ones had been detained for "offenses" such as driving while Black, having a mental health crisis while Black, even breathing while Black. They also explained how broader political and cultural forces aligned against anyone ever being held accountable for such killings—thanks to an array of protections such as qualified immunity, police union advocacy, and biased media narratives.

For the attendees, movement veterans, dedicated citizen-activists, and recently activated advocates, the terrain we traversed was grimly familiar, except for one distinguishing feature: the Black lives that were snuffed out in the deadly encounters we discussed that evening belonged to women—Michelle Cusseaux, India Kager, Kayla Moore, Shelly Frey, Korryn Gaines, Breanna Taylor, Sandra Bland, Aiyana Stanley Jones, Alberta Spruill, India Kager, Alicia Chrisian, and Atatiana Jefferson.

We do not mean for that list to be exhaustive. As you know from reading prior chapters, particularly chapter 5, the list of Black women killed by the police is a long one. What's striking about these stolen lives is that while they are remarkably diverse with respect to class, sexuality, gender identity, political engagement, region, profession, marital status, and parenthood, they are similar along one critical dimension: their stories of police violence were largely (though not entirely) unfamiliar to the general public. Although their killings had mostly followed the same tragic arc of needlessly sacrificed Black men and boys, there had been no corresponding moment of mass political organizing on their behalf. Bland's death while in police custody after a traffic stop in Texas, and now Taylor's, were the only exception to this pattern. As a result, the families of these victims were left alone in their grief and struggled to cope with unimaginable circumstances: the loss itself, yes, and the public's suppressed capacity to see Black women as subjects of police violence. Holding space to address this *unimaginability* is what #SayHerName has become.

By now you know that #SayHerName was born of a need to end the public silence surrounding the murders of Black women and address the isolation in its wake. You also know that the #SayHerName Mothers Network brings together Black women whose daughters, and in some cases sisters, have been killed by the police. You have read their individual stories and their memories of their precious daughters. I surmise that many of you are now sitting with the grief left in the wake of their loved ones' deaths, the anger and frustration at a system that refuses to accept accountability or provide justice for mourning families. You may even be thinking about the loss of the loss, as the names and lives of Black women killed by the police go largely forgotten, by the media, by the wider public, and sometimes by social justice movements as well.

But what I want you to understand as well is that when you read the mothers' and sisters' accounts of their loved ones' lives, their passions and loves, their commitment to their own children, their mothers, and siblings, you were honoring their too-short lives that were and the lives that should have been. You were enacting the imperative of the #SayHerName campaign to bear witness to unspeakable tragedies and to stand in solidarity with survivors' search for justice.

#SayHerName must continue. And subsequent iterations will continue to support the mothers and families of Black women murdered by police, continue to address the multiple traumas that overwhelm the communities police killings leave in their wake, and continue to bear witness to the multiple dynamics that create the disproportionate risks that Black women's police encounters will be both lethal and invisible to the public at large.

We bear witness to make our collective vulnerability legible, which in turn directs our advocacy to the conditions that must change for us to survive. We listen to and retell the stories we have heard, reckoning with the proximate causes of stolen lives and the broader structural forces that compromised those lives, and rendered them vulnerable to state-sanctioned violence. We hold space for the mutual recognition, support, and permissions that only women who have experienced this particular loss can fully understand and give to one another.

Bearing witness calls us to address all the ways that Black women die at the hands of police. It means we listen to the dying words of Kayla Moore, Natasha McKenna, Tanisha Anderson, and Michelle Cussaux—"I can't breathe," "You promised not to kill me," "Go away, I'm fine," or simply, "Momma!" They haunt, they traumatize, and they leave no doubt about the consequences of law enforcement being the first responders to mental health crises. These last words tell us that justifications routinely offered by police to rationalize their use of lethal force are grossly overused, that cruelty and dehumanization are the tools of policing based on enforcing order rather than enhancing well-being. They show in sharp relief that compassionate supportive intervention that could save lives remains a low priority in the current culture of law enforcement. These women's words beckon us to understand how the toxic interplay of ableism, racism, and misogyny shape these fatal encounters and the willingness of too many people to look away.

Bearing witness to the deaths of Black women and girls in their own homes is a reminder of a point we made earlier: Black women's homes are not our castles. The deaths of Breonna Taylor, Atatiana Jefferson, Aiyana Stanley-Jones, Kayla Moore, Tarika Wilson, Alberta Spruill, and so many others underscore the inescapable fact that there is no escape, no safe space, no place free of the threat of police violence. We will not be safe behind our own walls until rules that permit police to invade our homes are reined in and the narratives that frame our defense of ourselves and our families as the justification for obliterating us are reversed.

Bearing witness means understanding the ways that routine acts such as running an errand or going to work can lead to police encounters that escalate into death. Korryn's incarceration, the miscarriage she suffered as a consequence, and her ultimate homicide began over traffic violations. Bland's death was the end of an encounter that began over an allegedly faulty lane change. Both Gaines's and Bland's deaths underscore the largely unregulated discretion of police to initiate encounters—facilitated by the wildly permissive interpretations of Fourth Amendment protections against unreasonable search and seizure—and by bootstrapping the most repressive expressions of state power onto these minor infractions to force compliance. As noted by legal scholar Devon W. Carbado, because of Fourth Amendment law, "ordinary police interactions often *do* result in a range of violence . . . If the police have fewer opportunities to stop and question Black people, they have fewer opportunities to kill us."[2]

Korryn's death points to the need to minimize the involvement of armed officers in serving warrants for minor offenses, while Bland's death illustrates how boundless discretionary power leaves Black women vulnerable to the punitive impulses of officers set on disciplining and controlling them. The deaths of both Miriam Carey and Michelle Shirley show us that police need much better training in assessing the danger posed by drivers who appear to be out of control. The deaths of Atatiana, Kayla, Korryn, Michelle, and Tanisha remind us of the urgent work to be done so that a 911 call for help is never again a motive for violence. Bearing witness means holding space for mothers to grieve and supporting them as they turn from grief to advocacy. This mother-centered approach to eliminating police violence against Black women reveals that women who carry the memories of their murdered daughters and sisters possess crucial knowledge about what change looks like. Bearing witness centers their sense of what would have prevented their loved ones' deaths, and what could and should have been done to support families when violence did occur. These experiences ground what we all must do to fight for justice while imagining a world where other families are not devastated by predatory police violence.

Part of our charge as we bear witness is to envision a world where Black women can live free from the threat of lethal and sexual violence by police. Part of our charge is to interrogate policing practices at the intersections of race, gender, sexuality, and class; and part of our charge is to develop policy advocacy agendas along those same lines. Guaranteeing the survival and safety of Black women must be premised on efforts to reduce the exposure of all Black people to police, and efforts to reduce the exposure of all Black people to the police must include the particular vulnerabilities of Black women.

Grounding our work in mothers' needs will necessarily mean that there is no singular demand or exclusive framework for justice. Every loss is unique, and thus the consequential realities that survivors must carry will yield different priorities. Some of what we've learned from sitting with the mothers is different from talking points derived from standard policy discourse, or distinct from what we might hear from a public town hall, a rally, or a news report. Bearing witness to the mothers' visions of what justice would look like for them elevates a variety of commitments to both microlevel changes and to the fuller rethinking of policing writ large.

For Sharon Wilkerson, the key to reform would be to make sure that security guards in stores like Walmart are unarmed. That way, a routine trip to Walmart for a shirt or some makeup wouldn't end in another funeral for a Black woman like her daughter Shelly. Deadly force is an entirely incommensurate response to either the perception or the reality of shoplifting. As Sharon reminds us, "We don't need guns to protect stuff. We need people to protect people." Unarmed private security guards would signal a commitment to valuing the lives of all people.

Rhanda Dormeus believes that the pathway to greater accountability is through taking on the structural dimensions of modern policing that provide police officers with qualified immunity and also allow them to repeatedly engage in lethal practices without legal, criminal, or financial consequences. Rhanda notes that members of no other professional group would be able to retain gainful employment if they engaged in the pattern of lethal encounters that police officers do. For Atatiana's sisters Ashley and Amber, justice means not only seeing the officer who murdered their sister go to trial but also structural changes at the level of law and elections. In Ashley's words, they discovered that "laws matter" and "local elections matter." This realization has led the sisters to get involved in educating citizens about the importance of local elections and voting. Ashley and Amber have also had their mother's street renamed Atatiana Jefferson Parkway. Justice also means remembering.

Other survivors' stories speak to the wider patterns of violence, collusion, and injustice that are at the core of the culture of racialized police impunity. But these kinds of stories, which have become more broadly recognized and debated in the wake of Floyd's murder, still remain intensely personal for each and every mother.

The loss of a vital family member also brings with it the sudden financial toll of funeral expenses and other costs associated with the police killing a family member, which the families are left to cover. For example, Gina Best was sent the bill for the destruction of the car that her daughter was driving when she was killed. Atatiana's sisters tell the horrifying story of having to pay a huge sum to have their deceased sister's blood cleaned up. And as Gina's painful tales of experiencing shaming for the illegal killing of her daughter shows, too often families must do so with little recognition or support from their own communities, and with precious few resources of their own to continue absorbing these life-shattering circumstances.

In addition to offloading financial burdens onto families in already distressing circumstances, police put tremendous and concerted bureaucratic resistance in the paths of grieving families. All the mothers talk about how difficult it is to get information from local police departments following police killings of their loved ones. Local cops are sometimes not even required to respond to bewildered and grieving family members for forty-eight hours after a lethal police encounter. This delay makes it impossible for families to get crucial information immediately after the deaths of their daughters, when they need it most desperately. And this is no accident: families require reliable information soon after the trauma of a daughter's death so that they can begin to think about holding officers and police departments to account, and to pursue justice in courts.

Further, it is no accident that when, finally, the police do speak, their accounts often change to suit their needs and to protect their own. The initial statements and internal police communications may say one thing, but by the time the accused officers get to trial, they're all saying the same thing. Acting under the generous legal and cultural protections afforded to the police, officers can retroactively coordinate the official record of police killings to minimize their own liability and accountability. The families of slain daughters, sisters, and mothers, meanwhile, are left out in the cold, deprived of the basic information they need in order to get justice for their daughters in court. In some cases, the information lockdown extends to information about whether their daughters are alive or not, as was the case with Korryn, Tamika, and Breonna, or the whereabouts of their grandchildren—as Gina learned when trying to locate India's infant son.

And while the police are withholding information from the families, they're *feeding* information to the media—with extreme and selective prejudice. They get their preferred story out into the public and ensure that it gains traction as the official version of events in press reports. They represent their interests forcefully—and misrepresent, and even lie about, the women they have killed. This stultifying regime of information lockdown fuels a common and toxic narrative that distorts public debate around racialized police violence—the myth that its victims, in one way another, invited their fates, by provoking the police directly or by acting in suspiciously criminal or deviant fashion. The uncritical and deferential posture of the media before prefabricated police narratives has enabled this myth to become powerfully rooted in public consciousness.

Debra Shirley, whose daughter Michelle was shot to death by police after she had a car accident in Los Angeles in 2016, describes the media's treatment of her and her family after Michelle's death:

> I think that has a lot to do with the media's relationship with police officers. Someone told me that, I don't know if that's true, that's where they get a lot of their stories. So they have this real tight-knit relationship. Someone that came to my house wanted to interview us. We're like, "We don't want to talk to him." I ran outside to tell him now is not the time. But one of the first things he said was, "She did rev up her engine." Or, "She did try to run over the police." What? Who are you watching? I couldn't believe it. So needless to say, I never called him because he already has it in his head, he's already driving a narrative the way he wants it to go.

It is not only the public who are fed sensationalist and inaccurate stories about Black women killed by the police. Too often families first hear news about their loved ones through the media. Debra and her family learned of Michelle's death hours after it happened, not from the police but "at 9:30 at night by the news media, of all people." After years of waiting for the officers who killed her daughter Tanisha to be convicted following homicide verdicts from two different coroners, Cassandra Johnson learned on television that a grand jury had failed to indict the policemen involved. Valarie Carey first heard of the death of her sister Miriam when a journalist called her and told her to watch the news. When she turned on the television, Valarie saw an image of what looked to be her sister's car and her young niece being held by a police officer. The footer to the image read: "Suspect killed."

Like their male counterparts, female victims are framed with innuendo and suggestions to render their characters vaguely suspect, often in ways that track the suspicious framing of men, and sometimes along gendered lines that paint them as responsible for their own deaths either through their associations or through non-normative gender behavior.

Headlines rehearse a familiar chorus of suspicion that merely amplifies subtextual assumptions that victims of police homicide were to blame for their own deaths.

"Videos Capture Deadly Stand-Off between Baltimore-Area Mother, Police"

"'I Took the First Shot because I Had No Choice,' Officer Royce Ruby Jr., Baltimore County Police."

"Slain Shoplifter's Family Sues Walmart"

"Korryn Gaines Was Passionate about Beliefs, Anticipated Violent Confrontation with Police"

"Cleveland Officers Respond to Lawsuit, Say Tanisha Anderson Contributed to Own Death"

"Breonna Taylor Shooting: Warrant Says Suspect Used Her Apartment to Hide Drugs"

"Maryland Police Shoot Woman after She 'Repeatedly Threatened Officers'—video"

"Police Charge Korryn Gaines's Boyfriend with Heroin Distribution, Firearms Offenses"

"Trooper Fired for Sandra Bland Stop: 'My Safety Was in Jeopardy'"

"Mother's Lawsuit against Virginia Beach Police Downplays Danger India Kager Placed Herself In"

The clear agenda behind such coverage is to fuel the strong predisposition of many consumers to align with cop-friendly narratives, making it appear that individual victims are in fact dangerous potential threats to public safety, often just by looking or seeming suspicious in the eyes of law enforcement.

Readers and viewers will often come away from such coverage thinking "Well, you know, that person who was killed was a bad person," or "That was a situation she had no business being in." The insidious impact of such coverage is to chloroform the public conscience before it's had the opportunity to awaken. Floyd's story escaped this narrative template because his killing was captured in real time—unfiltered by self-justifying police narratives—on social media.

For the families who have to grapple with the loss and with the media's role in aiding and abetting the tragedy, these headlines are painful reminders that behind a stolen life is often a fabricated story.

For Gina, the path toward something like justice must involve a full and public recognition of the misinformation, distortion, and outright fabrication so as to short-circuit the character assassination of her daughter that replays over and over again. #SayHerName is not a simple hashtag for her but also a mandate to recognize and correct defamatory narratives that cruelly deprive Black women and girls of their stories.

The #SayHerName mandate stands as an eloquent and powerful rebuke to the racially driven lies and hate that have leveraged their way from social media platforms into our national politics. The viral power of saying her name lifts up unique and powerful stories of these women's deaths and also of their lives.

If we are committed to bearing witness, to learning, to amplifying, advocating, activating, and donating, we can resist the erasure of these stories, and we can support families who have lost loved ones and are continuing to fight for justice today. In order to get out the truth about Black women's lives, we need to insistently tell and circulate the stories behind those lives. Doing so both talks back to the collusive efforts between policing and reporting to fabricate a suspect character for Black women and girls killed by police and foregrounds the injustice done to them and their families.

Finally, and far from least, mothers often are left alone to bear the terrible personal fallout from police violence. They must carry their own grief as they also worry about the downward emotional spiral that their immediate and extended families will almost certainly endure, especially in the face of the ever-present threat that the lives of loved ones may be similarly at risk. These mothers are caught in an unexpected and sudden storm of trauma—and are charged, virtually in the same moment, with shoring up their beleaguered, grieving families against a hostile justice system, police culture, and media consensus. And alongside these unyielding obstacles, they also often find themselves contending with mounting financial struggles and potential family dislocation.

In a recent interview with several of the mothers, they were asked to raise their hands if they had suffered health consequences, family disruption, and lasting emotional trauma that impaired their ability to carry on normal daily activities. Every last one raised her hand in response. Clearly, the killing of their daughters and sisters began a journey through the multiple layers of trauma and grief that will continue to afflict their immediate and extended families, sometimes in ways that are even more destructive because the nature and depth of the grief cannot be named. Although researchers have recently brought a renewed focus to the effects of intergenerational trauma on Black families and communities, the intersectional and structural dimensions of the cataclysmic experience of state violence fall far beyond the margins of existing knowledge and expertise. Herein lies the tragedy of intersectional failure.

Racial justice advocates have brought attention to the residual effects of chattel slavery and structural racism on the mental health of people of color. And gender justice advocates have likewise highlighted the psychological effects of sexism on women. But rarely do researchers or policy makers consider how race and gender intersect with structural violence—notably extrajudicial police killings—to threaten the psychology and overall well-being of Black women survivors. To take one common example, many survivors in cases of police killing perform multiple roles in their families: caregivers to their children and grandchildren, financial breadwinners, spiritual leaders, and community leaders. Overextended and traumatized mothers and caregivers may well contend with mental and physical challenges that don't conventionally register as the fallout from police violence—even though they clearly are. Beyond that, little is known about how carrying these burdens in the face of institutional betrayal and communal abandonment affects the overall physiological and emotional health of mothers and sisters who must grapple with the consequences with precious little support or recognition.

As we explore the scale on which the experience of grief and loss afflicts Black women survivors, we must also weigh the follow-on traumas that such violence creates for families, neighborhoods, communities, and society in general. Currently, trauma experts focus on grief and loss in the context of readily recognizable expressions of trauma such as shame, guilt, sadness, and physical pain. Because the interpersonal violence that occurs at the intersections of race, class, and gender is firmly grounded in a documented legacy of generational structural violence in the United States, too many Black women survivors' expressions of grief may be simply invisible or otherwise unfathomable to traditionally trained trauma experts.

Bearing witness to the wider impact of trauma rooted in the theft of their daughters' lives underscores the need for a more comprehensive approach to such care, one that would promote compassion and grace toward the victim and survivor, anchored in the full recognition of the dignity and worth of the mother, and that of other family members. Such therapeutic interventions have to be understood, in turn, in the context of Black survivors' ongoing struggle against racial oppression, and the attendant stresses facing all of us who openly advocate for racial and gender justice in the face of police- and state-sanctioned violence. A more comprehensive intervention must embrace the mental safety and well-being of Black family members who cope with the loss of a loved one while fighting for justice.

For policy makers and trauma professionals, bearing witness must entail how race and gender, social class and social context, history and psychology, and behavior and health intersect to create complex trauma symptoms and adaptations to such symptoms. As we begin to understand the effects of trauma on the human psyche, we must advocate for more specific scrutiny of how police violence creates multilayered trauma for those living at the intersections of race, gender, class, *and* grief.

To recognize and understand the most visible and dramatic forms of Black women's trauma requires thorough grounding in the deeper sociocultural wellsprings of Black women's experience, its roots in history, and its transgenerational impact. This is the work of specialists and healers from various backgrounds, work that must be informed by and developed in response to bearing witness.

We have multiple ways to #SayHerName. We have found a wide range of settings in which we've come to #SayHerName together—in the streets, in our chants and our songs, in our writing and our artwork, on our social media pages and in our podcasts, in our day-to-day conversations with one another, with friends and family, with strangers. All of this is the work of solidarity: the sharing, the carrying of the weight, the determination to give back what we can. And we are moving forward together, with the mothers and the memories of their lost daughters, to an imagined world in which our lives, the lives of Black girls and women, really matter.

We performed this carrying and return from the very first #SayHerName vigil in 2014, in which we brought "the body" forward and recognized her lost life: seeing her, returning her to her family, accompanying the family to the mic, helping to conduct her and her loved ones through the trauma, and to another world. We performed this witnessing, and will continue to chant their names through the moving, inspiring, and activating song, "SayHerName (Hell You Talmbout)" with Janelle Monae, Beyoncé, Alicia Keys, and other artists and activists. We sit with and rise up to the drumbeat of lost lives that speak their presence through our cacophonous chanting their names.

In just seventeen minutes, we lift up sixty-one of hundreds of names. There are more. And there will be more until violence against Black women ends.

For some, seventeen minutes is a lot. For others, bearing witness for seventeen minutes is the least we can do to carry the weight that some of our sisters will now be carrying for a lifetime. Bearing witness is the least we can do when we realize that silence is part of the permission that leads to Black women's early violent deaths. The least we can do is say that we do not agree with, affirm, or accept the conditions that led to their daughters' deaths. The least we can do is break the conspiracies of silence that have created the plague of police violence against Black women—to dispel the social myths of distancing and dispassionate complacency. The least we can do is recognize that the conditions behind the vulnerabilities and state-sanctioned victimization of Black women do not simply dissolve when we choose not to ignore them.

The time devoted to bearing witness is negligible in comparison to that required to hear all of the names that we know, all of the names that we don't know, and all of the lives that have been harmed by the centuries of silence. It's the minimal act of repair—the moments in which we finally start redressing, in our public life and our daily routines, centuries of being valued only for what we could produce rather than for who we are.

To bear witness—either through our own artivism and activism or through listening, watching, and sharing the work of others—is to refuse the posture of the onlooker or bystander. It is a principled refusal to live out the scripts furnished by the state, the media, and the justice system that shore up and extend the distance between those who suffer the devastating trauma of police violence, and the rest of us, who have not yet had this horror visited upon us.

It is to give ourselves over to the message that we will not accept the failure of the state to grant recognition and justice, that we will not stand down and stand by. It is to say that we recognize ourselves to be family, both in the sense of shared histories and shared destinies, and in the sense that we honor our mutual obligations in the intimacies of grief and are committed to living out their full implications and opportunities.

When we do not bear witness, we signal that the consequences for taking a Black life will be minimal. We #SayHerName because we refuse the alternative. We refuse to accept violence, the silence, or the belief that there is nothing to be done to lessen the weight on those left behind. To #SayHerName is to affirm that the consequences of the collective, transgenerational, institutionalized trauma claims the lives and futures of Black women, including brokenhearted mothers.

Michelle Shirley

Epilogue

Brokenhearted

"You think you do everything right, raising your kids. Trying to give them a better life than you had. And then something like this happens. And I dare say it was because of the color of her skin."

Debra Shirley, mother of Michelle Shirley
(May 20 1977–October 31 2016)

Michelle was the oldest of seven children. Full of life, so full of life. She had big dreams, big aspirations, and she was so responsible.

I never realized how much of an influence she had on her six sisters and brothers. And I just recently figured out that Michelle was such a big part of her siblings having such drive and such successes. She was a hard worker. She pushed herself in school, in everything that she did. If it was being a leader, team leadership at church, whatever it was, she pushed herself. And I didn't realize how much her other siblings looked up to her and how that made them wanna be better and better students.

Recently, I just listened to them as they talk. And so many of them would say, "Michelle was so smart. That's why I worked so hard in school. And I tried so hard." And it just floors me now just to know how much they looked up to her and how much they admired her.

She graduated from high school a year early. She spoke two languages, Spanish and English. She graduated from UCLA, went on to law school. She did that herself, all by herself. She graduated from Loyola, and I remember there was a time when she was here visiting in San Diego, and she said "Mom, when I finish law school, I think I'm going to go back and I'm going to get my MBA." "Whoa!" I said, "Girl!" And she just laughed because she knew that she probably better slow down.

It was a surprise to me when she wanted to go to law school, because she had always excelled in science. She participated in every science fair in her school from the time she was eligible. I would drive her up to Los Angeles where she would compete in the California State Science Fair because she would win her division here in San Diego. She competed in that two years in a row. I even flew to Tennessee with her because she competed in the NAACP ACT-SO awards for students of the academic and something in excellence. And so I took one of her friends under our wing, and we got a hotel, and I took both girls, and they had the time of their life. I've never seen so many gifted and talented young people together.

Michelle had one son. His name is Harold. He's going to turn eighteen in September [2020]. He's in Chicago. He's in Crystal Springs, Illinois, where his father is. He's with his father, new mom, and his sister.

You know sometimes, when I'm really having a rough go of it, sometimes it helps to remind myself that Michelle did probably more living in her thirty-nine years of life than I've done in my entire life. And I get a little bit of peace with that, knowing how much she went after life with a gusto, and she never would give up. If you wanted to make sure she'd succeed, tell her she couldn't do something, and she would do it. She was just a hard worker always, from the time she was little.

She wanted to be a judge, of all things. And ironically she was a patrol officer at school that got awarded from police officers. I couldn't believe that, but then you have to look at the time. It was almost like alike, the perfect stew coming to a boil. It was five days before the election, and she was murdered in Torrance, California, where their department has, historically—there had been other shootings. And it was five days before the 2016 election.

She was in Torrance, California. She had started a business while she was in Oklahoma. And she came here from Oklahoma to get her car fixed. And then she thought, well, I'm gonna go make some money in Los Angeles, driving Uber, and use that to buy more materials—for her business that she started. But she never gave up on the dream that she was going to take the California bar.

She knew she could pass the bar anywhere else, but it was the California bar that she wanted to pass, which is a tough bar. So on this one particular day was October 31, 2016. It being Halloween, all our focus was on the kids and what they were going to be, the costumes and stuff. And just out of nowhere, two police officers knock on my door, and I answered the door, and they asked me, "Ma'am, we want to know what you know about an abandoned car in Torrance, California." And I said, well, my husband co-signed for my son's car. There might've been a few more words, but they got in their car and they laughed. And in the meantime, I call Michelle's dad, and I said, "What kind of car is it?"

He said, "I cosigned to get Michelle a new car." And he told me what kind, but I saw the police drive up the block and turn around immediately. So they get back here, and they said, "Ma'am, it's this kind of car." And so I hand the phone. So they're still not telling you at this point what they think has happened. Nothing. They talked to him. And they're not even the police department that's responsible. So they're basically doing a favor for someone. I later find out that it's against the law for the Torrance police to call the San Diego police. So that had to be the Fraternal Order of Police, which operates like mob bosses for the police.

So all during the day, I'm scared. I'm worried, because they come back and they say, "Ma'am, it's a female." So you're thinking, "What the heck is going on?" As it turns out, she's already been killed when they're doing this.

Later on that night, I get a call from another daughter who said, "Mom do not watch the long version video." We, we found out from the news media calling the house late that evening. I jumped on the internet. My brain is spinning fast. My brain is racing, and I see "Black." I see "Female." I see "Shot." I'm just like losing it, and there's the video. And so my daughter taps it and we watch the short video, and we just see them police running to get out of shooting range.

And then just fire.

The last thing I ever would have thought I would be dealing with. I had watched the DNC [Democratic National Convention], and I remember seeing the mothers on the steps. And Philando Castile [a Black man killed by police in his car in July 2016]. I was at home, and I watched that. I had the news on, the livestream of her [Castile's girlfriend, Diamond Reynolds], "Please tell me you did not do this to my boyfriend. Please tell me you just didn't." And tears just came flooding out my eyes. I was on the telephone trying to take care of my son who at the time was attending UC Irvine. So I was on the phone, and I just started bawling. I had to explain to the lady on the phone: "I just witnessed the most horrible thing I've ever seen in my life." So when I saw these mothers on the floor at the DNC I remember looking at them, I remember feeling so bad for them. Trayvon Martin, I remember thinking, "God, I wish I could do something to help them." Not realizing within a couple of months that our lives would be turned upside down and I'd be one of them.

I couldn't fathom that. Not in a million years. You think you do everything right, raising your kids, trying to give them a better life than you had. And then something like this happens, and I dare say it was because of the color of her skin. Because that's the law, the officers take the time to run by her vehicle. Her airbag was exploded. She had been hit by a truck. We did not know that. So when the media descended on us, we thought, "Well, you know, she suffered from bipolar disorder." And they took that and ran with it.

And then, I see the real video. I watched it that one time, I couldn't watch it again. But that video was a long version video, and it shows her car. It doesn't show a car that's recklessly running people off the road. It shows a car barely traveling, emergency flashers on, the airbag had exploded, and it's driving really really slow, but it's zig-zagging because she can only see out the side mirrors. You can't see anywhere. So I'm like, "Oh my God. She was really under stress but smart enough still to know to look out the . . ." So she just glided like that.

When I look at that, I look at a person in need, a person that needs help. So, I watched her pull into the gas station, the corner—whatever it was—and the officers pull in, take position. But rather than get her out of the car, break the window, like they did for somebody that day who was speeding, driving eighty miles per hour through the city and the freeway . . . They busted his window and dragged him out of that car. Instead of doing that for her and getting her out of that car, they told someone on the radio, "We're going to take her out." And there was a gasp, "You're going to what?" Like that. This is what the lady who gave me a hug told me.

The officer behind her gets out of his car, because he knows they're getting ready to start shooting. Runs right by her, doesn't look at her, doesn't try to help her, doesn't think twice that there's a human being in there. Somebody's child, somebody's mother, somebody's sister, somebody's aunt, somebody's grandchild. They didn't think like that. They thought, "We're going to kill her, take her out." That's what you're saying, "We're going to kill her." They could have shot her tires out to make sure she could never drive. They shot their guns, taking them out.

So when that runs by, and then you see her, what I've only ever heard in war movies, what you imagine to hear when you're fighting a war, directed on a citizen. And the only way that I can cope, I don't know what these officers look like, I don't have their names up here. And I think it might be a good thing, because I know what the officer that kneeled on George Floyd's face looks like. I know what it looks like. And if George Floyd was my son, having to have those pictures in my head might not be the best thing. So I don't know, I don't know their names. I can go back and find the email that was sent to me when the report came out, which is just riddled with lies.

But it's probably a good thing that I don't know what they look like and I don't have their names in my head because it would play back. It would be a loop in my head constantly. The only way I can deal with even thinking about what they did is to feel sorry for them. Feel sorry for them because to me they'll never be whole. How could you be when you just so easily take a gun out and take someone's life, a human being? How could you be whole? How could you love your children whole, your wife whole? It almost makes you a monster.

To me, I just think there will be a day when there will be a reckoning. Someone will realize what you've done. And what I mean by that, I saw [CNN presenter] Anderson Cooper on TV once being told about his family. And he was told about someone in his family that was murdered by a slave. And Anderson was like, "Well, he probably deserved it." It was a slave that had ran away from Anderson Cooper's relative, and his reply was, "He probably deserved it."

After a while, even members of your own family can't respect you, respect what you're doing. So I think, still someday there will be a reckoning. It's just like back in the day, remember the hippies and you know the struggle there, the generational struggle, they didn't believe what their parents believed. And I think that's going to happen with a lot of these gun-wielding police officers.

There has been an ongoing case for almost four years now, and the next court date that's set is for September 2021. A new attorney came to the firm [representing the Shirley family] and said, "Oh, you need to drop this case." They are just spending too much money on this case. And it kind of cut [our lawyer's] budget, and he left. But he never gave up on this case, and he still is looped in somehow. He's the only one that communicates with us right now. There was an appeal a few months ago. Back in April or February [2020], it was in Pasadena, and the city won. They won their appeal. So the attorneys felt like they did not violate her civil rights. And [the attorney] texted me to let me know the decisions and stuff, and I told him, I said . . .

I have to grab some tissues.

I said, "I'm sorry," I said, "but I've seen the law work one way for people of color and another way for people who are wealthy. It means nothing to me that the judges are following the law because the law is so flexible, bendy, and windy, and unpredictable when people want to get the outcome they want to get. And when the client is a different color or the client is from a different background or the client has wealthy parents. I'm sorry, there's no way you can tell me they didn't violate her civil rights."

They wanted to appeal it to the Supreme Court, and I gave him the thumbs up. I would rather see justice than anything, so I thought, "Do it." If they did it, the Supreme Court did not pick it up. So it's kicked back to whatever court it was in that ruled favorably, and that's where it stands right now. As far as I know right now, the officers, nothing happened to them. Nothing at all. I never even heard if they were on desk duty or anything like that. Ultimately whoever was the head of their precinct was let go because they had been after him for a while for spouting racist remarks internally in the division. So he got let go.

[There was no criminal trial.] No charges were brought against the officers.

So that's hard, dealing with the police. But I recently had a correspondence with Jackie Lacey, the district attorney in LA. I had written her this letter right after this happened. She sent me this cute note, the letters where all you got to do is fill in the name. She sent that to me and I wrote her back, but I didn't mail it because my youngest daughter who lives in the city says, "She doesn't have anything to do with what happened. It's not going to make a difference." But then I started looking, recently after everything that has come to light after the George Floyd, Ahmaud Arbery, Breonna Taylor, and all of their killings. The district attorney has a lot to do with why this behavior is perpetuated. Because no one ever charges the police, no one ever brings charges. Oftentimes, they're friends.

I thought, "No, I'm sending this letter." And so I wrote a letter telling her I wrote this letter two or three years ago, "But I'm sending it now." And I told her a few more things that I needed to get off my chest. She wrote me back, she sent me a card that she filled in. And it was a nice card, and she said she thinks about her case. She said there just wasn't enough evidence to bring charges and get a conviction, or something to this effect. But that she sees that there is definitely a need for reform and if I would be interested in working with her on that. And she gave me an open invitation to hear my input and then signed off on it.

So I didn't write her back right away because I like to let things settle first, so I don't say anything too bad that I wish I could take back. But after a week I couldn't take it anymore, and you know what I said? "Thank you for the kind words." But I said, "They rang hollow." I said, "There are still several things that are bothering me. There's things that are bothering me. Like the fact that one of these officers ran by her car door, her airbag was exploded, her flashers were on, she couldn't go no place. That bothers me that no one tried to help her.

"The fact that we were never contacted, that we had to learn about it at 9:30 at night by the news media of all people," I said, "that bothers me." I said, "The fact that the San Diego police department came here snooping on behalf of the police to see if we knew about an abandoned car, knowing that it wasn't abandoned. They got to the corner and came right back and said, "Oh, it's a female." Because they got back in touch with the police, who . . . then told them, it's a woman.

And I went through the list, the list of things that to me were totally wrong. Wrong to be treated this way. And I said, "I don't see how that is good policing." I said, "I don't see how that is good police policy."

And I said, "And I certainly, I don't understand how you're okay with it. Thanks but no thanks," and signed off on that. Haven't heard a word from her since. Not a word.

And when this happens, I thought it's going to make a change, things are going to change. It's like they don't care how many of us they kill. They don't care. So, that's where the hurt comes from. But I do understand and am genuinely happy to see the protesters in the streets on behalf of all the people who were murdered because, I mean, Ahmaud jogging, Breonna sleeping, and you just look at the things they're killed for. It makes no sense. Nobody knows about my daughter, no. But I do think that gender does play a part of it. Listening to a team, a panel, that was assembled, and they'd all be talking about our men, and they're shooting, and, and I'd be sitting here, "And women. Hey! They're not just doing this to the men."

And I've been shocked when [Kimberlé?] just named the names that she named. And the mothers. I just wanted to cry because I had no idea that it was even that many. I have heard Sandra Bland. Mike told me about Sandra Bland, and I watched the video, and that was hurtful and painful. I did not know there was another Michelle.

I just wanted to bawl.

Debra Shirley

Say Her Name is more than a chant and it's more than a hashtag. It is an imperative that requires that we see, we listen, and we move. As we do so, we must recognize that the lives that have been lost to police violence are not only those the police have killed. The casualties of lethal police violence also include those who have succumbed to the emotional and physical toll of their daughters' loss. We want to end with their stories, their words.

As outlined in the conclusion, an ongoing and overwhelming consequence of police violence against Black women is the devastating impact on survivors. In the aftermath of a police homicide, trauma wreaks havoc on the bodies of surviving mothers and across the families devastated by the loss of a daughter, a mother, or a sister. In the words of Valarie Carey, Miriam's sister, *when they kill a Black woman—a daughter, a sister, a mother—the police "dismantle a family with her death."*

Families who are already overcome with grief must grapple with the consequences of anger, injustice, and trauma. All the mothers in the network talk about how their daughters' deaths have impaired their own health and their ability to hold their families together, including the next generations. As Sharon Wilkerson's story of her breakup with her husband after her daughter Shelly was killed attests, bonds of love and family can be tested and frayed by trauma. Rhanda Dormeus speaks of the enduring anger and fear for his life that haunts her son after his sister Korryn was shot by police in her own home.

On top of losing their daughters, mothers are also confronting the loss of their grandchildren as fathers of single women who are killed are the next of kin and the presumptive custodial parents of their children. In some instances, these women have lost access to their daughters' children entirely, an exceptionally tragic circumstance for these children in light of the death of their mothers. A few have faced heartbreaking scenarios in which their daily interactions with their grandchildren—sometimes members of their own household—are terminated when the children are ripped from their homes by fathers who had played little to no role at all in the children's lives prior to the deaths of their children's mother. This was the case with Miriam Carey's daughter who was with her mother when she was killed. In the chaos following Miriam's death, custody was granted to her father, who was not in a relationship with Miriam when she was killed. The closest Miriam's sister Valarie has come to seeing her niece since her sister was killed is on FaceTime. Similarly, Gina has lost regular contact with India's son Roman, a heartbreaking separation from the living connection to her slain daughter. As next of kin, fathers have sometimes exercised their rights to take the children from the only homes they ever knew and deposit them with their own mothers, leaving children who are already devastated by their mothers' death even more injured by the separation from their maternal grandmothers. Already strapped with unexpected expenses associated with their daughters' deaths, the mothers are thrust into drawn-out battles for visitation rights that compound the emotional and financial fallout from police homicides.

With these relentless strains, it's little wonder that many mothers find that their own physical and emotional health become unacknowledged casualties of police violence. Coming on top of the cumulative effects of a lifetime of racism and sexism, profound grief can make women sick physically, as well as emotionally and mentally, particularly as the battle for justice inevitably involves reliving the trauma through the endless repetition of the neglect and aggression that led the police to take their daughters' lives in the first place.

Gina Best sums up the devastating impact on the mental health of the mothers when she says of her life since her daughter India was killed:

I walk around with an amputated heart.

The heart is more than a metaphor for love and loss. It is the organ that keeps us alive. To say that the mothers are brokenhearted when their daughters are killed by the police, that they "walk around with an amputated heart," is also to signal the physical impact of the desolation they face. Stressed by the hostility they must bear from law enforcement and the character assassinations of the media, and overwhelmed by the weight of responsibilities, the mothers must tend to wounded family members shattered by an unimaginable event as well as to the sometimes deadly impacts on their own health. Black women, already prone to premature death from stress-related causes, face compounded risks in facing the horrific consequences of their daughters' and sisters' deaths.

In early 2023 as this book was getting ready to go to press, we had to say farewell to one of the most recent members of the #SayHerName Mothers Network, Amber Carr. Amber had been recovering in hospital from open-heart surgery at the time that her sister, Atatiana Jefferson, was killed by a single shot from a police officer in their mother's home in Fort Worth, Texas, in October 2019. Amber's son Zion had been at home playing video games with his Aunt Atatiana when she was killed. Not long after Atatiana's death, the sisters' mother, the family matriarch, also died. In the face of so much loss, and in the midst of the COVID-19 pandemic, Amber and her sister Ashley founded the Atatiana Project in their sister's honor. Amber's death leaves Zion, his brother Zayden, Ashley, and their brother to hold together a family shattered by the brutality and aftermath of police violence.

Amber was empathetic, loving, and fierce. She was a woman of strong faith and commitment to her family. During her short life, Amber dedicated herself not only to raising her sons but also to supporting other Black women and young people. In the words of African American Policy Forum's Shermena Nelson, "Amber was clear about her mission and that was evident in how she showed up as a new member of the Mothers Network. Amber didn't just show up—she looked great while doing it. That was important to Amber. She held on tight to the things that she loved, even in what one would call the darkest of moments—she remained a light. We will carry Amber's light with us."

Amber is only the latest of the members of the Mothers Network to die in the midst of the pain following the death of a family member to police violence. Jennifer Johnson, sister of Tanisha Anderson, chronicled the many health challenges that their mother Cassie experienced after Tanisha was killed: stroke after stroke—thirteen in all. Jennifer felt helpless as she watched her mother's physical health deteriorate after each disappointing confrontation with the fact that no one would ultimately be held accountable for Tanisha's killing. A devastating blow came from

television when the family learned that the officers who pinned Tanisha to the ground until she died would not be criminally charged. The prosecutors did not tell the family in advance to at least give them time to prepare.

Jennifer also chronicled her own struggles to preserve her well-being as she helped her mother contend with the continual disappointment of her quest for justice and closure. The toll on Cassie and Jennifer came to a head in the middle of the pandemic when Cassie suffered her eleventh stroke. It was a catastrophic event, not only because it left Cassie in complete paralysis; it placed her in a care facility in the middle of COVID. As Jennifer recalls:

> While she was in the facility for physical therapy, she had stroke ten and eleven. Stroke eleven basically wiped her out, where she was unable to do anything for herself. She had to be fed. And once her vocals and everything, the muscles started to get weak, she was no longer able to swallow food. So they had to put what they call a PEG tube in, so she could get fed that way.
>
> During that time COVID hit, so we were unable to go into the facility to actually see her. I had to have window visits with her. And that was our only communication, and I didn't know when she was looking at me, if she even knew that I was still there every other day to go see her. Since I wasn't able to go in, I couldn't tell you how she was treated. But what I do know, finally, when the COVID was lifted a whole year later, and we were able to go into the facility, and that's when they were telling us that she had developed a bed sore. But they never mentioned anything about the bed sore

> until after the COVID and we were actually able to go and see her.
>
> So due to that, my mother ended up developing an infection, and the infection that she developed while she was in there, when they told us about the bed sore, finally, had already went to her bones. But at that point, there was nothing else that they could possibly do for her but suggest for us to bring her home on hospice and make her as comfortable as possible. So, that's exactly what we did. My mother would be here if my sister hadn't have passed.

Without the loving care of family members, Cassie, like too many others dependent on understaffed and low-paid health aid workers, languished and faced the pressures of the preexisting inequalities that make Black women and their families disproportionately vulnerable to ill health—cumulative inequalities that continued to the point where she ultimately could not survive.

Cassie died in her home, just steps away from the place where the Cleveland police, answering a call to help her daughter Tanisha, took her daughter's life seven years earlier. Cassie had fought for years for justice for Tanisha, with faith that ultimately justice would be done.

Some months after Cassie's death, Jennifer reflected on why her mother died so young:

> My mother's strokes leading up to her passing, it was all connected. My mother had a clean bill of health before all this started. She never even had colds, and the flu, or anything. She was fine. Until the death of her daughter. My mother's heart was broke. It was broke

> and she wanted her child back. And during that time, when you are going through something like that, it starts to affect different things as far as in your body. Stress, blood pressure. You can develop diabetes and all the other things that could go on with you. Because you don't know how to release what's going on in you, and you holding this.

Cassie's spirit lives on now in Jennifer and her other children, and her grandchildren, including Tanisha's daughter Mauvion. It survives in her passion to keep Tanisha's story alive. Cassie spoke powerfully as a voice of the Mothers Network, recalling Tanisha's life and death, testifying what it means to be the Black mother of a woman killed by police. In what would turn out to be her benediction, she spoke of how that profound loss changed her forever and placed her on a new mission, stressing both what she learned and what we can learn from her:

> You will never be the same person you were. But do you let it change you for the worse or the better? Because if you're thinking of them, your child, you should be thinking of what I can do to change something, in her honor. Since she's not coming back, how can I live on through her? We want them to be treated like human beings.
>
> If it hadn't have been my daughter, would I give it this much fight, this much thought? Of course not. It has to take something to wake you up. So since she's not coming back, how can I live on through her? Speak. How can she live on? Speak. Wake up the minds. Do something about it. Because it's like a domino effect. It's going to trickle on down to somebody else and

> somebody else and somebody else. Because the people are listening. And the people are what make the world.
>
> Just because she's not here doesn't mean we can't speak for her. We can be her mouthpiece. So that's my goal: To speak for her and to make her dreams a reality for other mentally ill people. Because their lives matter.
>
> Remember this day, because I'm on a mission, and I'm going to fulfill this mission for Tanisha Anderson and the rest of the mentally ill. My name is Cassandra Johnson.

Cassie wasn't the first mother of #SayHerName to have had strokes and other life-threatening conditions. Vicky McAdory, brokenhearted over the killing of a niece she raised as her daughter, India Beatty, channeled the fire behind #SayHerName with her body and soul. Vicky embodied everything the Mothers Network grew to become. At any point, Vicky could turn a somber moment into raucous laughter, and she was absolutely fearless about getting in anyone's face who got in the way of our mission. At the same time, her grief was never hidden. Through marches, vigils, playing cards, drinking, and doing "grown folks stuff," the mothers have seen Vicky literally laugh and cry at the same. As mom to everyone, even through her own disappointments, it was Vicky who led the mothers to leave the Women's March in disappointment after their daughters' names were not said. It was Vicky who gathered everyone up that day and cooked a brunch to soothe the aching hearts of the mothers and their allies. Rising up from despair, learning to live with it while reaching beyond it became the credo of #SayHerName. That's why when she too was hospitalized with a stroke, we just knew that this new trial would not vanquish her indomitable spirit.

Vicky called from her hospital room, and we spoke for several minutes. She was herself, and I teased her a bit about cheating the last time we played cards together. That banter could always get Vicky riled up, and I counted on it to lift her spirits. But her spirits didn't need lifting; the call was for another purpose. "I want you to keep moving. No matter what happens to me, the mission of #SayHerName must not end." She demanded a promise. I didn't want to give in to what was sounding to be like a goodbye. I deflected, and she caught me. "Promise me." I went to the edge, I promised, and quickly beat a retreat to the safe harbor of banter about what we were going to do when she got released. We ended the call with love. Four hours later, Vicky McAdory, auntie-momma of India Beatty, the heart and fire of #SayHerName, was dead.

Vicky, like Cassie, was prophetic. Like Cassie, she bequeathed to us a vision of the justice she demanded that transcended the moment, her own loss, and even her own life. She, like Cassie, implored us to keep fighting, understanding this work in the historical arc of all that has come before, and all that is yet to be. It is fitting that we end with her words:

> For so long, for so many years, almost from the beginning of time, we as women were not allowed to have anything to do with battle, or taking up for ourselves or for somebody else, protecting our communities, protecting our country. We didn't have a voice. We were just somebody else's other half. And when that other half didn't agree, we were quieted, we had to shut up and not be heard or seen. I refuse. I refuse as a woman, I refuse as a Black woman, I refuse as a human being, a citizen of this world, to shut up any longer. Especially when it comes to the senseless and vicious murders of

our babies. I'm not just a soldier for India Beatty, I'm a soldier for every one of our children who've been unjustifiably taken away from us, and I will stand up if it means my death. I will not stop speaking out until I have no voice. And being a soldier for a cause that I know is needed and that can be accomplished if enough voices stand up and speak out—that's everything to me. Because even in death—going to that march and walking with all my sisters, thousands and thousands of my sisters—even in death, I will be a part of history. And I know for a fact India is so proud of me. I know she's proud of me, because she knows I didn't just fold, and I'm not gonna fold. My biggest fear would be not to march. My fear would be how I would feel not realizing that I didn't put my all into something that's right, something that's deserved, something that we were born into a right of having.

How could I not? How could I not?
#SayHerName.[1]

Acknowledgments

#SayHerName has been nurtured and maintained by an active community of family members, supporters, advocates, and friends. Our deepest gratitude and respect goes to the courageous members of our Mothers Network who have shared the most precious and painful memories of their loved ones with us. Honoring your love for them, and now, your bonds with each other, is the reason we wrote this book. Gina Best, Rhanda Dormeus, Frances Garrett, Sharon Wilkerson, Maria Moore, Valarie Carey, Ashely Carr, Jennifer Johnson, Debra Shirley, and Chelsie Rubin, we stand in awe of all you have done in the memory of your daughters, sisters, and mothers. In spite of the unthinkable losses you have borne, your willingness to bear witness in the hopes that we can one day live in a world in which no other family experiences what you have is the special light that you each carry in this world.

We give honor to our sisters who vowed to fight for justice until their last breath and have bequeathed their indomitable spirit to keep the legacy of their loved ones alive. We acknowledge and honor Cassandra Johnson, Vicky Coles-McAdory, Amber Carr, and others who we cannot name but whose lives were surely cut short by the grief and injustice that the #SayHerName campaign seeks to end.

#SayHerName would not exist without dozens of people who have answered the call to encircle the Mother's Network with care, offering encouragement and support along the journey to justice. We are grateful to all, and especially to Barbara Arnwine, V., and Lisa Gissendaner whose midwifery nurtured a need into a living, breathing entity, and to Shermena Nelson and Glenda Smiley who have lovingly nurtured the bonds that this book memorializes.

This book was informed by the pathbreaking *Say Her Name* report, a joint effort undertaken with Andrea J. Ritchie, Rachel Anspach, Rachel Gilmer, Luke Harris, and Julia Sharpe-Levine. Thank you all for lighting the pathway for this project through the #SayHerName campaign.

Thank you also to Anthony Arnove, Maya Marshall, Jenn Baker, Eric Kerl, Rachel Cohen, and the team at Haymarket who saw the unlikely possibility that a book could capture the disparate, disturbing, and inspiring stories that ground the simple call to Say Her Name. We are also grateful for the research and thinking of those who have tirelessly contributed to the development of this project over the years: Dajourn Anuku, Gregory Bernstein, Andi Dixon, Venus Evans-Winters, Aniah Francis, Sana Hashmi, Alanna Kane, Michael Kramer, Amy McMeeking, Nadia Ncube, Allison Monterossa, Emmett O'Malley, Marina Reis, Nioshi Shah, Darci Siegel, Vineeta Singh, Alex van Biema, Judith Williams, Tanishia Williams, Cecile Yezou. A very special thank you goes to Kevin Minofu and Carrie Hamilton who held the reins on a project full of must-haves that would have faltered in less capable hands. Devon Carbado's incisive editing never fails to cut a path that integrates mind and heart to fully capture the wholeness of the experiences being rendered. And our enduring appreciation goes to all of our artivists who have curated, memorialized, and expressed all that #SayHerName represents. From our visual and graphic artivists—Ashley Julien, Julia Sharpe-Levine, Destiny Spruill, Rebecca Scheckman—to our performance artists and producers—Awoye Timpo, Abby Dobson, Dina Wright-Joseph, Gina Loring, and Afia Walking Tree. And of course the unseen but deeply appreciated work of our programs and operations team provides the support that allows #SayHerName to be. Thank you Yvonne Davenport-Perkins, Michael Kramer, and Myles Olmsted for holding us up in the work.

Finally, we acknowledge our #SayHerName partners and donors: the WNBA/WNBPA; Janelle Monáe and the Wondaland team; V-Day; Players Coalition; Pivotal Ventures, LLC; Collective Futures Fund; The Open Society Foundation; Tides Foundation; and Gucci Chime for Change; and the countless others who have supported a vigil, marched, borne witness, and answered the call to Say Her Name.

African American Policy Forum
and Kimberlé Crenshaw
May 2023

Notes

Prologue: Her Name

1. Throughout this book, the word "women" includes gender nonconforming people, femmes of different genders, and trans women.
2. The sources for the stories were AAPF gatherings, both in person and online, of the #SayHerName Mothers Network; interviews by me and other members of the AAPF; and videos produced to highlight the urgency of the work we do together to counteract the impacts of police violence on daughters, sisters, and other Black women. The stories are told in the family members' (mostly mothers') own words, with some reordering and added text where necessary. The stories have been read and approved by the mothers and/or close family members.
3. Ruth Wilson Gilmore, *Golden Gulag: Prisons, Surplus, Crisis, and Opposition in Globalizing California* (Berkeley: University of California Press, 2007), 247.

Introduction: Unheard Stories

1. Coauthored by Kimberlé Crenshaw and Andrea Ritchie, with AAPF's Luke Harris, Rachel Gilmer, Rachel Anspach, and Julia Sharpe-Levine.

Chapter 1: Breaking Silence

1. Chaz Arnett, "Race, Surveillance, Resistance," *Ohio State Law Journal* 81 (2020): 1103, 1106; Tammy Rinehart Kochel, David B.

Wilson, and Stephen D. Mastrofski, "Effect of Suspect Race on Officers' Arrest Decisions," *Criminology* 49, no. 2 (2011): 473, 490.

2. Devon W. Carbado, "Introduction" in *Unreasonable: Black Lives, Police Power, and the Fourth Amendment* (New York: New Press, 2022), 13.
3. See Devon W. Carbado, "Colorblind Intersectionality," *Signs: Journal of Women in Culture and Society* 38, no. 4 (Summer 2013): 811–45.
4. Shubham Kalia and Kanishka Singh, "Police Ignored George Floyd's 'I Can't Breathe' Plea: Transcript," *Reuters*, July 9, 2020, https://www.reuters.com/article/us-global-race-usa-floyd-idUSKBN24A0KX; Katie Benner, "Eric Garner's Death Will Not Lead to Federal Charges for N.Y.P.D. Officer," *New York Times*, July 16, 2019, https://www.nytimes.com/2019/07/16/nyregion/eric-garner-case-death-daniel-pantaleo.html; Maria Moore, "Under the Blacklight: The Fire This Time," interview by Kimberlé Crenshaw, *Intersectionality Matters!*, June 10, 2020, https://soundcloud.com/intersectionality-matters/19-under-the-blacklight-the-fire-this-time; Karl Etters, "Dash-cam Video of Barbara Dawson Case Released," *Tallahassee Democrat*, January 6, 2016, https://www.tallahassee.com/story/news/2016/01/06/dash-cam-dawson-case-released-today/78347194.
5. Marisa Iati, Jennifer Jenkins, and Sommer Brugal, "Nearly 250 Women Have Been Fatally Shot by Police since 2015," *Washington Post*, September 4, 2020, https://www.washingtonpost.com/graphics/2020/investigations/police-shootings-women.
6. Gerry Everding, "Police Kill Unarmed Blacks More Often, Especially When They Are Women, Study Finds," *The Source*: Washington University in St. Louis, February 6, 2018, https://source.wustl.edu/2018/02/police-kill-unarmed-blacks-often-especially-women-study-finds/.
7. For more detailed discussion of the circumstances in which police kill Black women, see Kimberlé Williams Crenshaw et al., *Say Her Name: Resisting Police Brutality against Black Women* (New York: African American Policy Forum and Center for Intersectionality

and Social Policy Studies, July 2015), https://static1.squarespace.com/static/53f20d90e4b0b80451158d8c/t/5edc95fba357687217b08fb8/1591514635487/SHNReportJuly2015.pdf.

8. See Oliver Wendell Holmes, *The Common Law* (Boston: Little, Brown, 1923).
9. Rory Kramer and Brianna Remster, "Stop, Frisk, and Assault? Racial Disparities in Police Use of Force During Investigatory Stops," *Law & Society Review* 52, no. 4 (December 2018): 960–93, 986.
10. See "1,046 People Have Been Shot and Killed by Police in the Past Year," *Washington Post*, August 23, 2022, https://www.washingtonpost.com/graphics/investigations/police-shootings-database.
11. See Joy James, *Resisting State Violence: Radicalism, Gender and Race in U.S. Culture* (Minneapolis: University of Minnesota Press, 1996).
12. Jada L. Moss, "The Forgotten Victims of Missing White Woman Syndrome: An Examination of Legal Measures That Contribute to the Lack of Search and Recovery of Missing Black Girls and Women," *William & Mary Journal of Race, Gender, and Social Justice* 25, no. 3 (April 2019): 741.
13. Sheri Shuster, dir., *Still I Rise* (Berkeley, California: Shuster Lab, 2021), http://www.stillirisethefilm.com/. This documentary details the stories of sexually trafficked Black women, girls, and femmes in California.
14. John Eligon, "A Black Officer, a White Woman, a Rare Murder Conviction. Is It 'Hypocrisy,' or Justice?" *New York Times*, May 3, 2019, https://www.nytimes.com/2019/05/03/us/mohamed-noor-guilty.html.
15. Eligon, "A Black Officer, a White Woman."
16. Julie Bosman, "After Minneapolis Police Shooting, Many Ask: Why Wasn't Body Camera On?" *New York Times*, July 19, 2017, https://www.nytimes.com/2017/07/19/us/body-cameras-police-shooting-video.html; Mitch Smith, "Minneapolis Police Chief Forced Out after Fatal Shooting of Australian Woman," *New York Times*, July 21, 2017, https://www.nytimes.com/2017/07/21/us/

minneapolis-police-chief-resigns-days-after-officer-fatally-shot-a-woman.html; Associated Press, "Minneapolis Police Officer Who Killed Justine Damond Given 12-year Jail Term," *Guardian*, June 7, 2019, https://www.theguardian.com/us-news/2019/jun/07/justine-damond-death-mohamed-noor-minneapolis.

17. Treva B. Lindsey, "Post-Ferguson: A 'Herstorical' Approach to Black Violability," *Feminist Studies* 41, no. 1 (2015), 232–37, https://www.jstor.org/stable/10.15767/feministstudies.41.1.232.
18. African American Policy Forum, "Breaking the Silence Town Hall," Columbia University, 2015.

Chapter 2: Stolen Histories

1. This account is based on that of Miriam's sister, Valarie Carey, as well as Jennifer Gonnerman, "How a Confused Mom Drove through a Whitehouse Checkpoint and Ended Up Dead," *Mother Jones*, March 12, 2015, https://www.motherjones.com/politics/2015/03/miriam-carey-whitehouse-rammer-police-death. This *Mother Jones* article is one of the two media accounts of Miriam's death that Valarie cites as objective.
2. See also Gonnerman, "How a Confused Mom."
3. A video of part of the performance is available on YouTube. aapfvideo, "Kim V-day Poem," Feburary 2, 2011, https://www.youtube.com/watch?v=Fdt88ElrJqo.
4. Kimberlé Crenshaw and Dorothy Roberts, "What Slavery Engendered: An Intersectional Look at 1619," *Intersectionality Matters!*, November 14, 2019, https://soundcloud.com/intersectionality-matters/what-slavery-engendered-an-intersectional-look-at-1619.
5. Sarah Larimer, "Ex-Oklahoma City Cop Daniel Holtzclaw Found Guilty of Multiple On-Duty Rapes," *Washington Post*, December 11, 2015, https://www.washingtonpost.com/news/morning-mix/wp/2015/12/08/ex-cop-on-trial-for-rape-used-power-to-prey-on-women-prosecutor-says/.

6. See Sarah Haley, *No Mercy Here: Gender, Punishment, and the Making of Jim Crow Modernity* (Chapel Hill: University of North Carolina Press, 2016), 6, 109–10.
7. Crenshaw and Roberts, "What Slavery Engendered."
8. The 1619 Project is a long-form journalistic initiative developed by Nikole Hannah-Jones of the *New York Times* and the *New York Times Magazine* that "aims to reframe the country's history by placing the consequences of slavery and the contributions of Black Americans at the very center of our national narrative." Nikole Hannah-Jones, "The 1619 Project," *New York Times Magazine*, August 14, 2019, https://www.nytimes.com/interactive/2019/08/14/magazine/1619-america-slavery.html.
9. Crenshaw and Roberts, "What Slavery Engendered."
10. Harriet A. Washington, *Medical Apartheid: The Dark History of Medical Experimentation on Black Americans from Colonial Times to the Present* (New York: Doubleday, 2006), 189.
11. Fannie Lou Hamer quoted in Washington, *Medical Apartheid*, 189–90.
12. Angela Y. Davis, *Women, Race & Class* (New York: Vintage Books, 1983).
13. Kazuyo Tsuchiya, "Johnnie Tillmon (1926–1995)," *BlackPast*, January 23, 2007, https://www.blackpast.org/african-american-history/tillmon-johnnie-1926-1995/.
14. Meritor Savings Bank v. Vinson, 477 U.S. 57 (1986), https://supreme.justia.com/cases/federal/us/477/57/.
15. Ryan Mattimore, "Before the Bus, Rosa Parks Was a Sexual Assault Investigator," *History*, December 8, 2017, https://www.history.com/news/before-the-bus-rosa-parks-was-a-sexual-assault-investigator.
16. Arlisha Norwood, "Rosa Parks," *National Women's History Museum*, 2017, https://www.womenshistory.org/education-resources/biographies/rosa-parks.
17. Combahee River Collective, "Black Feminist Statement," *WSQ: Women's Studies Quarterly* 42, no. 3/4 (Fall/Winter 2014): 279, https://www.jstor.org/stable/pdf/24365010.pdf. Originally published

in Zillah R. Eisenstein, ed., *Capitalist Patriarchy and the Case for Socialist Feminism* (New York: Monthly Review Press, 1978).

18. Audre Lorde, "Age, Race, Class, and Sex: Women Redefining Difference" in *Sister Outsider* (Berkeley, CA: Ten Speed Press, 2013), 118.

Chapter 3: Disposable Lives

1. The remainder of this chapter is adapted from Kimberlé Crenshaw, "Breonna Taylor and Bearing Witness to Black Women's Expendability," October 9, 2020, *Medium*, https://level.medium.com/breonna-taylor-and-bearing-witness-to-black-womens-expendability-472abf5f6cee. Published by Abolition for the People, a collaboration between Kaepernick Publishing and Medium.
2. Kentucky is a "stand-your-ground" state, meaning that the state's "law allows its residents to use deadly force against intruders they believe are breaking into their home. For an explanation on why Kenneth Walker was charged with attempted murder in spite of this law, see Andrew Wolfson, "'No-knock' Searches vs. 'Stand Your Ground' Laws: A Deadly Duo in Breonna Taylor Shooting," *Louisville Courier Journal*, May 15, 2020, https://eu.courier-journal.com/story/news/2020/05/15/breonna-taylor-shooting-no-knock-searches-stand-your-ground-laws-deadly-combination-civilians-police/5193854002.
3. Scott Glover, Colette Richards, Curt Devine, and Drew Griffin, "A Key Miscalculation by Officers Contributed to the Tragic Death of Breonna Taylor," *CNN*, July 24, 2020, https://www.cnn.com/2020/07/23/us/breonna-taylor-police-shooting-invs/index.html; Tessa Duvall, "FACT CHECK 2.0: Separating the Truth from the Lies in the Breonna Taylor Police Shooting," *Louisville Courier Journal*, June 16, 2020, https://www.courier-journal.com/story/news/crime/2020/06/16/breonna-taylor-fact-check-7-rumors-wrong/5326938002.
4. Rukmini Callimachi, "Breonna Taylor's Life Was Changing. Then the Police Came to Her Door," *New York Times*, August 30, 2020,

https://www.nytimes.com/2020/08/30/us/breonna-taylor-police-killing.html.

5. Taylor's death certificate lists the official cause of death as five gunshot wounds, which is different from what was stated in the family's lawsuit. The autopsy report indicated six gunshot wounds. Tessa Duvall, "Breonna Taylor Autopsy Report Reveals How Louisville Police Bullets Killed Her," *Louisville Courier Journal*, September 25, 2020, https://www.courier-journal.com/story/news/local/breonna-taylor/2020/09/25/breonna-taylor-autopsy-report-reveals-how-police-bullets-killed-her/3537839001.
6. Duvall, "FACT CHECK 2.0"; Richard A. Oppel and Derrick B. Taylor, "Here's What You Need to Know about Breonna Taylor's Death," *New York Times*, July 31, 2020.
7. Tessa Duvall and Darcy Costello, "Breonna Taylor Was Briefly Alive after Police Shot Her. But No One Tried to Treat Her," *Louisville Courier Journal*, July 17, 2020, https://eu.courier-journal.com/story/news/crime/2020/07/17/breonna-taylor-lay-untouched-20-minutes-after-being-shot-records/5389881002.
8. Ta-Nehisi Coates, "The Life Breonna Taylor Lived, in the Words of Her Mother," *Vanity Fair*, August 24, 2020, https://www.vanityfair.com/culture/2020/08/breonna-taylor; Tamantha Gunn, "Breonna Taylor's Mom Says She Found Out Police Killed Her Daughter from News," *Revolt*, August 26, 2020, https://www.revolt.tv/2020/8/26/21402921/breonna-taylor-mom-recalls-death-news.
9. "Say Her Name: Breonna Taylor Was Killed by Police in March. Why Haven't the Officers Faced Charges?" *Democracy Now!*, June 4, 2020, https://www.democracynow.org/2020/6/4/sadiqa_reynolds_breonna_taylor.
10. Callimachi, "Breonna Taylor's Life."
11. Coates, "The Life Breonna Taylor Lived."
12. Callimachi, "Breonna Taylor's Life."
13. Breonna Taylor (@PrettyN_Paidd), "I wonder what my life would be like if I never moved here from Michigan? Like what tf would I be doing right now? Where would I work? Would I have kids?

Etc.," Twitter, February 19, 2020, 5:08 a.m., https://twitter.com/PrettyN_Paidd/status/1230071605998518280.

14. Callimachi, "Breonna Taylor's Life."
15. Elisabeth Gawthrop, "The Color of Coronavirus: COVID-19 Deaths by Race and Ethnicity in the US," *APM Research Lab*, November 22, 2022, https://www.apmresearchlab.org/covid/deaths-by-race.
16. "Breonna Taylor's Mom Worried ER Tech Daughter Would Get Coronavirus before Police Killed Her," *People*, June 11, 2020, https://people.com/crime/breonna-taylor-mom-worried-daughter-coronavirus-before-police-shooting.
17. Rachel Treisman, Brakkton Booker, and Vanessa Romo, "Kentucky Grand Jury Indicts 1 Of 3 Officers in Breonna Taylor Case," *NPR*, September 23, 2020, https://www.npr.org/sections/live-updates-protests-for-racial-justice/2020/09/23/914250463/breonna-taylor-charging-decision-to-be-announced-this-afternoon-lawyer-says.
18. Nicholas Bogel-Burroughs, "What Is 'Wanton Endangerment,' the Charge in the Breonna Taylor Case?," *New York Times*, September 23, 2020, https://www.nytimes.com/2020/09/23/us/wanton-endangerment.html.
19. Steve Almasy, Aaron Cooper, and Eric Levenson, "Ex-officer Brett Hankison Was Found Not Guilty of Endangering Breonna Taylor's Neighbors in a Botched Raid," *CNN*, March 4, 2022, https://edition.cnn.com/2022/03/03/us/brett-hankison-trial-closing/index.html.
20. Sam Johnson, "AP Was There: 2 Men Acquitted of Murder in Emmett Till Case," *AP*, July 12, 2018, https://apnews.com/article/f6e82e2661424204b0f1920c313fa307.
21. Timothy B. Tyson, *The Blood of Emmett Till* (New York: Simon and Schuster, 2017), 19.
22. Tyson, *The Blood of Emmett Till.*
23. Jury nullification is a jury's knowing and deliberate rejection of the evidence or refusal to apply the law either because the jury wants to send a message about some social issue that is larger than

the case itself, or because the result dictated by law is contrary to the jury's sense of justice, morality, or fairness.

24. Carl L. Hart, "We Know How George Floyd Died. It Wasn't from Drugs," *New York Times*, June 25, 2020, https://www.nytimes.com/2020/06/25/opinion/george-floyd-toxicology-report-drugs.html.
25. See, for example, ABC13, "Suspected Shoplifter Shot by Deputy Dies at Apartment," *ABC13 Eyewitness News*, December 7, 2012, https://abc13.com/archive/89-1-1831.
26. Barbara Arnwine, *OKC Video* (AAPF).
27. Callimachi, "Breonna Taylor's Life."
28. Yoruba Richen, "The Police Can't Be Judge, Jury and Executioner," interview by Amy Goodman, *Democracy Now!*, September 8, 2020, https://www.democracynow.org/2020/9/8/new_details_breonna_taylor_nyt_documentary.
29. For example, Callimachi, "Breonna Taylor's Life Was Changing."
30. Coates, "The Life Breonna Taylor Lived."
31. Clayborne Carson et al., *The Eyes on the Prize Civil Rights Reader: Documents, Speeches, and Firsthand Accounts From the Black Freedom Struggle* (New York: Viking Penguin, 1991).
32. Christina Carrega, "Breonna Taylor's Death Brings Police Killing of Black Women into Focus," *ABC News*, June 6, 2020, https://abc7.com/breonna-taylors-death-brings-police-killing-of-black-women-into-focus/6235052.
33. In all sixteen law enforcement agencies studied by the ACLU, Black people were at least four times more likely than white people to be the target of SWAT raids. The most dramatic disparity was in Burlington, North Carolina, where Black people were forty-seven times more likely to be targeted. American Civil Liberties Union (ACLU), *War Comes Home: The Excessive Militarization of American Policing* (New York: ACLU Foundation, 2014), 36–37, https://www.aclu.org/sites/default/files/assets/jus14-warcomeshome-report-web-rel1.pdf. Other studies, including in Cincinnati, Ohio, and Louisville, Kentucky, have also found that no-knock warrants are disproportionately issued for houses in Black neighborhoods and that most people arrested under such

warrants are Black; Jolene Almendarez, "No-Knock Warrants: Black Cincinnatians More Often the Focus as Use Decreases Overall," *WVXU*, February 17, 2021, https://www.wvxu.org/post/no-knock-warrants-black-cincinnatians-more-often-focus-use-decreases-overall#stream/0; Matt Mencarini, Darcy Costello, and Tessa Duvall, "Louisville Police's 'No-knock' Warrants Most Often Targeted Black Residents, Analysis Shows," *USA Today*, December 1, 2020, https://www.usatoday.com/story/news/2020/12/01/louisville-police-no-knock-warrants-mostly-targeted-black-residents/6456241002.

34. Rukmini Callimachi, "Louisville Deal Tightens Reins on Police Force," *New York Times*, September 16, 2020, https://www.nytimes.com/2020/09/15/us/breonna-taylor-settlement-louisville.html.
35. Rebekah Riess and Theresa Waldrop, "Louisville Council Passes 'Breonna's Law' Banning No-Knock Warrants," *CNN*, June 11, 2020, https://www.cnn.com/2020/06/11/us/louisville-breonnas-law-no-knock-warrants-ban/index.html.
36. The United States Department of Justice (DOJ) FY 2021 enacted budget was $16,166 million, and the FY 2022 requested budget was $16,145 million. "U.S Department of Justice FY 2022 Budget Request at a Glance" Washington DC, US DOJ, https://www.justice.gov/jmd/page/file/1398931/download. President Biden's FY 2022 budget for the Community Oriented Policing Services (COPS) hiring program—a DOJ grant program that provides funding to state and local police forces—totaled $651 million, which is more than double that of President Trump in 2021.
37. According to Vaidya Gullapalli, the policing budgets available for public examination are not an entirely accurate reflection of the totality of state money spent on police-related activities. For example, New York City has a policing budget of more than $5 billion, but the city also paid out nearly $40 million to settle police misconduct cases in the first half of 2019 alone. Vaidya Gullapalli, "Spending Billions on Policing, then Millions on Police Misconduct," *Appeal*, August 2, 2019, https://theappeal.

org/spending-billions-on-policing-then-millions-on-police-misconduct.

38. Scott Calvert and Dan Frosch, "Police Rethink Policies as Cities Pay Millions to Settle Misconduct Claims," *Wall Street Journal*, October 22, 2020, https://www.wsj.com/articles/police-rethink-policies-as-cities-pay-millions-to-settle-misconduct-claims-11603368002.
39. Robyn Mowatt, "Hours of Body-Cam Footage Exposes Gaps in Investigation of Breonna Taylor's Death," *OkayPlayer*, October 2020, https://www.okayplayer.com/news/body-camera-footage-breonna-taylor-death-investigation.html.

Chapter 4: Building Community

1. Human chorionic gonadotropin, a hormone produced by the placenta.
2. The total amount is reported some places as $37 million and other places as $38 million. For a breakdown before the appeal, see Jay Connor, "Judge Overturns $37 Million Wrongful Death Award to the Family of Korryn Gaines," *The Root*, February 16, 2019, https://www.theroot.com/judge-overturns-37-million-wrongful-death-award-to-the-1832673900; Alex Horton, "He Watched Police Kill His Mother. A Jury Just Awarded His Family $37 Million," *Washington Post*, https://www.washingtonpost.com/news/local/wp/2018/02/17/he-watched-police-kill-his-mother-a-jury-just-awarded-his-family-37-million. For information post-appeal, see Tim Prudente, "Appeals Court Finds Judge Erred in Wiping Out $38 Million Verdict Over Police Shooting of Korryn Gaines," *Baltimore Sun*, July 1, 2020, https://www.baltimoresun.com/news/crime/bs-md-cr-korryn-gaines-verdict-reinstated-20200701-joywm4ravzcy3pu4k3d24i6rku-story.html.
3. Nicole Young, "Why We Say Her Name," #SayHerName special edition of *CHIME Zine*, September 2020, https://equilibrium.gucci.com/zine-issue-say-her-name/.

4. Toni Morrison, “Rootedness: The Ancestor as Foundation,” in *Black Women Writers (1950–1980): A Critical Evaluation*, ed. Mari Evans (New York: Doubleday, 1984), 339–45.
5. Thandiwe Newton, “Scripts for Sexual Violence in Person and on the Screen,” #SayHerName special edition of *CHIME Zine*, September 2020, https://equilibrium.gucci.com/zine-issue-say-her-name.
6. Abby Dobson, “SayHerName,” LadyBraveBirdMusicWorks Publishing, 2015.
7. Gina Loring, “#SayHerName,” #SayHerName special edition of *CHIME Zine*, September 2020, https://equilibrium.gucci.com/zine-issue-say-her-name.

Chapter 5: In Memoriam

1. “An Act about the Casuall Killing of Slaves,” October 1669, Act I, *Statutes at Large*, ed. William Waller Hening, 2 (1823): 270, http://www.virtualjamestown.org/laws1.html#15.
2. Robert A. Brown, “Policing in American History,” *Du Bois Review: Social Science Research on Race* 16, no. 1 (2019): 190.
3. Saidiya Hartman, *Scenes of Subjection: Terror, Slavery, and Self-Making in Nineteenth-Century America* (New York: Oxford University Press, 1997), 79–82.
4. Saidiya Hartman, “Venus in Two Acts,” *Small Axe* 12, no. 26 (June 2008): 2.
5. Fatal Encounters, founded by journalist D. Brian Burghart, began in 2013. “Why FE Exists,” *Fatal Encounters*, https://fatalencounters.org/why-fe-exists2. The *Washington Post* Fatal Force Police Shootings Database has been tracking fatal shootings by police since 2015. “Fatal Force: Police Shootings Database,” *Washington Post*, https://www.washingtonpost.com/graphics/investigations/police-shootings-database. Mapping Police Violence, a project of We the Protesters, was also founded in 2015, *We the Protesters*, http://www.wetheprotesters.org/.
6. Brown, “Policing in American History,” 193.

7. Death in Custody Reporting Act of 2000, *Public Law* 106–297, § 2(4).
8. Ethan Corey, "How the Federal Government Lost Track of Deaths in Custody," *Appeal*, June 24, 2020, https://theappeal.org/police-prison-deaths-data.
9. Office of the Inspector General (OIG), "Review of the Department of Justice's Implementation of the *Death in Custody Reporting Act of 2013*" (Washington, DC: DOJ OIG, 2018), 3, https://oig.justice.gov/reports/2018/e1901.pdf.
10. Bureau of Justice Assistance, "Agency Information Collection Activities; Proposed Collection Comments Requested; New Collection: Death in Custody Reporting Act Collection," *Federal Register* 81, no. 243 (December 19, 2016), https://www.federalregister.gov/documents/2016/12/19/2016-30396/agency-information-collection-activities-proposed-collection-comments-requested-new-collection-death.
11. Bureau of Justice Assistance, "Agency Information Collection Activities; Proposed eCollection eComments Requested; New Collection: Death in Custody Reporting Act Collection," *Federal Register* 83, no. 112 (June 11, 2018), https://www.federalregister.gov/documents/2018/06/11/2018-12503/agency-information-collection-activities-proposed-ecollection-ecomments-requested-new-collection.
12. OIG, "Review of the Department of Justice's Implementation of the DCRA," i.
13. "Mortality in Correctional Institutions (MCI) (Formerly Deaths in Custody Reporting Program (DCRP))," (Washington, DC: Bureau of Justice Statistics), https://www.bjs.gov/index.cfm?ty=tp&tid=19.
14. Joe Davidson, "DOJ Slammed by Senators over Poor Reporting on Deaths in Custody," *Washington Post*, September 21, 2022, https://www.washingtonpost.com/politics/2022/09/21/doj-deaths-in-custody-gao-report-hearing.
15. Kim's words.

Chapter 6: Art Activism

1. For more information and resources on 5150 calls see Family Education and Resource Center, https://ferc.org.
2. Mobile Crisis or Mobile Crisis Rapid Response Teams are a mental health service that supports a community by providing immediate response emergency mental health evaluations and crises services. To learn more, see City of Berkeley, "Crisis Services," https://www.cityofberkeley.info/Health_Human_Services/Mental_Health/Mobile_Crisis_Team_(MCT).aspx.
3. James Baldwin, *The Fire Next Time* (New York: Dial Press, 1963), 118.
4. Abby Dobson, "Singing to Remember, Singing to Resist: Singing to Say Her Name," #SayHerName special edition of *CHIME Zine*, September 2020, https://equilibrium.gucci.com/zine-issue-say-her-name.
5. Augusto Boal, *The Rainbow of Desire: The Boal Method of Theatre and Therapy*, trans. Adrian Jackson (London: Routledge, 1994), 16, https://doi.org/10.4324/9780203820230.
6. Aidan Ricketts, "Theatre of Protest: The Magnifying Effects of Theatre in Direct Action," *Journal of Australian Studies* 30, no. 89 (2006): 75, https://doi.org/10.1080/14443050609388094.
7. Dobson, "Singing to Remember."
8. Ntozake Shange, *For Colored Girls Who Have Considered Suicide/When the Rainbow is Enuf: A Choreopoem* (Oakland, CA: Shameless Hussy Press, 1975).

Conclusion: Bearing Witness

1. Atatiana Jefferson was killed by a single shot fired by Officer Aaron Dean after a neighbor of Jefferson's called the police expressing concern that both her house doors were open. Following the killing, Dean resigned from the Fort Worth police. His trial for the murder of Atatiana finally started at the end of November 2022. William Joy, "Timeline: Three Years Later, Fort Worth Officer Aaron Dean Goes to Trial for Death of Atatiana Jefferson," *WFAA*, November 22, 2022, https://www.wfaa.com/article/news/

special-reports/atatiana-jefferson/timeline-atatiana-jefferson-aaron-dean/287-9cdacd1f-599b-4a0b-b948-6d2409a5a059.

2. Devon W. Carbado, *Unreasonable: Black Lives, Police Power, and the Fourth Amendment* (New York: New Press, 2022), 13.

Epilogue: Brokenhearted

1. If you have been touched by the stories in these pages, inspired, angered, or motivated to get involved, there are many ways that you can do so. The #SayHerName Mothers Network and a variety of other organizations and networks that address various dimensions of the criminalization of people of color more broadly offer opportunities to learn and do more.

   We know that only a few people who are moved to act are prepared to shift their life mission to take up this work, but meaningful contributions can be made in minutes, hours, or days. The key is that your voice matters.

   AAPF operates on the belief that we all can contribute to #SayHerName by taking up tasks that fit the time we are motivated and able to dedicate to this work. Below is just a sample of actions, broken down into time-blocks, that can help you find a way to contribute to the movement. You can also visit AAPF's website to find up-to-date information about how to get involved: https://www.aapf.org.

About the Authors

Kimberlé Crenshaw, professor of law at UCLA and Columbia Law School, is a leading authority in the areas of Civil Rights, Black feminist legal theory, and race, racism, and the law. Her work has been foundational in two fields of study that have come to be known by terms that she coined: Critical Race Theory and Intersectionality. She cofounded and serves as the executive director of the African American Policy Forum

Founded in 1996, the **African American Policy Forum** is an innovative think tank that connects academics, activists, and policy makers to promote efforts to dismantle structural inequality. We utilize new ideas and innovative perspectives to transform public discourse and policy. AAPF promotes frameworks and strategies that address a vision of racial justice that embraces the intersections of race, gender, class, and the array of barriers that disempower those who are marginalized in society. AAPF is dedicated to advancing and expanding racial justice, gender equality, and the indivisibility of all human rights, both in the United States and internationally.

Janelle Monáe is a Grammy-nominated singer-songwriter, performer, producer, actor, and activist.

About Haymarket Books

Haymarket Books is a radical, independent, nonprofit book publisher based in Chicago. Our mission is to publish books that contribute to struggles for social and economic justice. We strive to make our books a vibrant and organic part of social movements and the education and development of a critical, engaged, and internationalist Left.

We take inspiration and courage from our namesakes, the Haymarket Martyrs, who gave their lives fighting for a better world. Their 1886 struggle for the eight-hour day—which gave us May Day, the international workers' holiday—reminds workers around the world that ordinary people can organize and struggle for their own liberation. These struggles—against oppression, exploitation, environmental devastation, and war—continue today across the globe.

Since our founding in 2001, Haymarket has published more than nine hundred titles. Radically independent, we seek to drive a wedge into the risk-averse world of corporate book publishing. Our authors include Angela Y. Davis, Arundhati Roy, Keeanga-Yamahtta Taylor, Eve L. Ewing, Aja Monet, Mariame Kaba, Naomi Klein, Rebecca Solnit, Olúfẹ́mi O. Táíwò, Mohammed El-Kurd, José Olivarez, Noam Chomsky, Winona LaDuke, Robyn Maynard, Leanne Betasamosake Simpson, Howard Zinn, Mike Davis, Marc Lamont Hill, Dave Zirin, Astra Taylor, and Amy Goodman, among many other leading writers of our time. We are also the trade publishers of the acclaimed Historical Materialism Book Series.

Haymarket also manages a vibrant community organizing and event space in Chicago, Haymarket House, the popular Haymarket Books Live event series and podcast, and the annual Socialism Conference.

Also Available from Haymarket Books

Abolition. Feminism. Now., by Angela Y. Davis, Gina Dent, Erica R. Meiners, and Beth E. Richie

Angela Davis: An Autobiography, by Angela Y. Davis

Black Women Writers at Work, edited by Claudia Tate, foreword by Tillie Olsen

Finding My Voice: On Grieving My Father, Eric Garner, and Pushing for Justice, by Emerald Garner with Monet Dunham and Etan Thomas

Her Word Is Bond: Navigating Hip Hop and Relationships in a Culture of Misogyny, by Cristalle "Psalm One" Bowen

Our History Has Always Been Contraband: In Defense of Black Studies, edited by Colin Kaepernick, Robin D. G. Kelley, and Keeanga-Yamahtta Taylor

Rehearsals for Living, by Robyn Maynard and Leanne Betasamosake Simpson, foreword by Ruth Wilson Gilmore, afterword by Robin D. G. Kelley

So We Can Know: Writers of Color on Pregnancy, Loss, Abortion, and Birth, edited by aracelis girmay

Printed in the USA
CPSIA information can be obtained
at www.ICGtesting.com
LVHW020420090923
756292LV00003B/43

9 781642 594942